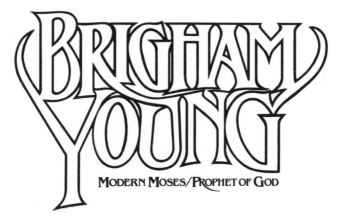

BRIGHAM YOUNG

MODERN MOSES/PROPHET OF GOD

FRANCIS M. GIBBONS

Deseret Book Company
Salt Lake City, Utah
1981

Library of Congress Cataloging in Publication Data

Gibbons, Francis M., 1921-
    Brigham Young, modern Moses, prophet of God.

    Bibliography: p.
    Includes index.
    1. Young, Brigham, 1801-1877. 2. Mormons—United
States—Biography.   I. Title.
BX8695.Y7G53   289.3'3 [B]   81-7766
ISBN 0-87747-858-9   AACR2

Contents

To Helen

Exodus

The plan was to leave in the spring, after the thaw, and after the wind and the sun had sufficiently dried the Iowa prairie. For months Nauvoo had pulsated with feverish activity as the Latter-day Saints prepared for their exodus—collecting animals and food, assembling and fitting out wagons, and carefully packing clothing and keepsakes.

Unlike their biblical counterparts, however, these modern children of Israel were uncertain about their destination. They had no Canaan, no specific land of promise as the object of their meandering trek. And unlike those unhappy slaves of Pharaoh, the Saints were not being restrained from leaving. Indeed, for some time the whole object of most Illinois officials and citizens had been to eject the Mormons from the state just as they had been ejected from New York, Ohio, and, more recently, neighboring Missouri.

But the Latter-day Saints and the Israelites, separated by centuries, were not without their similarities. Both were complex societies uprooted from one place and planted in another. Both groups had a sense of destiny and cohesiveness, and enjoyed frequent spiritual manifestations. Not the least of the similarities, making the two groups appear as branches growing from a common root, were the character, the methods, and the dominating authority of their leaders.

To mention Moses and Brigham Young in the same breath, to compare their attributes and work, or to ascribe their qualities of character to each other, is a compliment to both. Throughout their lives they were natural leaders, and their personalities and conduct exuded an air of authority and self-confidence. They

1

were deeply spiritual and acquired knowledge and instruction not only by study and observation, but from
heavenly sources. They played their historic roles
against a backdrop of injustice and oppression imposed upon their people.

The decisive link in the chain of events that led
each man to his destined role was a homicide. Moses
killed an Egyptian to defend a Hebrew brother. This
forced him to flee to the land of Midian, where, on
Mount Sinai, God called him to lead the children of
Israel out of Egypt. Joseph Smith's death in the
Carthage, Illinois jail on June 27, 1844, catapulted
Brigham Young into the leadership of The Church of
Jesus Christ of Latter-day Saints.

At the time of the martyrdom, Brigham was in the
East furthering Joseph's campaign for the United
States presidency. Devastated by news of the Prophet's
death, he returned to Nauvoo.

After a series of confrontations with men and factions who pretended to have succeeded to Joseph's
leadership, most Church members recognized the authority of the Quorum of the Twelve Apostles to lead
the Church. Since Brigham was the President of this
quorum, he inherited the reins of leadership that had
been held so firmly and capably by the martyred
Prophet.

The eighteen months following the martyrdom
were a nightmare. Church members were filled with
apprehension about the mob that had slaughtered
Joseph and Hyrum and boasted that the Mormons had
not seen the last of bloodshed. Members were uncertain about their destination after they would leave
Nauvoo, and they were burdened with fatigue and
harassment as they worked around the clock to finish
their beloved temple. Added to these traumas and
alarms was the pressure exerted by their ever-
increasing economic needs: to sell their Nauvoo properties (on a depressed market) and to accumulate the
supplies, equipment, and food to sustain them in the
wilderness.

Despite these and numerous other difficulties,

Brigham Young and his people worked with a deliberate assurance that was at once misleading and annoying to their enemies. To those not imbued with the spiritual fervor and dedication of the Latter-day Saints, it was incomprehensible that they would devote so much time and incur such heavy expense to complete the temple if they did not intend to remain and enjoy it. Thus, while the gentiles in and around Nauvoo had been told that the Mormons intended to leave, and while they had observed some activity toward this end, still there was the anomaly, the puzzle of the temple.

The Mormon-haters decided upon a ploy to hasten the exodus of the Saints, one that had proved so effective in destroying Joseph and Hyrum—an unsubstantiated criminal charge. At the December term of the United States District Court in Springfield, Illinois, enemies of the Church, through perjury, obtained indictments against Brigham Young and eight other Apostles for counterfeiting. The Brethren found themselves in collision with the United States government, a circumstance that raised a host of new problems and cast an entirely different light on the timing of the exodus. Reports that federal troops would be deployed up the Mississippi to block the departure of the leaders also caused concern.

A hint of what lay in store surfaced a few days before Christmas, 1845, when word came to President Young, who had joined the high council and members of the Twelve in the temple for a prayer circle, that federal officials were at the door with a warrant for his arrest. Demonstrating his aptness for impromptu strategy, Brigham directed William Miller to put on Brigham's cap and Heber C. Kimball's cloak; ordered his coachman, George D. Grant, to bring his carriage to the front door; and sent Brother Miller, deceptively capped and cloaked, to get into the carriage. The officers rose to the bait, arrested the man entering the carriage on the assumption that he was Brigham Young, and spirited him away to Carthage amidst his protestations of innocence. It was not until they were settled in

Hamilton's Tavern in Carthage that the chagrined officials discovered their blunder.

While the "Bogus Brigham" incident was the source of much hilarity in Nauvoo and Carthage, it had serious implications. As Brigham and his brethren weighed their options, they came to the realization that this episode was only the beginning of the government's attempts to arrest Church leaders. As they prayed for direction, they reached the unanimous conclusion that the exodus could not wait until spring, as they had originally planned, but that it must be undertaken immediately, in the dead of winter.

Within a month two thousand Saints were prepared to depart from their beautiful city, leaving behind their comfortable homes, farms, businesses, and, above all, their beautiful temple, in which they had received the special blessings that were to be a solace to them in the hard years ahead. At a special meeting in the temple on Monday, February 2, 1846, it was "agreed that it was imperatively necessary to start as soon as possible."[1] Thirteen days later Brigham Young, Willard Richards, their families, and Elder George A. Smith were ferried across the Mississippi River. After reaching the Iowa side, the party traveled four miles to the bluff whose steep sides presented the first real challenge to both horses and men. At this obstacle, the first of thousands Brigham was to face in the next three decades of pioneering, he exhibited one of the qualities that would make him preeminent among the great colonizers of the world. He wrote, "I would not go on until I saw all the teams up. I helped them up the hill with my own hands."[2] The following day at Sugar Creek, five miles beyond the bluff, where the fledgling pioneers had made their first camp, this paternal concern for those under his charge again surfaced. "I walked up the valley with Amasa Lyman and Willard Richards," Brigham later recorded, "where we united in prayer, and read to them a communication received two days previously, then returned to camp and continued the organization, acting the part of a father to everybody."[3]

In the months and years ahead, whether struggling along the pioneer trail, combating grasshoppers, contending against an armed invasion, repelling Indian attacks, or wrestling with the other myriad problems of planting a new civilization in an untamed land, Brigham Young never relinquished his role as the benign patriarch of modern Israel. And the feelings of kindly interest he manifested toward all were reciprocated by those who were the objects of his concern.

Yet the face a father shows toward his children is not always one of beaming approval. Often the exigencies of the moment, or the recalcitrance or neglect of the children, require stern reproof and, in some instances, discipline. As if by design this other side of Brigham Young's character was revealed the next day when he felt constrained to condemn laxness in the camp. Mounting his wagon, the President cried with a loud voice, "Attention! the whole Camp of Israel." (Research has failed to reveal an earlier instance when this phrase was used to identify the Mormon pioneers.) After the camp had assembled and Brigham had made preliminary remarks, he proceeded to the subject that weighed upon his mind: "I wish the brethren to stop running to Nauvoo, hunting, fishing, roasting their shins, [and] idling away their time, and fix nosebaskets for their horses, and save their corn, and fix comfortable places for their wives and children to ride, and never borrow without asking leave, and be sure and return what [is] borrowed, lest your brother be vexed with you and in his anger curse you, and then you would be cursed according to the power of the priesthood that brother possesses, and evil will come upon you. That all dogs in the camp should be killed, if the owners would not tie them up; and any man who would keep a horse in camp, that had the horse distemper, ought to forfeit all his horses. We will have no laws we cannot keep, but we will have order in the camp." The postscript added to these admonitions reinforced the implication they carried: "If any want to live in peace when we have left this, they must toe the mark."[4]

Anyone blessed with a sense of history who stood in the snow at Sugar Creek that cold winter day, listening to this unusual man, earnest and forthright, speaking in plain, unadorned words, would have recognized this as one of those pivotal episodes marking the close of one phase and the opening of another phase of a great life. Ahead lay a tortuous trail, steep and rugged, whose end was shrouded by a mist of uncertainty. Yet there was something about Brigham, something about his stance, his attitude, and his address, that imbued his listeners with confidence that although the destination and the means of reaching it were unclear, they could safely entrust themselves to his leadership.

That confidence must have been reinforced by a knowledge of the trail that lay behind, a trail marked by experiences and training that had prepared Brigham for the role he was now to play. He had discovered the reality and power of the spiritual world that lies beyond man's physical vision, a world that became more important to him than the work-a-day world in which he spent his mortal days. Indeed, as Brigham matured in his spiritual perceptions, as he became more disciplined, more persistent, and more successful in using the tools of other worldly power that had been placed in his hands, he seemed to those who knew him best to be more a resident of that world than of the world in which he performed his earthly labors. It was there, exposed to celestial influences, that he gained the knowledge and the will to accomplish the work of exodus and colonization that has made this world stand in awe of him.

Chapter One

Beginnings

Brigham Young first saw the light of day in a rough-hewn log cabin in Whitingham, Windham County, Vermont on June 1, 1801. His arrival swelled to nine the number of John and Abigail Howe Young's children, divided unevenly into five girls and four boys. Brigham's mother, fondly called "Nabby" by those who knew her well, had been carrying the yet unborn baby for four months when, at the height of a severe New England winter, with its blizzards, ice, and biting winds, she accompanied John and her eight children on a one-hundred-mile trip from their former home in Hopkinton, Massachusetts to Whitingham, Vermont. Thus, the second President of the Mormon Church was conceived in Massachusetts, but was born in Vermont, not many miles from the birthplace of Joseph Smith.

The ease and speed with which these hundred miles can be traveled today in the warm comfort of an automobile over smoothly surfaced roads obscure the privations and discomfort the Young family endured in making the same trip in a horse-drawn wagon over a rutted trail, alternately muddy and frozen, that meandered through forests and meadows only partially tamed by the ax and the plough.

But the difficulties of this trip, appearing so extreme to us, were an accepted part of life for people habituated to the rigors of farm life in rural New England in the nineteenth century. They had become tough and resilient under the imperative demands of a lifestyle yielding little more than a bare subsistence, even during the most fruitful years, and that was devoid of the amenities and comforts found in even the most modest households of today. Even so, life was characterized by a surprising mobility—the agrarian populace moved frequently as word came of the existence of land "further on" that supposedly was richer and cheaper and easier to work.

So in and of itself there was nothing of special significance in this mid-winter trip of the John Young family. We can surmise the timing was thought to be essential to avoid the deep mud of a spring thaw, to permit comfortable settlement in a new home before Nabby's pregnancy was too far advanced, and to enable John to commence planting and clearing as early as possible. It is interesting that Brigham Young was pioneering, was on the trail, even before he left his mother's womb.

The migratory impulse that prompted the Young family's move from Massachusetts to Vermont lay dormant for three years, during which John was engaged in "opening up" farms. Although but an infant during this period, the Young's baby doubtless imbibed subconsciously the tensions and the joys that frontier life produced in his parents and in his brothers and sisters who were old enough to comprehend the tenuous nature of their existence.

Survival under these conditions depended entirely upon one's industry and upon the vagaries of the weather. Thus, the farmer of that day, indeed, of any day, looked to himself and to forces beyond his control for the harvest necessary to sustain life. These exterior forces usually revolved around the idea of a supreme being, a creator, who controlled them and who would, under given conditions, exercise them in the farmer's behalf. The farmer is usually more susceptible to the idea of God than are those in most other occupations, especially as he witnesses the recurring miracle of life and growth in the planting, nurturing, and maturing of his crops. And this particular farmer, John Young, was especially susceptible to this idea because of his strict religious upbringing. His wife, Nabby, was no less devoted than he, and consequently the two of them raised their children in an atmosphere of faith.

Inculcating the ideas and doctrines of their adopted religion, Methodism, in their children, the parents taught them to pray and, according to Brigham, "to live a strictly moral life."[1]

By the time John Young left Whitingham in 1804, impelled again by the urge to move west, to find more fertile land and more congenial surroundings, the pattern of baby Brigham's life had been set. Although he was still too young to reason, he had begun to feel the spirit and attitudes of his family, especially his parents, whose example was to exert a life-long influence for good upon him.

The next stop in the Young family's western migration was Sherbourne, New York, a rural village in the Cherry Valley. There John was to wield his ax and his plough for nine years, during which he saw his family enlarged by the birth of his tenth and eleventh children, Louisa and Lorenzo Dow, and diminished by the death of Nabby, his second child and his wife's namesake, in 1807 at age fourteen.

From Sherbourne the migratory urge led John and his family to Aurelius, Cayuga County, New York, where in 1813 they settled into the last home Nabby was to occupy. Careworn with bearing eleven children in twenty-two years and mothering them under the harsh conditions of an almost nomadic farm life, she passed away two years later. Although by the standards of the day, fourteen-year-old Brigham was practically a man at the time of his mother's death, he mourned her passing like the teenaged child he actually was. There had been an especially close bond between this future prophet and his mother, and their spiritual affinities were not severed with her burial. Brigham's frequent and kindly references to her throughout his life poignantly reflected the depth of the love he had for her and of the lasting influence she exerted upon him.

Aside from his mother's death, which was the most important event that occurred while Brigham Young resided at Aurelius, there were other events that held significance for the future. Among these were the marriage of his sister Rhoda to John P. Greene and the marriage of his brother John to Theodosia Kimball. These nuptials brought Brigham into a personal relationship with two families that were to play a key role in his future following the organization of The Church of Jesus Christ of Latter-day Saints in 1830. But that event lay many years ahead.

With Nabby's death, the centripetal force that had welded the John Young family together was spent, which produced an inevitable diffusion and, in a sense, a disintegration. This is not to imply that there was dissension in the John Young family after her passing. It only suggests that with the heart of the household gone, its members began to reach out for other emotional ties. This included John Young, who two years later married a widow, Hannah Brown. By this time Brigham was a robust sixteen-year-old, already well along in learning the skills of a carpenter, joiner, painter, and glazier by which he would earn a livelihood during much of his adult life. While always in demand, these skills were especially useful at this time and place, as an economic boom brought on by the construction of the Erie Canal strained the capacity of contractors and artisans to the limit.

Brigham worked for a while in Auburn, a small village near Aurelius, where he plied his carpentry skills in the construction of a prison. From there he moved to Port Byron, a few miles to the north on the route of the Erie Canal. There he used all his artisan's skills, but chiefly painting. Employed for some time by a furniture manufacturer, he designed and constructed a water-powered paint crusher to facilitate the mixture of the pigment powder with oil and lead. He used a cannon ball acquired by his father during the American Revolution as a pestle, with an iron pot serving as the mortar.

While Brigham Young's neighbors in Port Byron failed to see in him the prophetic character that was to emerge with such powerful distinction in the years ahead, they did recognize qualities that were destined to elevate him above the crowd. He was intelligent, energetic, and tough-minded. Standing five feet ten inches tall and weighing 190 pounds, he was an imposing physical specimen, broad-shouldered and powerful from years of toil on his father's farm. His hair had a reddish tint and framed a high forehead. His blue eyes looked out on the world with a steady gaze that to some had a defiant quality, accentuated by his strong, determined jaw.

One seeing Brigham for the first time knew instinctively that here was a man not to be trifled with, a man who would assert his rights vigorously, although not in a way as to intrude upon others. Yet there was a tender, almost poetic quality about him that was evident in the loving relationship he bore to his mother, in his musical ability, and in his search for cultural development. The latter aspect of his character surfaced in Port Byron, where he joined a debating society. This leisure activity not only helped to develop his forensic skills, but broadened his intellectual interests as he researched the subjects the society had under debate.

Also during this period Brigham first formally affiliated himself with a church. At age twenty-two, he joined the Methodist Church, following the pattern set by his parents and by his older brothers, who were itinerant preachers for this sect. Also about this time he began to court Miriam Works, who was soon to become his bride. Miriam, like Brigham, traced her ancestry to Hopkinton, Massachusetts. Her parents, Asa and Abigail Works, had lived there and were well acquainted with Brigham's family. A few days less than a year after their marriage, Miriam gave birth to their first child, a girl, whom they named Elizabeth.

In 1829, when Elizabeth was four, Brigham and Miriam decided to move to Mendon, New York, a decision that had far-reaching consequences and that set the stage for their affiliation with the Mormon Church, which had not yet been organized. Mendon was a small village near the Erie Canal, less than a hundred miles west of Port Byron. In addition to the prospects of increased work that drew the Youngs to Mendon was the presence there or in nearby areas of several of Brigham's family, including his father, John; his brother, Joseph, who was still living at home; his sister Rhoda and her husband, John P. Greene; his brother Phineas and his family, who lived in nearby Victor; his sister Fanny Young Carr, who lived with Heber C. Kimball and his wife Vilate; and his brothers John Junior and Lorenzo Dow.

As they settled into their new home in a choice farming community, amidst close relatives who loved and appreciated them, near a major public works with its satellite industries and commerce, and with their health and strength, the Brigham Young family felt fortunate and happy indeed. They could look forward with anticipation to the peaceful years ahead in which they could expect to reap the harvest of industry and thrift, develop their talents, and practice their religion. The only disruption they might have foreseen was the possibility of another move, and this appeared less arduous as the canal approached completion.

But as they contemplated the future in the fateful year 1829, powerful forces were at work which would combine to engulf the Youngs, the Kimballs, and the Greenes, along with many other families in and around Mendon, and would carry them to heights of joy and depths of despair. In the early part of 1829 Oliver Cowdery, a young schoolteacher who was living with the families of his students in and around Palmyra, just a few miles east of Mendon, learned that Joseph Smith, Jr., a former resident of Palmyra, was in Harmony, Pennsylvania, translating a set of gold plates that had been delivered to him by an angel. Intrigued by this story and its astonishing implications, the young schoolteacher sought out Joseph Smith and became his scribe in translating the record that was published the spring of 1830 as the Book of Mormon. Soon thereafter, The Church of Jesus Christ of Latter-day Saints was organized against a background of heavenly manifestations unparalleled in earthly history in their scope and variety. These events ultimately carried Brigham Young to a destiny far beyond anything he or his new Mendon neighbors had imagined.

Chapter Two

Conversion

The trail that led Brigham Young into the Mormon Church was opened by his brother Phineas who, in the spring of 1830, set out from Victor on his preaching circuit. His visit to the Tomlinson farm coincided with the visit of another itinerant preacher, Samuel H. Smith, who carried in his backpack several copies of the Book of Mormon, which his brother, Joseph, had translated. Although Phineas was impressed with Samuel Smith's sincerity and noticed from a statement in the book that he was one of eight men who testified they had seen and handled the plates from which the book had been translated, he could not help but believe the young man was misled by an excess of zeal. So he purchased a copy of the book out of curiosity and with the intention to publicize the flaws he confidently expected to find in it.

Phineas placed the book with his gear, completed his preaching commitments, and upon returning to Victor advised his wife he intended to devote a week to cataloging the book's errors. What began as a search for error ended as an affirmation that the book was, as represented, a revelation from God. Not only did Phineas devote a week to studying the book once—he spent a second week going through it again with meticulous care. The errors and distortions he expected to find were missing. In their place he found a harmonious consistency with biblical doctrine. Also, the book shed important light upon concepts and incidents in the Bible that previously had been sources of speculation and doubt. As a consequence, when Phineas mounted his pulpit the second Sunday after returning home to discuss the book his parishioners had heard he was studying, instead of the harsh denunciation they had expected, they heard instead a lively endorsement. Indeed, after only a few minutes of analytical discussion, he launched into a spirited defense, during which he supported the claims of the Book of Mormon with biblical references and ended with the assertion that he believed the book to be true.

This incident, involving a man of substance who was held in high repute by his neighbors, created no small stir in and around Victor and Mendon. Having received such an unequivocal endorsement from a man to whom many looked for spiritual guidance, the book took on new meaning and importance as it was passed from home to home during the summer of 1830. Father John Young was the first to read it after Phineas, and he declared it to be as free of error as any book he had ever read. Then Brigham's sister Fanny read it and declared it to be a revelation from God. Then the Greenes, the Kimballs, and the Brigham Young family read it, all expressing their convictions about its truth and power except Brigham and Miriam, whose silence at this time about the book that was to have such a profound influence upon the Brigham Young family in the years ahead is anomalous. But the reason for the anomaly is apparent: on June 1 Miriam gave birth to her second child, a daughter who was named Vilate in honor of Miriam's best friend, Vilate Kimball. More than that, however, Miriam was not well. She had a nagging cough and severe congestion of the lungs that sapped her strength and made it difficult for her to carry out her normal household duties, and Elizabeth was still too young to help Miriam to any significant degree. When the new baby arrived, the problems of managing the household rested chiefly upon the shoulders of Brigham, who was under the necessity of working to provide the means to live and, in the early morning hours and late at night, of caring for an ailing wife, a new baby, and a six-year-old child. Thus Brigham had his hands full merely keeping his domestic ship afloat, and had little time to devote to the Book of Mormon.

It is evident, however, that the book had made an impact upon this man who was later to become one of its chief advocates, for it was not long thereafter that he confided in Phineas that he believed Mormonism had substance to it. But he was a man of deliberate and orderly habits and was not one to act precipitately upon new ideas presented to him. In fact, Brigham had known about the claims of Joseph Smith for almost a year before Phineas's copy of the Book of Mormon fell into his hands. As soon as the book came off the Palmyra press in the summer of 1829, the whole area was alive with stories and rumors about the "Gold Bible" and the miraculous way in which it had been translated and published. As Brigham was later to tell an audience in the old tabernacle in Salt Lake City, these stories and reports "were circulated as quick as the Book of Mormon was printed, and began to be scattered abroad."[1] Mendon, just a few miles from the epicenter of this religious bombshell, received the news within a matter of weeks after the story broke. But the first concrete evidence the Youngs had from which to judge the accuracy of the conflicting reports they had heard was the book Phineas acquired from Samuel H. Smith.

Although many townspeople in Mendon and Victor soon were convinced that the Book of Mormon was the authentic record of an ancient people who had inhabited the American continent and that it had been preserved and translated by divine means, they felt no need to join the Mormon Church. Their attitude reflected the prevailing view among protestant sects that it made little difference which church one belonged to because the various denominations were like different roads, all of which led to the same heaven. Thus, as long as those in Mendon entertained this idea, they could accept the Book of Mormon unquestioningly without feeling the slightest compulsion to convert to Mormonism.

Phineas was the means by which these families became aware that mere belief in the Book of Mormon
was insufficient. In August, 1830, he and his brother
Joseph set out on one of their many circuit jaunts in the
interests of the Reformed Methodist Church. While
on the circuit they stayed at the home of an old friend,
Solomon Chamberlain, who, since the last visit of the
itinerant preachers, had been converted to The
Church of Jesus Christ of Latter-day Saints. Solomon
expounded an idea that had never before occurred to
Phineas: that to act for God, as one did in the performance of religious ordinances, required priesthood
authority conferred by one who had himself received
it in a direct line from heavenly sources. The acceptance of this idea automatically eliminated all protestant sects from possessing divine authority, since they
were founded upon the rejection of a church they
claimed was apostate and not upon any investiture of
heavenly power.

Once this idea had taken root in Phineas's mind, he
lost all enthusiasm for preaching. Not long after, while
attending a conference of the Reformed Methodist
Church at Oswego, Solomon Chamberlain offered the
Book of Mormon as representing a revelation of the
Divine Will, whereupon both he and the book were re-
soundingly rejected by a voice vote. At this Phineas
rose to his feet and bore witness of the truth of what his
friend had said.

The catalyst that brought to a head the spiritual
stirrings which the Book of Mormon had produced in
Mendon and Victor was the appearance there in the
fall of 1831 of five Mormon elders. These young men,
Eleazer Miller, Elial Strong, Alpheus Gifford, Enos
Curtis, and Daniel Bowen, were members of an isolated branch of the Church in Columbia, Pennsylvania, and were passing through the Mendon area on a
"mission" in the interests of the Church they had but
recently joined.

What these missionaries lacked in formal education and social polish they more than made up in spiritual fervor. The meetings they conducted were filled

with a spirit the people at Mendon had never before encountered. Among the phenomena they experienced was the gift of tongues and interpretation of tongues. The residents of upper New York had long been exposed to the gibberish in local camp meetings that were held from time to time. In these meetings numerous people, some in a frenzied state, made incomprehensible sounds, all in a confused babel that they erroneously called "speaking in tongues." There was little, if any, resemblance between these camp meeting spectacles and the ordered yet spiritually powerful meetings the five elders conducted. Evidence of the effect of their teachings is found in the response of those who attended, men and women of substance who were not prone to being misled. "As soon as I heard them," Heber C. Kimball wrote later, "I was convinced they taught the truth, and that I had only received a part of the ordinances under the Baptist church. I also saw and heard the gifts of the spirit manifested by the Elders, for they spoke in tongues and interpreted, which tended to strengthen my faith. Brigham Young and myself were constrained, by the Spirit, to bear testimony of the truth, and when we did this, the power of God rested upon us."[2]

In a powerful sermon delivered in Salt Lake City five years after the exodus, Brigham Young gave voice to the same sentiments: "When I saw a man without eloquence, or talents for public speaking, who could only say, 'I know, by the power of the Holy Ghost, that the Book of Mormon is true, that Joseph Smith is a Prophet of the Lord,' the Holy Ghost proceeding from that individual illuminated my understanding, and light, glory, and immortality were before me. I was encircled by them, filled with them, and I knew for myself that the testimony of the man was true."[3]

The actual conversion of Brigham Young and Heber C. Kimball, who were later to be called as two of the original Twelve Apostles of the last dispensation and who were to play the leading roles in the exodus, dated from the 1831 meeting in Mendon where they spontaneously affirmed the truth of what the elders

had said. From that point on, their actual induction into the Church was only a matter of the maturing of
events.

In January, 1832, several months after the Columbia elders had visited Mendon, and after Brigham,
Phineas, and Heber C. Kimball had thoroughly digested the spiritual fare they had received in such abundance, they decided upon a perilous midwinter trip to
confirm the conclusions they had reached and to obtain new insights into the course they should follow.
"We travelled through snow and ice," he recorded
later, "crossing rivers until we were almost discouraged; still our faith was to learn more of the principles
of Mormonism." They remained with their new
friends about a week, conferring with them, attending
their meetings, and hearing them preach. After assimilating all the elders had to offer, and after reveling in
the spiritual feelings their conversation and actions
aroused, the visitors left for home "still more convinced of the truth of the work, and anxious to learn its
principles and to learn more of Joseph Smith's
mission."[4]

Although he was not yet a member of the Church,
Brigham was moved by a proselyting urge that took
him into Canada to confer with his older brother
Joseph, who was acting there as a Methodist circuit
minister. "After finding my brother Joseph," Brigham
noted, "and explaining to him what I had learned of
the Gospel in its purity, his heart rejoiced, and he returned home with me, where we arrived in March."[5]

The Youngs seemed determined to make their entry into the Church as a family. So, shortly after
Brigham returned from Canada, his father and his
Brother Joseph, guided by Phineas, made a pilgrimage to Pennsylvania, where they received further instruction from the faithful elders in the Columbia
branch. By this time they were thoroughly convinced
and were prepared for entry into the Church. Father
John and Phineas were baptized on April 5, 1832.
Joseph was baptized the following day, and on the day
after, the new members, accompanied by one of their

teachers, Eleazer Miller, began the 120-mile return trip to Mendon. There they found Brigham waiting expectantly, caring for Miriam and the two girls. Eleazer lost no time in completing the most far-reaching piece of missionary work he would ever perform, baptizing the future President of the Church on April 14, 1832 and confirming him at the water's edge. A jubilant Brigham recorded the last significant event of the day he was later to celebrate as his "re-birthday": "We returned home, about two miles, the weather being cold and snowy; and before my clothes were dry on my back he laid his hands on me and ordained me an Elder, at which I marvelled."[6]

Chapter Three

The Seeds of Power

The fire lighted in Brigham Young by his conversion and entry into the Church was to burn with an undiminished intensity during the remaining forty-five years of his life. It was never to die out or to flicker, even in the most tempestuous wind or storm. Indeed, the adversities through which he passed only made it glow brighter, as if fed by a vast reservoir of celestial energy. The cause of Brigham Young's vital power and drive lay deep within his spiritual being. And while it may never be possible to comprehend its full scope and depth, there are hints and shadows of its general outline.

One element can be found in an incident that occurred several weeks after his baptism. The occasion was a prayer circle held at the home of Heber C. Kimball. Present, in addition to the Young and Kimball families, was Alpheus Gifford, who was visiting from Columbia. While the prayer was being offered, Elder Gifford, moved upon by the Spirit, spoke in tongues. No sooner did this occur than Brigham was also moved upon by the Spirit. "I spoke in tongues," he was to report matter-of-factly," and we thought only of the day of Pentecost, when the Apostles were clothed upon with cloven tongues of fire."[1]

It is impossible to fully understand or overemphasize the effect of this experience upon Brigham Young. It was the first time heavenly power had been exerted through him. He had previously witnessed similar phenomena exhibited by the elders and he had felt and heard the inner promptings and whisperings that had caused him to testify of the truthfulness of the things the Columbia missionaries had taught and that had ultimately led him into the Church. But he found there was a vast difference between being a spectator and being a participant, between merely observing the marvelous effect of a spiritual phenomenon and of having it act through him.

But Brigham not only found himself speaking in a tongue he had not learned in mortality, a fact that of itself was awesome in its implications, but he also found that accompanying it, although quite apart from it, came a sure knowledge that Jesus Christ was and is the Savior, and that his Church had been restored to earth by heavenly means through the instrumentality of the Prophet Joseph Smith. From that moment to the end of his days Brigham was to speak of sacred things from an entirely different viewpoint. Thereafter he would not speak from mere belief, hope, or faith, but from absolute knowledge.

This knowledge alone would have been sufficient to set Brigham Young apart from the great mass of mankind. But its combination with his distinctive personal qualities of endurance and loyalty put him into a class by himself.

His endurance was hinted at in the earlier description of his physical appearance—the steady, unabashed gaze and the determined cut of his jaw. It was also suggested in the account of his first winter trip to Columbia, when he was "almost discouraged" by the foul weather, but hung on and completed the journey because of his thirst to learn more about "Mormonism." It comes into even clearer focus from a self-appraisal he made as he explained the agonies through which he passed in learning to speak in public: "When I think of myself, I think just this—I have the grit in me, and I will do my duty any how. When I began to speak in public, I was about as destitute of language as a man could well be. . . . How I have had the headache, when I had ideas to lay before the people, and not words to express them; but I was so gritty that I always tried my best."[2]

His other outstanding quality, loyalty, was always a Brigham Young trademark. It was evident in every as-

pect of his life—in his family and business relationships, in his social contacts, and especially in his relationship to the leader of his adopted church. When
Brigham came into the fold, Joseph Smith acquired
the most ardent supporter and disciple he was ever to
have outside the circle of his immediate family.
Brigham was often heard to say that he considered
himself fortunate even to have known the Prophet.

Even more than his words, Brigham's actions be-
spoke an almost worshipful loyalty toward his leader.
While Joseph lived, Brigham stood ready to respond
to any call, whether to walk to Missouri with Zion's
Camp, to direct the flight of the Saints into Illinois, to
preach abroad without purse or scrip, or to advance
the Prophet's presidential candidacy. And, invariably,
his response to these varied and frequent calls was enthusiastic, prompt, and unequivocal. After the
Prophet's death the whole object of Brigham's ministry seemed to represent a deliberate effort to execute,
in the most minute detail, the plans and programs of
his predecessor. Thus, extending from Canada to
Mexico, along the ribs of the towering Rockies, will be
found Mormon communities that reflect a plan of urban development devised by Joseph. The temples built
or commenced by Brigham Young reflected a basic design originated by Joseph, and the ordinances performed in them sprang from the inspiration of
Joseph's fertile mind. In like manner, the doctrines expounded from the hundreds of Mormon pulpits that
sprang up in the West were based upon the inspired
utterances of Joseph, doctrines that Brigham insisted
be taught with orthodox precision. Thus, in all his
manifold duties as the President of the Church,
Brigham Young followed the path laid out by his
predecessor. There was little, if any, deviation from it.
The special distinction of Brigham's own ministry
arose from a knack for organization, discipline, and
motivation.

It is apparent, then, that the relationship between
these two giants was not unlike the relationship of architect to builder. Joseph designed. Brigham execut-

ed. And the builder, throughout life, recognized his dependence upon the plan and in a thousand ways demonstrated his loyalty to the one who designed it.

Chapter Four

Beginnings in the Ministry

The ardor and enthusiasm touched off by Brigham's entry into the Church was temporarily dampened by an alarming deterioration in Miriam's health. The lung congestion that had troubled her for many months was at last diagnosed as consumption, the same ailment that had taken Brigham's mother to an early grave. Although Miriam shared her husband's convictions about Mormonism, her infirmity made it unwise to join him in baptism during the snow and wind of a cold April. Within a month, however, the weather had moderated to the point that her open-air baptism did not produce too great a shock upon her frail system.

The couple and their two daughters were to spend only a few months together as a Latter-day Saint family. Miriam passed away on September 8 after having spent a bittersweet summer—bitter because of the sure signs of approaching death, and sweet because of the exalted concepts of life and the hereafter she had gained from her new religion. Despite the sadness of her passing, the end was tinged with an elevated sense of joy and peace.

At this moment of grief, it was providential that Brigham had the Kimballs to rely upon. They were true friends indeed, always willing to share, always loyal, and always available to help in an emergency. So, in this time of dire need, Brigham turned to his staunch friend Heber, with his dark, searching eyes, and to his gentle wife, Vilate, after whom Brigham's baby daughter had been named.

The need of the moment related to plans laid during the summer to visit the Prophet Joseph Smith.

From the moment of his conversion, if not before, Brigham was impelled by an insatiable desire to meet, face to face, the man who had seen and talked with the creator of the world. More than this, he must have understood that his affiliation with the Church had set him upon a course whose direction and ultimate end were intertwined with those of the Mormon Prophet. Once Miriam had been lovingly laid away, there was all the more reason to bring his plan to fruition in order to provide an antidote for the grief and loneliness he felt at her passing.

Prior to his departure for Kirtland in company with his brother, Joseph, and Heber C. Kimball, Brigham performed a symbolic act that demonstrated his absolute commitment to the ministry he instinctively felt lay ahead. He divested himself of all earthly possessions that he "might be free to go forth and proclaim the plan of salvation to the inhabitants of the earth."[1] He did not want to be encumbered by material possessions that would distract him from the goal of dedicated service to God. More than that, he seemed to strive for a condition of abject poverty from which to begin his ministry to demonstrate that any achievements attained were traceable to God's power and influence and not to his own efforts. "When I went to Kirtland," he said, "I had not a coat in the world. . . . Neither had I a shoe to my feet, and I had to borrow a pair of pants and a pair of boots."[2]

Leaving his two daughters in the care of Vilate Kimball, Brigham left for Kirtland in his borrowed clothing, riding in Heber's wagon. Armed with letters of introduction, the three travelers visited branches of the Church along the way. "We exhorted them," Brigham wrote, "and prayed with them, and I spoke in tongues."[3]

The Kirtland visited by Brigham Young and his two companions on this occasion bore little resemblance to the sleepy village Joseph Smith had founded a little less than two years before. The arrival of the Mormon Prophet in January 1831 had signaled the beginning of an unprecedented growth, triggered by the

vigorous propensity of the Mormons to proselyte acquaintances and strangers alike and by the Prophet's
clarion call to "gather" there. "The gathering" was a
phenomenon peculiar to the Latter-day Saints, rooted
in the teachings that scattered Israel would ultimately
be restored and that America is Zion, the home and
gathering place of the wandering ten tribes. Moved by
these scriptural imperatives and by the summons of a
man whom they sustained as a prophet, the new Mormon converts had gravitated to Kirtland in an ever-
increasing flood, anxious to learn of God's will and to
be an intimate part of a movement that presaged the
Second Coming and the beginning of the Millennial
reign. Bursting at the seams for the lack of housing to
accommodate the hundreds of newcomers, Kirtland
was in the midst of an almost frantic building boom.
Many Saints were temporarily living with friends or
relatives or in makeshift shelters as they awaited the
completion of their homes.

The three visitors were fortunate to have relatives
in Kirtland with whom they were able to stay, Mr. and
Mrs. John P. Greene, Brigham Young's brother-in-law
and sister, who had joined the Church in Mendon and
had already migrated to Kirtland.

Despite their lengthy trip, lengthy for that day, at
least, over unsurfaced roads in a wagon without
springs, the visitors rested but briefly and then started
in search of the Prophet Joseph Smith. Directed first to
the home of Joseph's father, they learned that the
Prophet and his brothers were in the woods chopping
logs for fuel and to help feed the hungry demand for
building materials.

It was a moment of high drama for Brigham
Young to find himself in the presence of a prophet of
God. He had no preconceived notions about how a
prophet should look or act or how his time should be
occupied. Others before him had expressed disap-
pointment to find that Joseph filled his days like most
of his contemporaries. Somehow they had the distorted idea that a prophet lived an aloof, remote life
apart from his fellows in a trance-like dream world,

where his sole object is to act as a conduit of heavenly communication. These had fallen prey to sectarian dogma and had lost sight of the fact that the Savior was a carpenter, Abraham a herdsman, the Apostle Paul a lawyer-tentmaker, and Matthew a tax collector. Brigham, who was a careful student of the Bible, was aware of these and other precedents that demonstrate that the prophetic mantle is not fashioned only for those of a certain trade or profession nor made only for those with certain physical attributes. On the contrary, he knew that a prophet is measured on the basis of his spiritual stature, upon the level of his obedience and discipline, and upon his receptivity to the mind and will of God.

Thus, as Brigham Young appraised the man identified as the Prophet Joseph Smith, who stood before him dressed in rustic clothing and with an ax in hand, he was not so much impressed with his powerful physique and handsome features as he was with the spiritual impression that his attitude and demeanor conveyed. Brigham's own words indicate how Joseph met this test: "Here my joy was full at the privilege of shaking the hand of the Prophet of God, and [I] received the sure testimony, by the Spirit of prophecy, that he was all that any man could believe him to be, as a true Prophet."[4]

One can only speculate about the unspoken thoughts and impressions, vague or explicit, that passed through the minds of these two young men as they shook hands that autumn day near Kirtland. It is enough to know that the prophetic insight Brigham received was to be a spur and incentive throughout his life. And an incident that occurred in the evening suggests that Joseph had similar impressions about his new disciple. The occasion was an impromptu dinner meeting at the Prophet's home to which the three visitors and others were invited. By now Joseph's long-suffering wife, Emma, had resigned herself to the unexpected intrusions upon her time and energy caused by her husband's hospitable and gregarious nature. Seldom did the Smiths sit at their dinner table alone,

especially at this time while Kirtland was undergoing
such rapid growth. So on this evening the hungry travelers from Mendon were welcomed into the heart of
Mormondom's first family, where there was good food
and lively conversation. Given the composition of the
group and the occasion that brought it together, the
conversation predictably centered upon spiritual
themes. This in turn set the stage for the electrifying
episode that followed when, during a prayer Joseph
asked him to offer, Brigham spoke in tongues. Although Joseph had witnessed almost every other kind
of spiritual manifestation, he had never before been
exposed to the gift of tongues, nor had others from
Kirtland who were present. Some asked the Prophet
about it, expecting him to denounce the gift as being of
satanic origin. Out of Brigham's hearing he answered
the questioners: "No, it is of God, and the time will
come when brother Brigham Young will preside over
this Church."[5] Joseph offered the explanation that his
new follower had spoken in the pure Adamic language. Knowing of the high spiritual sensitivity he
manifested throughout his brief career, it is not surprising to learn that Joseph also exhibited the gift of
tongues during the short visit of the three converts
from Mendon.[6]

Their encounter with the Prophet, and the spiritual outpourings manifested then and during the trip
to and from Kirtland, so imbued the Youngs with missionary zeal that upon returning to Mendon they left
almost immediately for Canada to preach the gospel.
The main target was the scattered congregation of Reformed Methodists for whom Joseph Young had
served as a circuit rider. That their destination lay 250
miles to the north, that it was mid-winter, and that they
had no means of conveyance seemed irrelevant to this
intrepid pair. A foot of snow that covered a layer of
mud did not deter them. Nor were they balked in
crossing from Gravelly Point to Kingston, a distance of
six miles, on thin ice that bent under their feet, creating pockets of water half a shoe deep. Arriving at West

Loboro, a rural village considered to be in "Upper Canada," the Youngs established their headquarters with Joseph's friends and began their work.

Having converted from the same sect, the missionaries had special insight into the mental processes of these Reformed Methodists. Moreover, the fervency of their preaching, the spiritual gifts they manifested, and their personal account of contact with a living prophet brought about the same results that occurred following the Columbia missionaries' visit to Mendon. Within a six-week period Brigham and Joseph Young baptized forty-five people in and around West Loboro, raising up several small branches of the Church. Judging from the experience of the Youngs, the Kimballs, and the Greenes in Mendon, it is also probable that the seeds planted during this brief mission later matured and bore fruit that was not evident at the time of their departure.

As the missionaries left for home in February, 1833, the newly baptized Saints pooled their spare resources and gave them five York shillings to cover their expenses on the 250-mile return trip. Also, one of the sisters gave Brigham a pair of worn-out gloves.

This missionary jaunt into Canada was to be repeated in a few months with like results. In the interval Brigham made his home with the Kimballs, plied his artisan skills, and spent his weekends and evenings in the surrounding countryside preaching the doctrines of his new faith. On his second swing into Canada as an ordained Mormon missionary, he concentrated first in the area around Lyons where he had found his brother Joseph the year before, following his trip to Columbia. There he organized a small branch, comprised mainly of his thirteen new converts, and ordained a young priest, Jonathon Hampden, who became his traveling companion. The pair crossed back into the United States, where, laboring near Indian River Falls, they baptized several more converts, including members of the family of David W. Patten, who was later to be one of the original Twelve

Apostles of this dispensation, and Warren Parrish, who was later to become one of Joseph Smith's personal secretaries.

The pair recrossed into Canada, visiting the small branches near West Loboro that Brigham and his brother Joseph had organized a few months before. Remaining there until the first of July, Brigham then accompanied three of his convert families, the James Lake and the David and Abraham Wood families, to Kirtland, where they were to settle in obedience to the call of the Prophet Joseph Smith to gather. No sooner had Brigham returned to Mendon from this last excursion than he and his two daughters joined the Heber C. Kimball family in a permanent move to Kirtland.

If Brigham did not arrive at this last destination breathless, it was not for want of a good reason. During the preceding year he had traveled more than 2,400 miles by boat and wagon, but mostly by foot. Much of his traveling had been during inclement weather through sparsely settled, if not untamed, areas. And this was merely the beginning of a life that was to keep him almost constantly on the move, often afoot.

Chapter Five

Kirtland—Remarriage

Lying near the Great Lakes, not far from the present metropolis of Cleveland, Ohio, Kirtland was the first community that was comprised largely of Latter-day Saints. Its origin as the first Mormon gathering place is tied to a mission Parley P. Pratt and others undertook only a few months after the Church was organized in 1830. Elder Pratt and his associates were sent from New York by Joseph Smith to the then western borders of the United States in Missouri to take the gospel to the Indian tribes there. En route they stopped in Mentor, a village near Kirtland, to visit some of Elder Pratt's acquaintances whom he had known while he lived nearby while serving as a lay minister of a minor protestant sect. There he introduced his former ministerial associate, Sidney Rigdon, to the Book of Mormon. As a result this eloquent and powerful man ultimately joined the Church, along with many of his followers. Emanating from this nucleus, the influence of the Mormon Church spread into Kirtland and the surrounding area, resulting in the baptism of many new converts. Among these were men of maturity and intelligence who comprised the backbone of the local society, merchants, farmers, and ministers. In addition to Sidney Rigdon this harvest included others who were to play leading roles in the Church in the years ahead, including Newell K. Whitney, W. W. Phelps, Edward Partridge, and Frederick G. Williams. It is paradoxical that all these men were many years older than Joseph Smith, some a full generation older, and were more experienced in business matters and in the ways of the world, yet they instinctively deferred to him in all things, including those that lay within the circle of their own competence.

In addition to these powerful local men of affairs who had joined the Church in the Kirtland area, there were many others who had migrated there or who would soon do so who played prominent roles in the early days of the Church and who were, or would be, men of influence and prestige in the community. These included Oliver Cowdery, the Whitmers, the Pages, and the Prophet's father and brothers.

Thus, when Brigham Young arrived in Kirtland as a new convert with comparatively little experience in the Church, penniless, with no education to speak of, and with no powerful friends or relatives to open doors for him, he was strictly one of the crowd. Except for the few who were privy to the prophetic insight into Brigham's future role in the Church that Joseph had provided on the day the two had first met, there probably was no one in Kirtland who recognized in him a future President of the Church and one of the great colonizers of all time.

It was not long, however, before this energetic newcomer began to manifest the qualities of character and the abilities that, within a few years, would elevate him to the highest Church leadership. Brigham first began to reveal himself when he faced the decision of how to provide for his family. His artisan skills clearly pointed the direction in which his livelihood lay. The question was in which locality they would be exercised. While the building boom in Kirtland was still very much alive, ready cash was in short supply. More often than not artisans were paid with bartered goods, and cash payments frequently were deferred for indefinite periods due to the tightness of money. Because of the lack of means and the consequent need to receive prompt payment for their services, many Saints who had migrated to Kirtland had begun to travel to nearby communities for employment. This sometimes took them away from Kirtland for extended periods of time, thereby removing them from the direct influence of Joseph Smith and the other leaders of the

Church. As Brigham wrestled with this dilemma, weighing the need for an assured income against his desire for close association with the Prophet, he reached a decision that typified his attitude throughout his career. Of the incident he wrote: "In the fall of 1833, many of the brethren had gathered to Kirtland, and not finding suitable employment, and having some difficulty in getting their pay after they had labored, several went off to Willoughby, Painesville and Cleaveland. I told them I had gathered to Kirtland because I was so directed by the Prophet of God, and I was not going away to Willoughby, Painesville, Cleaveland, nor any where else to build up the Gentiles, but I was going to stay here and seek the things that pertained to the kingdom of God by listening to the teachings of his servants, and I should work for my brethren and trust in God and them that I would be paid. I labored for brother Cahoon and finished his house, and although he did not know he could pay me when I commenced, before I finished he had me paid in full. I then went to work for father John Smith and others, who paid me, and sustained myself in Kirtland, and when the brethren who had gone out to work for the Gentiles returned, I had means, though some of them were scant."[1]

In this tenuous, uncertain way Brigham Young began to get an economic toehold in Kirtland. In the process he learned lessons that schooled him for the maze of problems that lay ahead. He learned that solutions often emerge from conditions of dark complexity merely by taking positive, self-confident action and by awaiting the maturing of events. He learned that there is safety in adhering to counsel. And he learned the skill of followership, a skill that was to be indispensable to him in the years ahead when the heavy responsibility of leadership would be thrust upon him. Once Brigham had shored up his economic position, he began to think seriously of matrimony. Miriam had been gone for over a year. Since her death the care of his two little girls had rested almost entirely upon Vilate Kimball. While this saintly woman was more than willing to continue to render assistance in caring for her departed friend's children, who by now seemed almost like her own, it did not seem fitting to Brigham that he continue to impose as he had upon Vilate and Heber C. Kimball. Moreover, he was beginning to feel the need of the love and support of a wife in whom he could confide and to whom he could turn for support and comfort in times of stress and challenge.

Pragmatist that he was, Brigham deliberately set about to find a mate who would at once provide the conjugal love and support he sought and the mothering care his daughters increasingly required. What began, however, as a somewhat practical and prosaic search for a wife and mother culminated in a tender and lasting love for a woman whose name aptly described her character—Mary Ann Angell.

This dignified and talented woman was first exposed to Mormonism in 1830 in Providence, Rhode Island, through the preaching of Thomas B. Marsh. She obtained a copy of the Book of Mormon from Elder Marsh and later testified that even before she had read it completely she became convinced of its truthfulness by spiritual means, a conviction that was to remain with her throughout her life.

The marriage took place on February 10, 1834, in Kirtland, joining a couple who were to exert an increasingly powerful influence upon their family and upon their associates in Kirtland and later in Missouri and Illinois.

Chapter Six

Zion's Camp

T he newlyweds had spent only two short weeks together when an incident occurred that was to introduce great upset and uncertainty into their lives. It was fortunate for them, and for the stability of their marriage, that their convictions rested upon a spiritual foundation.

On February 24, 1834, the Prophet Joseph Smith received a revelation directing him to organize a force of men to go to Missouri for the relief of the members of the Church there who were the victims of a lawless and brutal mobocracy. Although the revelation was not directed to Brigham Young by name, it was explicit enough to cause him to volunteer immediately. "Say unto the strength of my house," the revelation enjoined, "my young men and the middle aged—Gather yourselves together unto the land of Zion."[1]

Obedient to this mandate, Brigham began immediately to prepare for a journey of over a thousand miles on foot (he had no horse) for a purpose that as yet had not been completely elaborated. It was enough that his brethren and sisters in Missouri were faced with extreme danger and that the direction had come from God through the medium of one whom he sustained as a prophet.

The group of men assembled for this novel undertaking traveled under the distinctive name "Zion's Camp." It was organized according to a pattern that invested its leader, Joseph Smith, with overall control, but that delegated broad responsibilities to the captains of twelve-man teams within the camp. Unlike any other military organization effected by Joseph Smith, the captain of each twelve-man team was elected by its members instead of being appointed by the directing head. The result, in most instances, was to elevate those whose native leadership ability was apparent and to give the captains more feeling of responsibility toward their respective teams. That Brigham Young was elected the captain of his twelve-man team indicates his stature in the eyes of his associates.

Each team included two cooks, two firemen, two tentmen, two watermen, two wagoners and horsemen, a runner, and a commissary officer. As there was no central food supply, each team had to be self-sustaining, gathering food as best they could along the line of march. Thus, teams led by men of energy and initiative like Brigham Young fared well, while others, led by men of lax habits and infirm will, were riven with dissension and discontent.

The excellence of Brigham's performance in Zion's Camp did not stem from past experience but from innate ability and his powers of observation and emulation. Using the parlance of another time and place, he was a "quick study." He carefully observed Joseph Smith's methods in leading men. He noted that Joseph was demanding but kind; that he was an accomplished delegator, never feeling compelled to do everything himself; that, above all, he had the spiritual perceptions and manifested in his conversation and demeanor the attributes that gave his followers complete confidence in his leadership.

During the march of Zion's Camp Brigham learned by observation the advantages of giving the housekeeping responsibilities to the leaders of the small units within the camp. He learned about the eroding effect of fatigue and hunger upon one's good nature and cooperativeness. He learned about the need for diversions and occasional change of pace to avoid the enervating effect of monotonous travel. At the same time he learned that too much diversion created an unwanted air of levity and carelessness. He learned, too, that without a governing head who is resilient and accommodating as to personal and inconsequential matters, but tough and unyielding as to matters of principle and objective, utter chaos reigns.

The lessons of leadership Brigham learned during the march of Zion's Camp were carefully stored away in memory, awaiting the day when they would be called forth for use on a vastly different and broader field of action.

But his experience in Zion's Camp not only served as a schoolmaster to help prepare Brigham for the exodus that lay ahead, it also revealed traits of character that both fed his self-confidence and magnified him in the eyes of his leader, the Prophet Joseph Smith. Before commencing the trek to Missouri, Brigham Young knew he was tough and gritty. He had had to be in order merely to survive. And the mid-winter trips he had taken afoot, both prior to and after his conversion, had demonstrated his physical endurance. But he had not been long on the trail toward Missouri before the realization dawned that the hardships of his past travels were inconsequential beside the monstrous adversity that then faced him. To walk a hundred miles in a few days with intermittent stops to rest and with no time pressures is a far cry from traveling a thousand miles on foot in less than thirty days under great pressures of time and without adequate clothing and subsistence. Since the camp had to average from thirty to forty miles a day over the entire period of the trip, there was time for little else than to walk, to scrounge food and eat, and to sleep. Occasionally those, like Brigham, who had no means of conveyance other than to walk, were given the opportunity to ride. These interludes enabled the walkers to conserve energy and to care for their feet. The lack of adequate laundering and sanitary facilities made it impossible for the marchers to give their feet the attention they required. Thus, it was more the rule than the exception that they lacked clean stockings and the medicines and supplies to treat adequately the extreme cases of blisters that often were agitated into infection and bleeding. On this account Brigham and other members of the camp often commented in later years that they had walked with blood in their boots en route to Missouri.

Tired, dusty, and footsore, the members of Zion's Camp ferried across the Grand River into Missouri on June 16, 1834. Here they were met by the Missouri brethren to whose aid they had come without understanding the extent of their need or how it could be satisfied. Joseph quickly ascertained that the duplicity of Missouri officials and the belligerence and armed power of the mobs that had driven his people out of Jackson County rendered Zion's Camp powerless to alter the conditions there. Moreover, Governor Dunklin, advised about the arrival of the force from Ohio and alarmed by the specter of possible armed conflict, had warned that the Mormons could go armed to Jackson County only on authority of the Commander-in-Chief. Against this background Joseph decided that the continued existence of the camp posed the threat of its destruction at the hands of Missouri troops and subjected the Saints in Zion to the threat of further attacks by the mobs.

Realist that he was, Joseph saw that he had no alternative but to dissolve Zion's Camp immediately. The order of dissolution was issued on June 23, and less than two weeks thereafter Brigham and his brother Joseph Young and several other members of the now disbanded camp had begun the thousand mile walk back to Kirtland. Twenty-five days later, after averaging forty miles a day, they were reunited with their families.

It was only natural that the members of the camp were later interrogated at length about their experiences by those who saw no value in what, on its face, appeared to have been an entirely sterile and unproductive enterprise. To those who questioned him thus, Brigham had a ready answer, revealed in this dialogue he quoted in a talk delivered years later in the Old Tabernacle in Salt Lake City. "When I returned from that mission to Kirtland, a brother said to me, 'Brother Brigham, what have you gained by this journey?' I re-

plied, 'Just what we went for; . . . I would not exchange
the knowledge I have received this season for the
whole of Geauga County; for property and mines of
wealth are not to be compared to the worth of
knowledge."[2] Still later, in a talk delivered in the
Bowery in Salt Lake, he elaborated on a specific kind
of knowledge to which he had made general reference
in the earlier sermon. Said he, "I told those brethren
that I was well paid—paid with heavy interest—yea
that my measure was filled to overflowing with the
knowledge that I had received by travelling with the
Prophet." More to the point, he added, "When companies are led across the plains by inexperienced persons, especially independent companies, they are very
apt to break into pieces, to divide up into fragments,
become weakened, and thus expose themselves to the
influences of death and destruction."[3]

Here is laid bare, in language that cannot be misun-
derstood, the vital role of Zion's Camp in preparing
Brigham Young for the exodus. It was the harbinger
of things to come. It furnished him with actual, living
precedents that were to be relied on time and again as
he struggled with the monumental problems of shepherding his people across the plains and directing
their settlement in the seclusion of the mountainous
deserts of the West.

Chapter Seven

Call to the Twelve

Training in the skills of leadership and pioneering, important as they were, did not constitute the sole benefit that followed in the wake of Zion's Camp. Equally if not more important was the growth in stature of Brigham and others like him whose ability and character were illuminated and magnified by the adversities through which they passed. Unlike the grumblers and complainers with which the camp abounded, these men stoically endured every inconvenience and hardship of the journey, faithfully executed every order given by the Prophet, and diligently prepared for the uncertain events that lay ahead in Missouri.

The acid test of Zion's Camp had separated the dross from the men of superior faith and tenacity. Joseph Smith, who was a shrewd judge of men, had had the opportunity to observe the attitude and demeanor of the members of the camp under the most adverse conditions and knew, therefore, who could or could not be trusted with authority and responsibility in times of stress. When, therefore, a few months following the march he felt impressed to organize the Quorum of Twelve Apostles pursuant to a revelation received in 1829,[1] he decided to do so in connection with a special meeting of those who had been members of the camp. Notification of the meeting was given through Brigham Young at the direction of the Prophet. As so often happened with Joseph, the decision to hold the meeting was made without premeditation as the result of a sudden spiritual impulse that came upon him. Following a Sunday service on February 8, 1835, he had invited Brigham and his brother

Joseph to come to his home to sing to him. This pair had melodious voices that harmonized well and they often sang together. On this occasion they sang for the Prophet "a long time," as Brigham later explained,[2] during the course of which Joseph, in a reminiscent mood, recalled many of the trying experiences through which the camp had passed. "Brethren," he said, "I have seen those men who died of the cholera in our camp; and the Lord knows, if I get a mansion as bright as theirs, I ask no more." At this, the Prophet wept "and for some time could not speak."[3] When he had regained his composure he turned to Brigham, saying, "I wish you to notify all the brethren living in the branches, within a reasonable distance from this place, to meet at a general conference on Saturday next. I shall then and there appoint twelve Special Witnesses, to open the door of the Gospel to foreign nations, and you will be one of them."[4]

In discussing this singular experience years later, President Young said, "He had a revelation when we were singing to him." Brigham related the Prophet's words: "He said, 'Brethren, I am going to call out Twelve Apostles. I think we will get together . . . and select Twelve Apostles . . . from those who have been up to Zion, out of the camp boys.' "[5]

News of the special meeting spread throughout Kirtland and neighboring communities with lightning speed. The members knew that some extraordinary event was at hand, and it was with a sense of high anticipation that they assembled on Saturday evening, February 14, 1835. They were not to be disappointed.

Early in the proceedings, Joseph, with characteristic flair, invited the members of Zion's Camp who were present to take seats together, apart from the congregation. He advised the assembly "that the meeting had been called, because God had commanded it; and it was made known to him by vision and by the Holy Spirit."[6] After rehearsing some of the tribulations and woe the camp had endured, the Prophet declared, "It was the will of God that those who went to Zion, with a determination to lay down their lives, if necessary, should be ordained to the ministry, and go forth to prune the vineyard for the last time."[7]

Following a recess, the witnesses to the Book of Mormon, who had been directed by the revelation given in 1829 to seek out the Apostles,[8] presented with Joseph's authorization and approval the names of twelve men, nine of whom had been members of Zion's Camp. Second on the list was Brigham Young, followed by Heber C. Kimball. Later the Apostles were assigned seniority in the Quorum of the Twelve on the basis of age, at which time Brigham was ranked third below Thomas B. Marsh and David W. Patten, and Heber C. Kimball, who was only thirteen days younger than Brigham, was ranked fourth.

Brigham took his seat in sight of the whole congregation to be ordained an Apostle under the hands of Oliver Cowdery, David Whitmer, and Martin Harris. These were the men to whom the angel Moroni had shown the gold plates from which the Book of Mormon was translated. And Oliver Cowdery, in company with Joseph Smith, had received the Aaronic Priesthood from John the Baptist, and the Melchizedek Priesthood from Peter, James, and John. The blessing given by these men, whose hands had touched the ancient plates, was calculated to arouse the most profound feelings of excitement, that were never to be stifled, but were to increase in fervor over the years. "He shall go forth from land to land and from sea to sea," the blessing promised, "and shall behold heavenly messengers going forth; and his life shall be prolonged; and the Holy Priesthood is conferred on him, that he may do wonders in the name of Jesus; that he may cast out devils, heal the sick, raise the dead, open the eyes of the blind, go forth from land to land and from sea to sea; and that heathen nations shall even call him God himself, if he do not rebuke them."[9]

Adding to the solemnity of the occasion, the First Presidency, Joseph Smith, Sidney Rigdon, and Frederick G. Williams, also placed their hands upon Brigham's head to ratify the ordination and blessings the Three Witnesses had previously conferred.

The final act in the drama of Brigham Young's induction into the Quorum of the Twelve took place later when Oliver Cowdery delivered a formal charge to the newly ordained Apostles. While it contained much important counsel, the essence of it was compressed into this single sentence: "You have been ordained to this holy Priesthood, you have received it from those who have the power and authority from an angel; you are to preach the Gospel to every nation."[10]

Obedient to this mandate, Brigham and several other members of the Twelve undertook a mission to the eastern United States soon after. Several conferences were held in western New York where members were trained in their responsibilities and where investigators were exposed to the doctrines of the Church. In the early part of June Brigham Young found it necessary to leave temporarily to return to Kirtland to testify in a lawsuit involving Joseph Smith. He then rejoined his brethren in the East, where they remained until the latter part of September proselyting and setting the local branches in order.

By this time Brigham and Mary Ann had reached an accommodation that enabled the new Apostle to come and go as the heavy duties of his office required. During the short periods he was at home between assignments, Brigham worked with a fury, earning money through the application of his artisan skills and providing for the necessities and some few comforts around the house. His domestic responsibilities had been measurably increased shortly before his call to the apostleship with the birth in October 1834 of his first son and third child, Joseph Angell Young, named in honor of the Prophet. This was only the first of his seventeen sons who would live to maturity. And twenty-seven more daughters who grew to maturity were later to join Elizabeth and Vilate. This does not take into account eleven other children who were to die in infancy.

For the moment, however, the knowledge of this large and vigorous family was shielded from Brigham's view by the curtain of futurity; obscured also was the knowledge of a domestic revolution that later would be wrought upon the Latter-day Saints by a revelation to Joseph Smith concerning the plurality of wives, a revelation the Prophet had already received by the time of Joseph Angell Young's birth, but which he would not confide to his disciples for many years.

Chapter Eight

The Zenith and Nadir at Kirtland

As buildings mushroomed in Kirtland, filling the needs of the swarms of immigrants who had gathered at Joseph's command, one building stood preeminent among all the others, not only because of its impressive size and stately appearance, but because of the spiritual significance the Latter-day Saints attached to it. This was the holy temple, whose cornerstone had been laid in July of 1833, two months before the arrival of the Young and Kimball families.

From the beginning Brigham's interest in this structure was almost obsessive. In the first place, the temple excited his artisan instincts. He was impressed by its simple yet classic architecture and by the insistence of Joseph Smith that the materials used in its construction were the very best available and that those who worked on it possessed superior skills. The other facet of the building that intrigued Brigham was the Prophet's oft-repeated prediction that when the temple was completed, the worthy Saints would receive a spiritual "endowment." This had aroused in Brigham powerful feelings of anticipation.

The exact nature and meaning of the endowment had never been explained by Joseph, but the magnitude of the spiritual phenomena already revealed by him, and the powerful confirmation of Joseph's prophetic status Brigham had received, were enough to bring conviction that what lay in store was something of extraordinary importance.

As work on the temple progressed, Joseph came to rely even more heavily upon the skills and native managerial ability of his disciple from Mendon. Indeed, in

the latter phase of the project, Brigham superin-
tended the painting and finishing work. The promptness and efficiency with which he filled this assignment, and the spirit of loyalty and brotherhood that
his whole manner conveyed, elevated him even higher
in the estimation of his leader.

It was intended from the beginning that the Kirtland Temple would serve a threefold purpose: as a
place of worship where the members could sharpen
their spiritual perceptions and draw closer to God; as a
school where the leaders could extend the borders of
their knowledge, whether in religious or secular subjects; and as an executive headquarters from which the
fast-growing Church could be administered.

Months before the formal dedication of the building in late March, 1836, the upper floor housed the
School of the Prophets, where the Church leaders
were instructed in doctrinal subjects by Joseph Smith
and his associates and in academic courses by professional teachers. A course in Hebrew was taught by a
Professor Seixas, a nonmember, who had been
brought to Kirtland for this purpose. And it was on the
upper floor that the Prophet maintained his office and
clerical staff. Here too, Joseph administered to
Brigham and other leaders of the Church the initia-
tory ordinances preparatory to receiving the full
endowment.

On January 21, 1836, in connection with this ordi-
nance, the Prophet recorded that "the heavens were
opened" to him and that he "beheld the celestial kingdom of God, and the glory thereof." He also saw "the
transcendent beauty of the gate through which the
heirs of that kingdom will enter, which was like unto
circling flames of fire; Also the blazing throne of God,
whereon was seated the Father and the Son."[1]

When the two lower floors of the temple were completed, final arrangements were made for the dedicatory services that began on Sunday, March 27, 1836.

In the evening of the first day of these services occurred a spiritual manifestation of pentecostal magnitude. Brigham Young was present on the occasion and

was never to forget the electrifying sequence of events
that began when nineteen-year-old George A. Smith,
who was later to become one of Brigham Young's
counselors in the First Presidency, arose and began to
prophesy. As soon as he spoke, "a noise was heard like
the sound of a rushing mighty wind, which filled the
Temple, and all the congregation simultaneously
arose, being moved upon by an invisible power; many
began to speak in tongues and prophesy; others saw
glorious visions; . . . the Temple was filled with angels,
which fact [was] declared to the congregation. The
people of the neighborhood came running together
(hearing an unusual sound within, and seeing a bright
light like a pillar of fire resting upon the Temple), and
were astonished at what was taking place. This continued until the meeting closed at eleven p. m."[2]

During the ensuing week many other spiritual
phenomena were manifested in the temple, mounting
toward the climax that occurred on Sunday, April 3,
when, in response to "solemn and silent prayer," four
visions were opened to the minds of Joseph Smith and
Oliver Cowdery and, in succession, the Savior, Moses,
Elias, and Elijah appeared to them.[3]

These and other events surrounding the dedication of the Kirtland Temple deeply impressed and
strengthened Brigham and other members of the
Church. Even so, beneath the surface of the extraordinary spiritual phenomena that pervaded the community lay the seeds of a volcanic dissension that, in less
than two years, was to erupt with such vengeful fury as
to force Joseph, Brigham, and other leaders and
members of the Church to flee Kirtland forever.

The irritant that produced such cataclysmic results, wholly unforeseen at the time of the temple dedication, was economic and political. At the time, the entire country was caught up in a wave of false prosperity
caused, in large part, by extensive speculations in land
and the absence of a sound banking system. Laxity in
controlling the organization and operation of banks
had created bedlam in the monetary field as new
banks, spawned almost overnight, glutted the market

with notes that more often than not were secured only
by land whose value was inflated out of all proportion
by the rank spirit of speculation that prevailed. It was
in the midst of this chaos that Joseph Smith and his associates organized the Kirtland Safety Society Bank.
When the Ohio legislature, through the imposition of
an overstrict standard it did not apply to non-Mormon
groups, refused to issue a charter, the bank was converted into the Kirtland Safety Society Anti-Banking
Company. The bank notes the organizers had had
printed, in anticipation the charter would be granted,
were salvaged merely by printing the prefix "anti" before and the suffix "ing" after the word "bank."

This unorthodox procedure, reflecting the casual
business practices of the day, merely postponed the
fate to which the venture was inevitably doomed.
Caught up in the financial panic that swept the country
in 1837, and that saw eight hundred bank failures in
the month of May alone, the company had no more
chance to survive than a raindrop in the desert. Its predictable demise was hastened by the embezzlements of
Warren Parrish, who occupied a position of trust on
the Prophet's administrative staff.

When it became apparent that the Kirtland Safety
Society Anti-Banking Company would go under,
many who had invested in it heaped the full blame
upon the shoulders of the Prophet. Forgotten for the
moment were the kindly, even adulatory, feelings they
had entertained toward him just a few months before.
In their place arose feelings of hostility and condem-
nation for what they considered to be Joseph's business ineptitude, if not dishonesty. For the most part
these attitudes were irrational and grew out of a fury
occasioned by the loss of investments.

Still, Brigham remained true to the Prophet. He
later told the Saints: "Once in my life I felt a want of
confidence in brother Joseph Smith, soon after I became acquainted with him. It was not concerning religious matters—it was not about his revelations—but it
was in relation to his financiering—to his managing
the temporal affairs which he undertook. A feeling

came over me that Joseph was not right in his financial management, though I presume the feeling did not last sixty seconds, and perhaps not thirty."[4]

Having thus suppressed a fleeting impression that Joseph might have been wrong, Brigham steeled his mind against criticism of his leader and thereafter adamantly refused to allow any such criticism to be spoken in his presence.

It made little difference who the critics were, whether of high or low station. For instance, several high leaders were once gathered in the Kirtland Temple—that holy place where they had experienced such marvelous pentecostal outpourings—to consider deposing the Prophet and installing David Whitmer as his successor. They received a forceful tongue-lashing from Brigham, "the Lion of the Lord." "I rose up," he later reported, "and in a plain and forcible manner told them that Joseph was a Prophet, and I knew it, and that they might rail and slander him as much as they pleased, they could not destroy the appointment of the Prophet of God, they could only destroy their own authority, cut the thread that bound them to the Prophet and to God, and sink themselves to hell."[5]

And a new dimension was later added to the meaning of Brigham's "forcible manner" when there appeared in Kirtland a zealot named Hawley who felt himself to be under a divine mandate to rebuke Joseph Smith and to advise him he had been rejected of the Lord. The bearer of this denunciatory message added a dramatic and, to Brigham, annoying flair to his mission when one night he paraded through Kirtland's empty streets in the wee hours, railing against Joseph and shouting in a loud voice, "Woe! Woe! unto the inhabitants of this place." One can imagine the shocked surprise with which Mr. Hawley discovered the impact his message had upon Brigham, who left us this account of the incident: "I put my pants and shoes on, took my cow-hide, went out, and laying hold of him, jerked him round, and assured him that if he did not stop his noise and let the people enjoy their sleep without interruption, I would cow-hide him on the spot, for we had the Lord's Prophet right here, and we did not want the Devil's prophet yelling round the streets."[6]

But the determined efforts of Joseph's fearless disciple, the Lion of the Lord, could not begin to stem the evil tide that soon was to engulf Kirtland and to drive and scatter the Prophet's loyal followers before its devastating flood.

The end in Kirtland came for Brigham three days before Christmas, 1837, when the pressures became so intense that he had to flee "in consequence of the fury of the mob and the spirit that prevailed in the apostates, who had threatened to destroy" him. He explained the reason for the mob's unfeeling rage: " . . . because I would proclaim, publicly and privately, that I knew, by the power of the Holy Ghost, that Joseph Smith was a Prophet of the Most High God, and had not transgressed and fallen as apostates declared."[7]

Less than a month after Brigham departed from Kirtland, Joseph left also under the impetus of a mob that forced him to go by horseback under cover of night. With him was his counselor Sidney Rigdon, who still had not fully recovered from the brutalities inflicted upon him a few years before in Hiram, Ohio, by a mob that had beaten and tarred and feathered him and Joseph. This pair rendezvoused with Brigham and other leaders of the Church at Dublin, Indiana, where they endeavored to earn money for the remaining trip to Missouri by cutting cordwood and sawing logs. This proving to be ineffectual, the Prophet one day caught Brigham off guard by seeking his advice as to what should be done. "You are one of the Twelve," said he to the Apostle, "who have charge of the Kingdom in all the world; I believe I shall throw myself upon you, and look to you for counsel in this case."

At first Brigham doubted that the Prophet was in earnest. The request was extraordinary because typically the members of the Church sought counsel from Joseph but did not give it. When Joseph assured him of his sincerity, Brigham responded: "If you will take my counsel it will be that you rest yourself, and be assured you shall have money in plenty to pursue your journey."[8]

The unwavering faith this answer implies was soon fulfilled through an unusual incident. A brother Tomlinson from Dublin was able to sell his farm as the result of counsel given to him by Brigham Young. Brigham suggested to Tomlinson that he aid the Prophet, which he did promptly and willingly by giving him three hundred dollars, an amount more than sufficient to see Joseph to Missouri.

Chapter Nine

Missouri Interlude

Brigham Young had mixed feelings about Missouri. Recognizing that it had been designated by revelation as Zion, the center of the Church, the place the great temple would be erected and the main gathering of the lost tribes occur, and where the Savior would reign after the Second Coming, he regarded it with reverential awe. Yet he could not restrain the feelings of repugnance and fear that it aroused. Missouri was the dumping ground for the dregs of American society. It was the jumping-off place into the vast, unsettled West, with its plains, mountains, and deserts. There congregated the adventurers who sought thrills in the unusual and bizarre; the lawless who lived by their wits beyond the pale of civilized society; the venal who sought easy wealth in gold, furs, gambling, or chicanery; and the bloodthirsty who reveled in violence and death. Intermingled with this collection of misfits and malcontents was a class of industrious, law-abiding farmers and merchants who had gone west to take advantage of the opportunities this fertile land afforded. Being in the minority, however, and being inclined to remain in the background and to tend to their own affairs, their voices either remained silent or were drowned out by the violent and venomous clamor of the unprincipled majority.

It was this raw element in Missouri that had robbed, pillaged, and burned the homes and businesses of the Saints in Jackson County, Missouri, that had beaten their men, raped their women, and had mercilessly driven them into Caldwell and Daviess counties to the north.

It was in Far West, Caldwell County, that Brigham Young decided to settle. He arrived there on March 14, 1838, and soon acquired land on nearby Mill Creek. Immediately he began to construct a cabin and build fences, anticipating that Mary Ann and the children would join him soon. The home he projected on Mill Creek would be more commodious than his Kirtland home, as his family had now grown to seven with the births of Brigham, Jr., and baby Mary Ann in 1836.

Because of the concern he had for his family, who had been required to more or less fend for themselves since his call to the apostleship, he was grateful for the direction given to him by Joseph Smith through a revelation received on April 17: "Let my servant Brigham Young go unto the place which he has bought, on Mill Creek, and there provide for his family until an effectual door is opened for the support of his family, until I shall command him to go hence, and not to leave his family until they are amply provided for."[1]

Mary Ann was sent for immediately and, with her five children, traveled by wagon to Wellsville and thence by river steamer to Richmond, Missouri, where Brigham met them and drove them by team to Far West.

Brigham and the other leading brethren nurtured the hope of remaining indefinitely at Far West. This hope was strengthened by a revelation received by Joseph Smith on April 26, 1838, which declared Far West to be "a holy and consecrated land" and which commanded that a temple be built "for the gathering together of my saints, that they may worship me." An interesting aspect of this revelation was the direction that the temple be commenced "on the fourth day of July next . . . and in one year from this day [April 26, 1838] let them re-commence laying the foundation of my house."[2] On July 8, 1838, the Lord directed the Twelve to "take leave of my saints in the city of Far West, on the twenty-sixth day of April next, on the building-spot of my house" on a mission "over the great waters."[3] Although the Saints had been driven again before the April 26, 1839, target date, this time into Illinois, and despite the boasts of the Missouri mobs that this revelation of Joseph Smith would never be fulfilled, several members of the Twelve, including Brigham Young, returned to Far West on the day appointed; held a meeting at the temple site; sang hymns; ordained those present who had been appointed to fill vacancies in the quorum; laid a cornerstone of the temple; took leave of some of the brethren who were still in Far West; and started on their mission, stopping for a time en route at Nauvoo.[4]

But all this lay in the dim future for Brigham Young as he settled into his new home on Mill Creek with his wife, Mary Ann, and his active brood of five children who then ranged in age from thirteen-year-old Elizabeth to two-year-old baby Mary Ann. Although there was still much unrest among the Missourians, who chafed at the presence of the industrious, aggressive Mormons, Brigham and the other leaders entertained the hope that they would be permitted to remain in peace, live their religion, provide for their families, and prepare a people fit for the society of the Messiah at his second coming.

These high aspirations, however, did not take into account the perversity of the people both within and outside the Church, nor the satanic forces that would be stirred up within such an unbelievably short time after the Kirtland expulsion. Beyond the unsettling effect of Mormon doctrine and the assured way in which Church members expounded it, the mobocrats were in almost constant agitation about the threat these newcomers posed to their political and commercial dominance. It did not require any special prescience for the Missourians to foresee that if left undisturbed, the Latter-day Saints, who were flocking into Missouri in droves as the result of their leader's call, would soon control the ballot box and with it the machinery of government that until then had been in their hands. And, knowing of the cohesiveness of these unusual people, coupled with their penchant for sobriety and hard work, the Missourians could envision a time when their own influence in commercial matters would diminish to nothing. Faced with these threats and believing that all other avenues of escape were closed to them, the mobocrats yielded to their most inhuman tendencies and began deliberately and methodically to plot the expulsion or, if necessary, the complete extermination of the Mormons.

The plotters' assault was diverse and complex. It was best described by General Moses Wilson, who commanded the brigade that escorted Joseph Smith and other prisoners to Independence from Far West. "We know perfectly that from the beginning the Mormons have not been the aggressors at all," said the general one evening as he sat by the fire with his prisoners. "As it began in '33 in Jackson County, so it has been ever since. You Mormons were crowded to the last extreme, and compelled to self-defence; and this has been construed into treason, murder and plunder. We mob you without law; the authorities refuse to protect you according to law; you then are compelled to protect yourselves, and we act upon the prejudices of the public, who join our forces, and the whole is legalized, for your destruction and our gain. Is not this a shrewd and cunning policy on our part, gentlemen?"[5]

But the enemies within the Church were more insidious than the gentile mobocrats outside it, precisely because they were not immediately recognizable as enemies. For the most part, however, these interior foes were merely weak and easily misled rather than malignant. This was certainly true of the most notorious apostate of the Missouri era, Thomas B. Marsh, then president of the Quorum of the Twelve Apostles. In the unsettled and somewhat chaotic conditions in Missouri, Marsh, who really had never been close to the Prophet, began to believe some of the exaggerated stories being circulated about him. The most frequently mentioned was that Joseph considered himself another Mohammed, with designs of empire that he intended to enforce by the sword if necessary. This fanciful myth originated with an ambitious, aspiring, and presumably insane man named Sampson Avard, who had organized a secret, oath-bound group of

Latter-day Saints later known as the Danites, whose object was to prey upon and to plunder the gentiles. "In this way," he had informed his disciples, "we will build up the kingdom of God, and roll forth the little stone that Daniel saw cut out of the mountain without hands."[6] For a while he was able to convince some of the more gullible members of the Church that his activities were being carried out at the direction of the Prophet. When word reached Joseph of what Avard was doing, he denounced him and pressed charges that resulted in his excommunication. With his plans exposed, Avard openly and aggressively asserted that Joseph was behind it all, and for evidence of the Mormon leader's militaristic ambitions, referred to the march of Zion's Camp, which was characterized as an abortive attempt to subjugate Missouri by armed force. Ludicrous though this charge was, it was believed by some, including Thomas B. Marsh, whose ardor for the Church had cooled because of a dispute in which his wife had become embroiled with some of her sister Saints over the right to milk strippings from a cow. Feeding on suspicion, innuendo, and misinformation, and nursing hurt feelings over the alleged mistreatment of his wife, Marsh at last came to accept as fact the malicious stories circulated about the Prophet. His final act of apostasy occurred when he swore out an affidavit that asserted Joseph was guilty of the false Mohammed charge. So convinced had he become of the culpability of his former leader that he momentarily swayed Orson Hyde, also of the Twelve, who had only recently returned from a successful mission to the British Isles.

The fall and subsequent excommunication of Thomas B. Marsh effected an important and lasting change in the leadership status of Brigham Young. Because of the unexpected death of David W. Patten in a skirmish with a band of mobocrats at nearby Crooked River, Brigham suddenly found himself the senior member of the Quorum of the Twelve Apostles. Joseph Smith, held under false charges in a gloomy, makeshift jail in Richmond, Missouri, summoned

Brigham to advise him of his appointment. With the new President of the Twelve was his trusted friend and fellow Apostle, Heber C. Kimball, who had likewise moved his family to Missouri from Kirtland.

The circumstances under which Brigham Young was elevated to a position of high leadership in the Church were both inauspicious and difficult. The Prophet and his first counselor, Sidney Rigdon, were then in custody, as were many of the men who had led the Saints in Missouri. Missouri Governor Lilburn Boggs had issued an order to exterminate the Mormons. And while the fury the extermination order unleashed had to an extent subsided with Joseph's arrest, there was still constant agitation to remove the Saints from the state, either in a coffin or at gunpoint.

It was providential for the Mormons and their jailed leader that Brigham was a comparative unknown to the mobocrats and Missouri officials. He had been in the state only a few months and had not, therefore, had time to impress himself on their consciousness. This relieved him of much anxiety and pressure he would otherwise have experienced and allowed him a freedom of action essential to accomplish the heavy task Joseph laid upon him. That task was to supervise, under the direction of the Prophet from Liberty Jail, the movement of the Latter-day Saints from Missouri to Illinois. In a sense, this was for Brigham a dress rehearsal for the massive exodus west he was to direct in less than a decade. All the same stressful elements were present: the urgency to leave ahead of the angry and impatient mobs that pressed from behind; the difficulty, if not impossibility, of disposing of property that could not be carried away in a wagon or backpack; the uncertainty about what lay ahead; and the constant daily upset of being on the move.

The relationship between the Prophet and Brigham Young at this time was reflected in a letter from Joseph, issued from the jail, that in effect gave Brigham and the other leaders blanket authority to act as they deemed best, while reserving in the Prophet a power of veto. "Now, brethren, concerning the places for the location of the Saints," he wrote, "we cannot counsel you as we could if we were present with you; and as to the things that were written heretofore, we did not consider them anything very binding." He then suggested that in his absence the affairs of the Church be directed "by a general conference of the most faithful and the most respectable of the authorities of the Church," a body that Brigham Young headed by reason of his position as President of the Quorum of the Twelve. The letter further directed that "a minute of those transactions . . . be kept, and forwarded from time to time to your humble servant; and if there should be any corrections by the word of the Lord, they shall be freely transmitted, and your humble servant will approve all things whatsoever is acceptable unto God."[7]

Operating within these guidelines, Brigham began to plan the move of the bulk of the Saints in Missouri to temporary locations in and near Quincy, Illinois. He had opened negotiations with a group known as the "Democratic Association" in Quincy that played a promotional role not unlike that of the modern-day Chamber of Commerce. Comprised of local businessmen and boosters, the association was endeavoring to lure capital and settlers into the area to broaden the tax base and to inject new life into its sagging economy. Having received assurance that the Saints would be welcome in Illinois, Brigham made final plans to evacuate Far West. On January 29, 1839, Brigham and 379 other heads of families signed a document that gave a committee of seven men the power to dispose of all the surplus property of the signatories in order to raise money to help finance the exodus. The committee was authorized to use the funds received from this source to assist the worthy poor.

There was special irony in the fact that the first section of a caravan of Latter-day Saints, led by Brigham Young, left Far West headed for Quincy on Saint Valentine's Day, February 14, 1839.

As with the later exodus from Nauvoo, the timetable of the exodus from Far West was accelerated by mob pressure. By this time, Brigham Young had become known to the Missourians through his outspoken defense of the Prophet and by his activity as a leader during Joseph's confinement. He therefore had become a marked man, subject to special harassment. So it was decided that he should go ahead to blaze the trail, as he would do in the trek west, and direct the movement of the Saints from the other end of the trail in Quincy.

Brigham decided to lead his group overland on an almost direct line east to a point across the Mississippi from Quincy. Some of the Saints who migrated later in the winter or in the spring followed Brigham's trail, although most of them went by steamer from Richmond down the Missouri to St. Louis and thence up the Mississippi to Quincy.

Brigham likely would have followed the river route had it not been for fear of detection at Richmond, where he was well known because of his visits there to see the Prophet in jail or on trial in the courtroom of the notorious Mormon-hater, Judge King. So he left Far West by wagon at the height of a cold Missouri winter. Aboard were his family and all their personal belongings except those that had been declared surplus and turned over to the committee for sale. In caravan with the Youngs were several other families.

The travelers had not been long on the road before Brigham learned a truth that most colonizers learn early, that a wagon train or caravan moves at the pace of its slowest member. But Brigham innovatively added an interesting variation to the procedure. Instead of moving at the snail's pace dictated by the slowest member of the caravan, he would travel at the fastest speed conditions would permit, establish a temporary base camp where his family could remain in comparative comfort, and then return along the trail on horseback to meet and shepherd the slower members along. In this way the caravan leap frogged across the heavily vegetated and rolling landscape of northern Missouri, adjusting by degrees to the damp cold that seemed to permeate their whole beings. In

the course of this trek Mary Ann and the children were
established for short periods of time at eleven different sites.

By mid-March the Youngs were temporarily
settled in Quincy, where they and the other Mormon
refugees had been received with warm hospitality.
While the "Democratic Association" had an ulterior
motive in inviting the Saints to settle in Quincy, the citizens responded with charitable compassion when they
saw the poverty to which the newcomers had been reduced by their enemies across the river.

At meetings held in Quincy on March 17 and 18
Brigham Young counseled with members of his quorum. Out of these council meetings came decisions for
the vast enterprise of moving thousands of Latter-day
Saints, many of whom were destitute, from Missouri to
the temporary gathering place on the east bank of the
Mississippi.

In the midst of these heavy exertions, as the Twelve
struggled day by day to solve the complex problems
that the Missouri exodus imposed, they were planning
to return to Far West on April 26, only a short month
away, to lay the cornerstone of the temple and to hold a
special council meeting before departing for their mission abroad.

Having created a suitable administrative mechanism to transport the refugees from Missouri to
Quincy and to care for them after their arrival, the
Twelve finalized their plans to return to Far West and
departed for that place on April 18. Four days later, on
April 22, 1839, Joseph Smith arrived unexpectedly
from Missouri, having escaped from the Liberty Jail
with assistance from Missouri officials who, as public
opinion mounted against them, had sought for a way
out of the "Mormon Dilemma." Joseph took up the
reins of leadership that had been handled so well by his
trusted subordinate who was then halfway to Far West.

About the same time Joseph arrived in Quincy,
Brigham, who was riding with Orson Pratt and Wil-
ford Woodruff in the latter's carriage, came upon
John Page, also of the Twelve, who was en route to

Quincy with his family. The three Apostles found Elder Page "on a sideling hill, with his load turned bottom side upwards." Brigham Young reported that Elder Page "had upset a barrel of soft soap, and he was elbow-deep in the soap, scooping it up with his hands." In that stressful situation, one in John Page's shoes likely would have expected a reaction from the three Apostles different from the one he received. At least he might have expected the offer of a helping hand to gather up his scattered belongings. Instead he was met with the injunction to leave his family and accompany his brethren to Far West! "He replied he did not see that he could, as he had his family to take to Quincy." That was hardly the response Brigham expected or the one he was prepared to accept. "I told him his family would get along well enough," the senior Apostle answered, "and I desired him to go up with us." Elder Page yielded the point but then pleaded for time to make ready to leave. The final shock came when Brigham advised he had "five minutes" to prepare.[8]

Brigham was not insensitive to Elder Page's condition, nor was he selfish or unwilling to assist those in need. Rather he found it imperative that all personal considerations of the Twelve be laid aside, that their personal needs be subordinated to the demands of their apostolic calling. Once Brigham found that Elder Page was prepared to follow directions, his whole attitude changed. "We assisted in loading his wagon," wrote Brigham. "He drove down the hill and camped, and returned with us."[9]

Brigham Young's obedience to the commands of God and insistence that all under his direction follow them emerged time and again as his career unfolded. The result was a sharp cleavage in the attitudes toward Brigham Young and his leadership. The spiritually weak and insensitive regarded him as arbitrary and unreasonable. But to the spiritually mature and farsighted, Brigham was an inspired leader called to guide the Church during a perilous time.

Chapter Ten

Mission to England

The nocturnal meeting of the Twelve held at the Far West temple site on April 26, 1839, heralded the beginning of an aggressive new phase of missionary work abroad. As has often happened in the history of the Church, the new demands came while the Saints were beset with immense personal problems. Many were destitute and were literally camping out at Quincy, waiting for their leaders to find a place to settle permanently. Meanwhile, the angry mobs that had driven them from Missouri were still near at hand, and although the Democratic Association and many of the residents of Quincy had extended the hand of friendship, the Saints perceived that the antagonisms that had flared up against them in New York, Ohio, and Missouri simmered just below the surface, posing a constant threat. Yet, amidst these and other perils, the Twelve self-confidently went about the task of preparing to depart for Great Britain.

After returning from Far West, Brigham Young moved his family up-river, settling them in an old army barracks at Montrose on the Iowa side across from Commerce, later called Nauvoo, Illinois. It was a relief and comfort to Mary Ann to have a roof over her head again, as she was carrying her fourth child, Alice, who would be born September 4, just ten days before Brigham crossed the river to leave for England.

The summer of 1839 was most trying for the Brigham Young family. The trouble was a compound of poverty, illness, and uncertainty. When the Youngs arrived in Illinois, their larder was practically empty. They had brought some stores with them, but not

enough to feed for long a family of seven—soon to be
enlarged to eight. And the temporary stay in Quincy
had not been long enough to enable Brigham to plant
and harvest a crop. The move to Montrose during the
growing season had further complicated Brigham's
task. His responsibilities weighed more heavily upon
him as he realized that according to the revelation the
Twelve's mission abroad had actually begun on April
26 at the Far West Temple site. His role as the president of that quorum multiplied the anxieties he felt.
And the conditions were worsened by an epidemic of
malaria caused by the swarms of mosquitoes that in-
fested the swamp areas near the river.

The situation became progressively worse as refugees continued to pour into the new gathering place,
either from Missouri, Quincy, or Ohio. Almost invariably they fell prey to the sickness and became charges
of the Saints who had preceded them there. By mid-
summer Joseph Smith's log cabin in Commerce over-
flowed with the sick and the dying as did a tent that had
been set up in his yard. The few other shelters in
Commerce and the rambling, decaying barracks in
Montrose across the river, where Brigham and many
other Saints had taken up temporary refuge, were sim-
ilarly littered. Joseph Smith had contracted the disease, which was characterized by alternating chills and
fevers. For days he lacked the energy to do little more
than satisfy his own needs and offer encouragement
and occasional sustenance to his family and to the refugees who had been invited to share his hospitality.
Having endured long enough the disease that had almost immobilized his people, Joseph, one sultry July
morning, arose from his bed, shook himself in the
manner of one ending a long hibernation, and, in effect, declared a holy war upon the disease that had so
dispirited his people. Beginning at his own house and
moving from there to the tent and to the other humble
dwellings in Commerce, the Prophet began to administer to the sick, rebuking their illness by the authority
of his priesthood. The results were astonishing. Many
were healed instantly. Others felt a new surge of vitali-

ty as they began to shake off the effects of the disease
that had immobilized and disheartened them. After
making the rounds in Commerce, the Prophet ferried
the river to Montrose, where the first call he made was
at the Brigham Young household. Joseph blessed his
disciple, along with his family, and Brigham, invigo-
rated by the spiritual power the Prophet had invoked
in his behalf, left his wife and children to accompany
Joseph in visiting and blessing the other Saints in and
near Montrose. Many were miraculously healed.

For many, the healing was merely a bright interlude in a dreary summer of illness. Brigham was
among these. The difficulty lay in the widespread nature of the disease and the seemingly inexhaustible
generations of mosquitoes that carried it. So while
Brigham Young was revived by the Prophet's blessing,
assisted him with vigor in administering to others, and
for several days afterward performed his work effectively, he soon fell prey to the debilitating illness again.
It had not left him by September 14, the day decided
upon for his departure. Brigham did not want to leave
his bed that hot, muggy morning, but he was impelled
by the constant pressure of the apostolic duties that
weighed upon him and by his love for the work and for
the people who had been and would be the recipients
of his ministry.

Brigham climbed from his bed, dressed, and
packed a small bag with clothing, a few toiletries, and
assorted Church literature. He then tidied up the
apartment with the help of the older children and
made Mary Ann as comfortable as possible. Still recuperating from the recent birth of Alice, Mary Ann was
quite weak, and unable to do much around the house.

Exhausted by this moderate activity that in days of
robust health would not have been worth recording,
Brigham was unable to walk to the river's edge, a mere
thirty rods away, where a small skiff waited to ferry
him to Nauvoo. There, by prearrangement, he was to
meet his companion, Heber C. Kimball. Seeing his dis-
ability, a generous neighbor, anxious to play a small
role in the senior Apostle's historic mission abroad,

helped him into his wagon and, after tearful goodbyes between Brigham and his family, drove him the short distance to the skiff.

The rhythmic movement of the small craft on the choppy waters of the Mississippi did little to improve Brigham's equilibrium, so that by the time he reached the other side he felt even less fit for the arduous mission that lay ahead.

He felt somewhat better on reaching shore, especially when he saw that the welcoming party consisted of his old friend from Mendon, Israel Barlow, who invited Brigham to mount his horse and ride to Heber C. Kimball's home. It required a supreme effort to climb aboard the horse behind Israel, where he clung to his friend until he was deposited at the front door of the Kimball home. There he was nursed by his friends for four days before he could muster enough strength to continue the journey toward England, a land that seemed so remote—it had already taken him five months to travel the comparatively short distance from Far West.

Word reached Mary Ann in Montrose that her husband's health had worsened after he reached Nauvoo. Leaving the older children in care of neighbors, she ferried the river with her new baby to offer comfort and help. She found that Heber was little better off than Brigham, as he too had contracted the river sickness.

On the eighteenth of September, despite the fact that neither of them was in any condition to travel, the intrepid pair decided they could delay no longer. Assisted by friends who had gathered to see them off, they mounted a wagon owned by Charles Hubbard and driven by his teenage son. As the wagon pulled away from the Kimball home, Vilate and Mary Ann were framed in the front door tearfully waving goodbye. So pitiful and forsaken did they look that the missionaries, desiring to break the spell of despondency that had settled upon the scene and to introduce a feeling of optimism and exhilaration, stood erect in the wagon, supporting each other to avoid falling. Removing their hats, they waved vigorously while shouting their good-byes.

We gain some insight into the penurious condition of these two Apostles when we learn that the hat Brigham clutched in his hand as he waved goodbye was made "out of a pair of old pantaloons." The "overcoat" he had packed in his bag consisted of a small quilt he had taken from a trundle bed in Mary Ann's austere apartment in Montrose. And between them, Brigham and Heber had cash totaling $13.50. Ahead lay a journey almost halfway around the world, at the end of which was a laborious mission that would require finances for self-maintenance, for the printing and distribution of vast quantities of Church literature, and for the organization and operation of a complex system for transporting to the United States the large harvest of converts they confidently expected to reap in the British Isles.

Brigham and Heber operated on no rigid timetable. They traveled only as far and as fast as their pinched finances and frail health allowed. On the first day, with Charlie Hubbard's willing boy at the reins, they covered only fourteen miles, reaching the humble dwelling of Brother and Sister Duel, where they were received warmly and spent the night. The following day Brother Duel drove them to Lima, and the day after that they were driven to Father Mikesells near Quincy. In this manner they were passed from one benefactor to another until, on October 1, they arrived at the home of Lorenzo Dow Young, who drove them to Springfield. There Brigham, who had been gaining strength along the way, suffered a relapse.

Although the Young brothers were not aware of it at the time, while Brigham waged an uphill but successful battle against poor health in Springfield, their aged father, John, was fighting a losing battle with death at Quincy. This grizzled patriarch, whose health had been broken during the brutal persecutions in Missouri and whom Brigham had seen and embraced for the last time as he and Heber passed through

Quincy, died peacefully on October 12 at age seventy-six. Characterized by Joseph Smith as a martyr for his religion, John Young was to exert an influence upon earthly affairs through the work of his children and their progeny. Their lives were to be profoundly affected by his granite-like character and integrity.

In some way as yet unexplained, the missionaries acquired a nondescript team of horses and a wagon at Springfield. They drove the team east with the help of George A. Smith, Theodore Turley, and Father Murray, Heber's father-in-law, who had joined them along the way. As Brigham had not fully regained his health by the time of their departure, he left Springfield flat on his back in a bed his friends had prepared for him in the bottom of the wagon.

By the time the party reached Terre Haute, Indiana, Brigham was much better and had begun to shoulder his share of the responsibilities, a fortunate circumstance, as it was here that Heber took ill again. At the time, the two Apostles were staying in the home of a Dr. Modisett, who, it was found later, was noted more for drunkenness than medical skill. On the evening Heber took ill, the doctor, who apparently held his liquor well, was seemingly sober, but was actually quite drunk. Observing Heber's condition, he prescribed a tablespoon of morphine. The remedy almost proved to be fatal. "A few minutes after he took it," Brigham wrote, "he straightened up in his chair, and said he felt very strange, and thought he would lie down; and on his making a motion to go to bed, he fell his length upon the floor. I sprang to him, rolled him over on his back, and put a pillow under his head." At this, Elder Kimball revived briefly and assured his companion, "Don't be scared, for I shan't die."

There were times during the hectic night that followed when Brigham had cause to doubt the accuracy of his companion's consoling words: "I changed his under clothing five times," he wrote, "and washed him previous to changing his clothes. I found him covered with sweat, at first like thin honey. This gradually wore out towards morning, and he sweat naturally. He was scarcely able to speak, so as to be understood, through the night."[1]

Heber's illness caused a breakup in the party, with Brigham and his fellow Apostle remaining behind while the other three went on with the team and wagon. As they parted, Elder Kimball, exhibiting the prophetic quality for which he was so widely known, predicted that he and Brigham, even without any sure means of transportation, would beat their companions to Kirtland. Like so many other of Heber C. Kimball's prophecies, the prediction was accurately fulfilled.

The pair began the trip from Terre Haute to Kirtland in the same way they had started from Nauvoo, with friends and fellow Saints alternating to give them rides from place to place. Beyond Pleasantville these rides ended. They decided to take the stage for whatever distance their meager funds would allow, both of them being too weakened by their illness to walk. But their lack of money was remedied by the unexplained appearance of money in their bags as the need arose. "On looking over our expenses," Brigham confided at the end of the trip, "I found we had paid out over $87.00, out of the $13.50 we had at Pleasant Garden, which is all the money we had to pay our passages, to my certain knowledge, to start on. We had travelled over 400 miles by stage, for which we paid from 8 to 10 cents a mile, and had eaten three meals a day, for each of which we were charged fifty cents, also fifty cents for our lodgings."[2]

Aside from his brother John and his sister Nancy Kent and their families, Brigham found little in Kirtland to please him. The spirit of apostasy and rebellion that had permeated the place in December, 1837, when he left was still present, although it had moderated to a small degree. This was evident from the fact that he and Heber were permitted to preach in the temple. But they were so vocal in defending Joseph Smith that the knot of apostates in control declared that the pulpits of the temple would never again be available to them. Because of the bitterness these malcontents felt toward Joseph, any praise of him was interpreted as being critical of them. And knowing of Brigham's and Heber's tendency to speak their minds, we may safely assume that their meaning was not left to mere inference, but that they addressed some words of blunt criticism and admonition to their uneasy listeners.

Barred from this building they had contributed so much to in erecting, they knew that in their day the Saints would never again be concentrated in large numbers in Kirtland. The city once so prominent in Church affairs had long since passed its zenith and now lay dwindling and decaying in the backwaters of history. All the faithful and dedicated members of the Church had already abandoned it, or would soon, leaving only the dead carcass of the temple and memories of the events that had occurred there. For Brigham and Heber there were other temples to build, other communities to establish, other worlds to conquer by the power of God and the unquenchable enthusiasm that burned within them.

The two Apostles and their companions left Kirtland with no regrets but the sadness of leaving loved ones. As they were now near commercial waterways, they sold their team and wagon and traveled by stage to nearby Fairport on Lake Erie, where they booked passage for Buffalo. Aboard the steamer one night a violent wind troubled Brigham, who was not yet accustomed to water travel. Going on deck he "felt impressed in spirit to pray to the Father, in the name of Jesus, for a forgiveness" of all his sins. "I felt to command the winds to cease," he wrote, "and let us go safe on our journey. The winds abated, and I felt to give the glory and honor and praise to that God who rules all things."[3]

Because of the need to stop along the way to replenish their funds and due to side excursions to visit family members or friends, Brigham and his companion took six weeks to cover the distance from Kirtland to New York. Arriving January 31, 1840, they were accommodated at the home of Parley P. Pratt at 55 Mott

Street. That night in his prayers Brigham thanked the
Lord for "having preserved us and brought us in safety so far on our mission to the nations of the earth."[4]

Brigham remained in New York and its environs
for almost six weeks preparing for his sea voyage. During this interval he spent his time profitably, visiting
and stirring up the local branches; arranging for his
fare and shipboard gear and food; and absorbing the
sights, sounds, and smells of the first metropolis he
had ever visited. He must have been fascinated by the
sense of throbbing energy the fast-paced life in New
York conveyed and by the indifference with which
New Yorkers seemed to regard each other and the
strangers in their midst. Anxious to broaden the scope
of his knowledge, Brigham visited the points of historic and cultural interest in New York—the famous bat-
tery, Central Park, the libraries and museums, and
other attractions.

On one sightseeing jaunt he suffered an injury
that, except for his quick thinking and iron nerves,
could have incapacitated him for weeks. Hurrying to
board a ferry headed for Manhattan, he lost his balance and fell on a heavy iron fitting connected to the
deck. The impact dislocated his left shoulder. While
prone on the deck, suffering intense pain, Brigham
gave explicit instructions about his care. "I asked
brother [Reuben] Hedlock to roll me over on my
back," he later wrote. "I directed brothers Kimball and
Hedlock to lay hold of my body, and brother [Parley]
Pratt to take hold of my hand and pull, putting his foot
against my side, while I guided the bone with my right
hand back to its place." With everyone performing exactly as Dr. Young prescribed, the shoulder slipped
back into its socket. His companions then made a sling
from a handkerchief in which he cradled his lame arm
until he reached home.[5]

The account of this painful incident, which another less stoic than he might have amplified to epic proportions, was distilled into a few terse sentences. In his
writing, as in his speaking, it was sufficient for

Brigham that he convey only the essence of his thoughts. He was as economical with his words as he was with his means.

It was foreign to Brigham's nature to ask for help, except that which he sought regularly and fervently from a divine source. So deeply ingrained were the habits of self-reliance and independence he had learned and practiced from infancy, that he called on others for assistance only in cases of dire emergency. And now such an emergency was upon him. He had frequently found it necessary to supplicate others as he traveled toward the Atlantic coast from Far West, gratefully accepting rides, food, and shelter from the kind Saints who had befriended him. In New York, as he prepared to sail to Liverpool, he found it necessary once again to throw himself upon the charity of the members, this time asking for money with which to pay his fare. Following a meeting with the Saints during which his need for financial help had been explained, $19.50 was placed in his hands. This was used to pay his steerage fare of $18.00 and his share of the cost of hiring the ship's cook, $1.00. The remaining 50¢ comprised his only cash surplus for the trip abroad.

In addition to the money, the Saints in the Manhattan branch had provided him with a straw-filled mattress and pillow and a supply of food, consisting mostly of dried fruits and vegetables, that was expected to see him through twenty-nine days at sea.

On March 29, 1840, Brigham and five companions, Heber C. Kimball; the Pratt brothers, Parley and Orson; George A. Smith; and Reuben Hedlock boarded a Black Ball Line packet ship, the *Patrick Henry*, which was loaded and ready to depart for England. On the wharf stood most of the Manhattan Branch, joined by members from the other New York burroughs, waving goodbye while singing "The Gallant Ship is Under Weigh." The missionaries joined in the refrain, singing loudly as long as they could hear voices from the shore. When these faded into silence, the missionaries, landlubbers all, except Heber C.

Kimball, who had been abroad once before, began to take inventory of their surroundings and to contemplate what lay ahead.

The ship had hardly begun to ride the comparatively gentle ground swells off the coast before Brigham was overcome with seasickness. It was unlike any illnesses he had experienced before. It began with a lightness of head and a violent nausea centered in the abdomen that soon infected his whole system with helpless agony. The fact that his steerage quarters were below deck in the bow of the ship did not help matters, as there the ventilation was poor, making the air stale if not fetid, and the movements of the ship were more pronounced there than anywhere else.

Often a sea voyager will adjust to the movements of a ship after a few days and lose his nausea. Brigham did not adjust, likely because of the residual effects of the malaria that had weakened him over a period of months and the dislocated shoulder he had suffered on the Brooklyn Ferry. As a result he spent most of the voyage in his bunk, tossed about by the pitching and rolling of the *Patrick Henry*. The movement became violent and terrifying eight days out when an angry storm tore away part of the bulwark of the ship and sent large volumes of water cascading below decks through the hatches.

Under these stressful conditions Brigham had little appetite for the meager shipboard fare that was served intermittently when the weather allowed. When he and his companions arrived in Liverpool on April 6, his loose-fitting clothes attested to the extraordinary weight loss he had suffered. The extent to which he had been emaciated is shown by the fact that Willard Richards did not at first recognize him.

Chapter Eleven

At Work Abroad

Preston was selected as the first headquarters of the Twelve because it was here Heber C. Kimball and his companions had established the first branch of the Church in England in the summer of 1837. On July 30 of that year these first missionaries baptized nine converts in the River Ribble in sight of thousands of curious watchers who had thronged the riverbank on a pleasant Sunday afternoon. The sense of drama and timing Heber and his associates injected into that service set the tone for the proselyting work that was to follow in Great Britain, including the work of the Twelve, now to be directed by Brigham Young. Knowing that outdoor baptisms were unusual in England and would therefore be an attention-getter, Heber and the brethren had set the service on Sunday, when they knew the nearby park would be swarming with people, and had given the event wide publicity several days in advance. The nine persons baptized that day formed the nucleus of the Preston Branch, which was later augmented by many other converts, most of whom had received their first exposure to the Church at this service or from the dramatic consequences that flowed from it.

Beginning with this auspicious event, the Church had steadily grown in Great Britain, resulting in first a trickle and then a stream of converts that flowed to the Mormon settlements in the United States, obedient to the call of the Prophet Joseph Smith to "gather" to Zion. But now the time had come to increase the stream to a veritable flood, and assembled in Preston to lay the groundwork for that enormous undertaking were seven members of the Twelve, the five who had

arrived on the *Patrick Henry* and Elders Wilford Woodruff and John Taylor, who had arrived in January and
had already enjoyed spectacular success.

These seven humble but powerful men met in
council April 14 to plan their proselyting assault upon
the staid and stolid Britons. With them was Willard
Richards, who previously had been called as a member
of the Twelve and who was now ordained and set apart
by his seven brethren. The eight then formally sustained Brigham Young as the President of the Twelve,
an action that had not been taken before due to the
scattered condition of the members of the quorum.

This organizational business having been disposed
of, the Brethren turned to important matters of policy
and procedure that were to govern their work in the
months ahead. Having been schooled by Joseph Smith
in the art of communication and publicity, they first
decided upon the publication of a monthly periodical
to be the official voice of the Church in Great Britain.
By this means they expected to interest investigators in
the doctrines of the Church and to instruct and unify
its members. Given the name *Millennial Star* at another
quorum meeting held on April 16, this publication became the literary provender for many generations of
Latter-day Saints in the British Isles. Parley P. Pratt,
who had a gift for words, was designated as the first editor of the *Star,* although he had much to learn from
the president of his quorum about the acumen and
daring essential to the success of a business enterprise.

A committee chaired by Brigham Young was appointed at the April 15 general conference to make a
selection of hymns to be used by the Saints in their worship services. At the April 16 council meeting he was
also appointed to chair a committee to obtain the British copyright for the Book of Mormon and the Doctrine and Covenants prior to their publication.

When these vital matters had been resolved, the
Apostles went in different directions to pursue their
proselyting. Brigham teamed up with Wilford Woodruff, who had already experienced phenomenal success in Herefordshire. En route there the pair stopped

in historic Worcester near the birthplace of Shake-
speare at Stratford-upon-Avon, where they attended
Church of England services in the great cathedral.
The Apostles were awed by the architectural grandeur
of this famous church, but were disappointed by the
cold, impersonal nature of the services, which were devoid of the spiritual warmth that characterized their
own. To them the contrast illustrated the difference
between a dead church and a living one. Theirs was a
dynamic organization, founded upon the principle of
revelation, whose energizing power, made manifest
through the Holy Ghost, was available to each member
for his personal guidance. It was precisely this difference, and the need to call it to the attention of every nation, that had prompted Joseph Smith to send the
Twelve abroad at a time when their spiritual strength
and dedication were sorely needed at home.

When Brigham and Wilford reached their destination on April 22, just sixteen short days after Brigham
and his companions had arrived at Liverpool, they
went first to the home of John Benbow, a wealthy
farmer in Ledbury, who, with hundreds of other
members of a group known as the United Brethren,
had been baptized by Wilford Woodruff only the previous month.

Now he had returned with the president of his
quorum, Brigham Young, who wanted to see the fruits
of the labors of his fellow Apostle and who was anxious
to capitalize on the new strength these converts added
to the work in England.

Brigham was pleased with what he found. Not only
had Wilford Woodruff's harvest been bounteous in
the number of converts, but also in the faith and dedication of the converts. When, for example, in meetings
held with the new Saints, it was made known that the
Apostles lacked the means to publish a hymnbook and
a British edition of the Book of Mormon, John Benbow and Thomas Kington came forward to offer £350
for this purpose, a substantial sum for that time and
place.

Brigham's month-long stay in Herefordshire was

not only marked by the temporal harvest of the
Benbow-Kington donations, but by a demonstration
of extraordinary spiritual power that healed the sick,
cast out devils, and made the lame to walk. This is best
illustrated by the remarkable case of Mary Pitt, who
had not walked for eleven years, and whose legs were
so crippled she had to be carried into the pool to be
baptized. On the evening of May 18, 1840, at the home
of Brother Kington in Dymock, Elders Young and
Woodruff, assisted by Willard Richards, who had followed them to Herefordshire, laid hands upon Mary
Pitt's head and blessed her. Wilford Woodruff recorded the results in his ever-present journal:
"Brigham Young being mouth, rebuked her lameness
in the name of the Lord, and commanded her to arise
and walk. The lameness left her, and she never afterwards used a staff or crutch. She walked through the
town of Dymock next day, and created a stir among the
people thereby; but the wicked did not feel to give God
the glory."[1]

A main source of the enormous spiritual power
Brigham Young exercised in the ministry derived
from his habit of frequent, fervent prayer. Whether
standing in the pulpit or the marketplace, whether
walking, sitting, or kneeling, he felt the need and the
freedom to implore God for guidance and sustenance.
He was never reluctant to invoke heavenly blessings
upon anything pertaining to his work or welfare, even
though the matter at hand was commonplace. He had
learned from Joseph Smith that because of free agency
God does not enter one's personal life unbidden, but
only in response to an invitation through prayer.

Brigham Young's commitment to prayer also extended into the public realm, where he insisted that
prayer be an unvarying element in any Church activity. Thus, all Mormon socials and entertainments,
whether dances, plays, parties, or athletic events, were
commenced with prayer.

More important, perhaps, to the work of his quorum were the group prayers offered when Brigham

assembled with the Apostles to counsel and to lay plans for the future. On these occasions the Brethren were able to focus attention upon problems of common concern and to pool their spiritual and mental resources in their solution. During the exodus, Brigham often invited members of the Twelve and other selected leaders to join him in group prayers in secluded places, where they implored God for special blessings.

In Herefordshire in the latter part of May, 1840, Brigham and his fellow Apostles Wilford Woodruff and Willard Richards felt a need to communicate with God in a solitary place. The site selected was Herefordshire Beacon, one of the higher peaks in the Malvern Hills, a low range of mountains near Worcester and Ledbury. Upon its slopes lay the ruins of an ancient fortification said to have been erected by the Britons of Saluria and later overrun and occupied by the disciplined legions of Rome. Here, amidst the decaying remnants of war, the three Apostles of peace knelt to offer thanks to God for his many blessings to them and to implore him for guidance. After their prayer and the lengthy deliberations that followed, the trio reached important decisions that were to have a lasting effect upon their labors in Britain. "[We] agreed," wrote Brigham, "that, since we had obtained £250 from brother John Benbow, and £100 from brother Kington, towards publishing the Book of Mormon and Hymn Book, I should repair immediately to Manchester, and join the brethren appointed with me as a committee, and publish 300[0] copies of the Hymn Book without delay. It was also voted that the same committee publish 5,000 copies of the Book of Mormon, with an index affixed. I started for Manchester (accompanied by Elder Kington a short distance,) and went to Wolverhampton."[2]

En route to Manchester, Brigham visited George A. Smith and Theodore Turley, who had been working with success in Burslem and the Potteries since May 9, when Elder Turley was released from the Stafford jail. He had been incarcerated ostensibly on a

stale and flimsy charge arising from an earlier contrac-
tual obligation, but actually to prevent him from
proselyting.

In Manchester, after receiving the affirming vote
of the members of the Twelve who were not present at
the "Beacon Council," Brigham went forward with the
negotiations to have the Book of Mormon printed and
to collect and arrange the music for the hymnbook.

His return nearly coincided with the publication of
the first issue of the *Millennial Star,* whose front cover
bore a poem composed by Parley P. Pratt, "The Morning Breaks, the Shadows Flee." This gifted man, whose
fruitful missionary labors in Canada in 1836 foreshadowed the later work in Great Britain, and whose productions were to grace the pages of the *Star* for many
months, was the last of the Apostles to leave the British
Isles after the concentrated proselyting effort in the
early 1840s. His literary skill, combined with Brigham
Young's hardheaded business acumen, established the
Millennial Star on a firm foundation that endured for
over one hundred and thirty years. Brigham's role in
this enterprise is best told in his own words: "I wrote to
brother Pratt [from Herefordshire] for information
about his plans, and he sent me his prospectus, which
stated that when he had a sufficient number of sub-
scribers and money enough in hand to justify his publishing the paper, he would proceed with it. How long
we might have waited for that I know not, but I wrote
to him to publish two thousand papers, and I would
foot the bill."[3]

In this aggressive, self-confident manner Brigham
Young, aided by the members of his quorum and
other leaders, laid the foundation for missionary work
in the British Isles. We gain an appreciation for the
magnitude of that work when we read the summary of
it Brigham included in his personal history: "It was
with a heart full of thanksgiving and gratitude . . . ," he
wrote at the conclusion of his British Mission, "that I
reflected upon [God's] dealings with me and my
brethren of the Twelve during the past year of my life,
which was spent in England. It truly seemed a miracle

to look upon the contrast between our landing and departing from Liverpool. We landed in the spring of 1840, as strangers in a strange land and penniless, but through the mercy of God we have gained many friends, established Churches in almost every noted town and city in the kingdom of Great Britain, baptized between seven and eight thousand, printed 5,000 Books of Mormon, 3,000 Hymn Books, 2,500 volumes of the *Millennial Star,* and 50,000 tracts, and emigrated to Zion 1,000 souls, established a permanent shipping agency, which will be a great blessing to the Saints, and have left sown in the hearts of many thousands the seeds of eternal truth, which will bring forth fruit to the honor and glory of God, and yet we have lacked nothing to eat, drink or wear."[4]

One unacquainted with the author of those words might consider him to have been boastful. Indeed, that charge has been leveled at Brigham Young both by those intent on blackening his name and those ignorant of the facts. While it is true that he was outspoken, hard-driving, and self-confident, it is equally true that in his attitude toward God and in his dealings with those in authority over him, he was as humble and submissive as a child. We see this aspect of Brigham's character more clearly from a statement he made in 1871 following a recital of the achievements of the Twelve in Great Britain thirty years before. Said he: "Was it our ability? No. Is it our ability that has accomplished what we see here in building up a colony in the wilderness? Is it the doings of man? No. To be sure we assist in it, and we do as we are directed. But God is our Captain; he is our master. He is the 'one man' that we serve. In him is our light, in him is our life; in him is our hope, and we serve him with an undivided heart, or we should do so.

"What do you suppose I think when I hear people say, 'O, see what the Mormons have done in the mountains. It is Brigham Young. What a head he has got! What power he has got! How well he controls the people!' The people are ignorant of our true character. It is the Lord that has done this. It is not any one man or set of men; only as we are led and guided by the spirit of truth. It is the oneness, wisdom, power, knowledge and providences of God; and all that we can say is, we are his servants and handmaids, and let us serve him with an undivided heart."[5]

To understand fully the character of Brigham Young, one must grasp the significance of this statement, for it reveals the mainspring of all his actions. At the heart of everything he did was his knowledge that God is a living reality, and that he had a personal responsibility as God's earthly mouthpiece.

During the year Brigham Young served in England, he presided at four general conferences. The last of these convened in Manchester on April 6, 1841, the anniversary of his arrival in Liverpool. On this occasion almost sixty-five hundred Saints crowded into Carpenter's Hall, a facility the Brethren had used as a permanent meeting place for several months. Included in this number, in addition to the Apostles, were over six hundred priesthood bearers. The reports given at this historic meeting illustrated the aggressive competence of the missionaries and the enthusiastic manner in which the British had taken to the Latter-day Saint doctrines. By this time there were missionaries in Scotland and Wales. The banners of Mormonism had also been carried into Ireland and the Isle of Man by John Taylor, and into London by Elders Kimball, Woodruff, and George A. Smith.

The British converts had been profoundly affected by the concept of "gathering," which had been assiduously taught by the elders from the beginning. This doctrine admonished all converts to migrate to Zion, meaning America, and more particularly, Nauvoo. This was not a difficult idea to accept for those who had been shackled by a relatively authoritarian society. Most of them were locked into an economic status that offered little prospect of rising above a mere subsistence level, and their educational status practically condemned them to perpetual ignorance. To those whose lives had taken on an aura of futility, the call of the elders to gather to Zion had a special appeal. "Yes, friends," an issue of the *Millennial Star* beckoned, "this glorious work has but just commenced; and we now call upon the Saints to come forward with united effort, with persevering exertion, and with union of action, and help yourselves and one another to emigrate to the Land of Promise." Then, warming to his subject, the eloquent editor implored: "Ye children of Zion, once more we say, in the name of Israel's God, arise, break off your shackles, loose yourselves from the bands of your neck, and go forth to inherit the earth, and to build up waste places of many generations."[6]

Impassioned pleas of this kind and the aggressive preaching of the elders had their desired effect. No sooner did converts enter the waters of baptism than they were imbued with a consuming desire to emigrate to Zion, to Nauvoo the Beautiful, the land of promise, where they could live constantly under the direct influence of a living prophet.

In June, 1840, only two months after Brigham Young and his companions arrived in England, the first company of Mormon emigrants sailed for America on the packet ship *Britannia*. Consisting of forty recent converts filled with excitement and anticipation, this vanguard company, departing from the same Liverpool docks that had welcomed Brigham Young, would mark the path so many other emigrant companies would follow across the turbulent Atlantic and around the tip of Florida to New Orleans. From there it was a comparatively quiet river trip up the Mississippi to Nauvoo.

As the proselyting work accelerated, the frequency and size of the emigrating companies increased proportionately. In February, 1841, for example, Brigham Young, assisted by John Taylor and Willard Richards, supervised the departure of two companies within two weeks, one consisting of 235 members that sailed on the *Sheffield* on February 7, and the other consisting of 109 members that left on the *Echo* on February 16.

Toward the end of Brigham's stay in Great Britain, emigration had become big business. The emigrant

companies were departing with ever-increasing frequency, and the accelerated tempo of missionary work
was such that the Brethren foresaw the need for a
long-range plan to handle the details of the emigration
and to provide temporary financial aid for the indi-
gent converts who wanted to gather to Zion. Thus was
laid the groundwork of the Perpetual Emigration
Fund, which was to remain in existence until the late
1880s, when it was dissolved pursuant to the
Edmunds-Tucker Act. Those who received aid from
this fund were expected to repay it as soon as their financial circumstances allowed, thereby making the
money available to other needy Saints planning to emigrate.

This novel concept originated in the fertile, inspired mind of Brigham Young. Typically, however,
the skeletal idea was fleshed out with a profusion of details that bore the clear imprint of his organizational
genius. It was not sufficient that the emigrants merely
be transported from England to Zion. They went in
true Mormon–Brigham Young style, fully organized,
instructed, and motivated. Passage for an entire company was booked by a Church representative, thus
protecting individual passengers from the depredations of dishonest shipping agents. Ordinarily, the
elders responsible for the conversion of emigrants
would accompany them to Liverpool, introduce them
to their new companions, and get them settled aboard
ship. Once on board, the passengers were divided into
smaller groups usually presided over by three men
comparable to a bishopric. During the long trip, these
men acted as confidants and advisers to those under
their supervision and directed social, cultural, and religious activities.

The cohesion and sense of purpose that characterized Mormon emigrant companies set them apart
from all others. And as word spread about them and as
their number and frequency increased, they became
an object of national interest and, in some quarters, of
concern. Especially agitated were the pastors of other
churches, who began to feel the strain as they saw

many of their members flock to the Mormon standard. What was even more distressing was the aggressive sense of evangelism that descended upon Mormon converts. They seemed bent upon converting all Britons and transporting them to Zion. In defense, many clerics and others who helped mold public opinion lampooned and caricatured the Latter-day Saints, portraying them as a group of misguided and gullible zealots. Occasionally the Saints retaliated in kind, as evidenced by this apocryphal story related by Joseph Smith of an Englishman who sought to deter an acquaintance from migrating to America:

" 'Your preacher preaches false doctrine,' exclaimed a sectarian in Manchester to one of the Saints. 'Ah!' inquired the other, 'wherein does he teach false doctrine?' 'Why, in telling the people to go to America, to be sure,' said the sectarian; 'and' continued he, 'there is nothing in the Bible that commands people to go to America.' 'Ah!' replied the other, 'and there is nothing in the Bible that commands people to stop in Manchester; so I wonder how you dare stay in so unscriptural a place another night; for certainly no one ought to live in England unless they can find scripture for it, any more than in America.' "[7]

Brigham and six other members of the Twelve, Heber C. Kimball, Orson Pratt, Wilford Woodruff, John Taylor, George A. Smith, and Willard Richards boarded the sailing ship *Rochester* in Liverpool on April 20, 1841, headed for home. With them were 123 converts. Left behind were two other members of the Twelve, Parley P. Pratt, who was to head the British Mission while publishing the *Millennial Star,* and Orson Hyde, who was preparing to leave for the Holy Land to fulfill a mission assigned to him by Joseph Smith.

Brigham enjoyed the first two days at sea like an experienced voyager. He strode the decks, wrote in his journal, read the scriptures, and gave assistance to the members of the company who had taken ill almost the moment the *Rochester* began to ride the ground swells. On the third day, however, Brigham joined the others

on the sick list as the ship encountered violent head-
winds that tore away the fore-topsail. By April 28 the
storm raged violently. The passengers did not sleep
much that night, as the pitching and rolling of the ship
loosened cargo and gear that was thrown about wildly,
endangering the passengers, many of whom were
thrown to the deck. Despite this chaos and terror, no
one was killed or seriously injured. The next day conditions improved when for the first time the *Rochester*
encountered fair winds.

This set the pattern for the balance of the voyage,
as the Rochester alternately encountered bad, then
good, weather. While the weather was good, Brigham
used his time profitably. His natural inquisitiveness
and intelligence led him to study the navigation and
management of the ship. He was especially interested
in the guidance mechanism, and during the time he
was aboard he learned how to box the compass.

Aside from the customary hazards and difficulties
that attended sea voyages of the day, the only tragic oc-
currence was the unexpected death of Peter
Maughan's six-week-old daughter. The incident was
made even more poignant for the father by the fact
that he had buried his wife just a few weeks before. His
daughter's tiny body was sewn in a canvas, weighted,
and buried at sea.

The *Rochester* arrived in New York harbor on May
20. A head wind made docking at Ellis Island impossible. This necessitated loading the passengers' gear on
lighters and transporting it to the customs house,
where it was unloaded, inspected, reloaded, and taken
to the docks on Manhattan Island. There pandemoni-
um reigned. "We found them covered with horses and
drays," wrote Brigham, "and a great crowd of dray-
men and pickpockets, who stood ready to leap on
board and devour all our baggage." The tough, resourceful dockhands, who often garnered business or
imposed on shy and frightened immigrants by their intimidating aggressions, were quite unprepared for the
resistance offered by the leader of this group. "Many
attempts were made to steal our baggage," Brigham

recalled. "I collared some of the thieves, and threatened to throw them overboard if they would not let it
alone. I was under the necessity of striking their fingers to keep them from carrying off the trunks they
laid hold of."[8]

Brigham and his fellow Apostles remained in the
New York area for several weeks, setting the local
branches in order and strengthening the Saints.

When it came time to travel on to Nauvoo, they
selected a route that took them by streamer up the
Delaware to Philadelphia. From there, by canal boat
and railway, they traveled to Pittsburgh and thence
down the Ohio River to the Mississippi. There they
caught a riverboat up the Mississippi to Nauvoo.

On the landing to greet Brigham were Mary Ann
and the older children, along with the Prophet Joseph
Smith and many of the Saints. It was then Brigham
learned that during his absence Mary Ann had moved
across the river from Montrose to a small cabin in Nauvoo.

Chapter Twelve

At Nauvoo

An absence of almost two years had wrought an enormous change in Brigham's family. Elizabeth, the oldest child, was now a mature sixteen, and, according to the mores of the day, almost of marriageable age. Alice, the youngest, who was a mere infant when her father left Nauvoo in September, 1839, was now a toddler, and the oldest son, Joseph, had reached baptismal age during the interval.

As for Mary Ann, her husband's absence had been both a trial and a blessing—a trial because of the loneliness she had felt with her companion gone, and a blessing because the added responsibilities she had had to shoulder had developed important qualities of competence and independence.

Wanting to be nearer the center of things, Mary Ann had left the barracks apartment in Montrose and had moved to an unfinished log cabin on a lot in Nauvoo that adjoined the residence of Vinson Knight, the bishop of Lower Ward. A block east and a short distance south of the new Young residence were the "Homestead," the original Nauvoo residence of Joseph Smith, and the site of the "Mansion House," the new, larger Smith home that was to be completed later. Also within a short distance from the Young residence were the homes of other leaders of the Church, who, along with the Saints, were involved in the exciting enterprise of building a new city destined to become the second largest and the most noted city of its day in Illinois.

Brigham soon discovered that his new home site was not yet an Eden. The lot was "so swampy that when

the first attempt was made to plow it the oxen mired."
However, after the flat was drained, it "became a very
valuable garden spot."[1]

Within ten days after Brigham's return to Nauvoo,
the Prophet received a special revelation that fully
compensated his obedient disciple for all the travail he
had suffered while filling his British mission: "Dear
and well-beloved brother, Brigham Young," it began,
"verily thus saith the Lord unto you: . . . it is no more
required at your hand to leave your family as in times
past, for your offering is acceptable to me. I have seen
your labor and toil in journeyings for my name. I
therefore command you to send my word abroad, and
take especial care of your family from this time, hence-
forth and forever."[2]

A radical change in the status of the Twelve occurred the following month. Up until this time, the
Twelve had had little, if anything, to do with the administration of Church affairs at home. Their responsibility had been proselyting in the world, away from
Church headquarters. Below the level of the First
Presidency, the stake presidencies, high councils, and
bishops had exercised the principal ecclesiastical authority at home. These leaders had not, therefore,
been subject to the direction of the Twelve.

On this occasion, however, Joseph Smith, who was
unable to attend because of the death of his infant son,
Don Carlos, sent word that Brigham Young was to
conduct a meeting scheduled on August 16, 1841. The
awkwardness the President of the Twelve felt in occupying this position is evident in the minutes of the
meeting: "The speaker [Brigham Young] hoped that
no one would view him and his brethren as aspiring,
because they had come forward to take part in the proceedings before the conference; he could assure the
brethren that nothing could be further from his
wishes, and those of his quorum, than to interfere with
Church affairs in Zion and her stakes. He had been in
the vineyard so long, he had become attached to foreign missions, and nothing could induce him to retire
therefrom and attend to the affairs of the Church at

home but a sense of duty, the requirements of heaven, or the revelations of God; to which he would always submit, be the consequence what it might."

Any question about the propriety or the meaning of the President of the Twelve taking charge of a meeting in the stakes was answered during the afternoon session. Taking his accustomed place at the pulpit, the Prophet Joseph announced to a surprised though supportive audience that "the time had come when the Twelve should be called upon to stand in their place next to the First Presidency, and attend to the settling of emigrants and the business of the Church at the stakes, and assist to bear off the kingdom victoriously to the nations."[3]

While the full import of what was done on this occasion was not readily apparent to the general membership of the Church, those close to the Prophet and who had studied the revelations understood it well. What he did was to make effective a conditional power and authority that had been given to the Twelve at the time they were first ordained. The revelations had made it clear that the Twelve comprised a quorum equal in authority and responsibility to the First Presidency, so that it had the inherent power to perform any act when assigned to do so by the Prophet, who held the keys. Those keys had now been turned, opening to Brigham Young and the Twelve a wide field of endeavor that would bring into play the full scope of their abilities and energies.

In retrospect we can see many reasons why such a radical shift in administrative emphasis occurred at this time. Joseph, whose chief strength lay in the spiritual realms, needed relief from the daily press of administrative detail to give him time to pray, to reflect, and to study. His dominant role was one of generalship, of strategic planning in accordance with divine revelation. In the short period the Saints had occupied Commerce, or Nauvoo, Joseph had set in motion an awesome train of initiatives that were in various stages of development or projection when Brigham and the Twelve returned from abroad. A model city was being built to accommodate the Ohio and Missouri refugees and the hundreds of converts now flocking in from abroad and elsewhere. A novel form of government had been devised for the new city, based on a broad charter granted by the Illinois legislature that invested Nauvoo with a power and autonomy never held before nor since by another American city. The charter authorized and projected an independent militia, the Nauvoo Legion; a university; and a court system possessing the authority to issue writs of habeas corpus. A magnificent temple was to crown the rise above the bottom lands, and a modern hotel was planned near the river to accommodate the ever-increasing flow of tourists.

All these and many more enterprises required the constant, disciplined attention of qualified managers and administrators. Where better to look for such men than among the Twelve, who had demonstrated their capacity and dependability in the British Isles?

Thus, following the pivotal August 16 meeting, Brigham and his brethren of the Twelve took their place next to the Prophet in the governing hierarchy of the Church, with worldwide authority and responsibility. With that crucial step Joseph began to groom and train these men for the role of pioneering leadership he foresaw for them.

The time between August, 1841, and June, 1842, was of momentous importance to Brigham Young. It was a period of learning and of testing and trial. Joseph Smith was the catalyst that produced both results.

The learning came from what seemed to be an endless round of meetings, councils, and consultations with the Prophet. The scope of his instruction on this and numerous other occasions was as broad as life itself. At the December 30 meeting, for example, he taught them about the operations and power of spiritual beings. At another meeting, he talked in the most practical terms about charity. At still another, he expounded on the Book of Mormon.

The testing came from the doctrine of the plurality

of wives. As early as April, 1841, Joseph Smith took his first plural wife. This fateful step was accompanied by much trepidation and foreboding, emotions that were not inspired by uncertainty as to the correctness of the action, but that grew from a knowledge of the catastrophic effect it would have upon the Church and its members.

Once Joseph had begun to live this principle, he also taught it to some of his close associates. After the Twelve returned from abroad, he taught them the doctrine. However, unlike many faithless brethren who had surrounded Joseph while they were gone, the Twelve accepted the principle to a man. But it was not easy for them, nor did they accept it blindly. They were men of experience and perception, and were well aware of the abuse and scorn that would be heaped upon them once they became polygamists.

At this time the law did not prohibit polygamous marriages. Therefore, the issues that confronted the Twelve when Joseph presented the doctrine to them were grounded in morality and conscience. Was it wrong for a man to have more than one wife? Would it offend his personal sensibilities to live as a polygamist? When the new doctrine was first presented to Brigham and the Twelve, these issues stirred up profound conflicts within them. The doctrine seemed to run counter to their background and to the Christian teachings they had expounded as missionaries. Yet the scriptures demonstrated that many ancient prophets who were polygamists had found favor with God. And the Book of Mormon, which they accepted as being of divine origin, made it plain that while monogamy is the customary marital relationship, polygamy is permissible when directed by God for the purpose of raising up "seed" unto him. (See Jacob 2:27-30.)

While these considerations made the doctrine intellectually acceptable, unqualified endorsement came about from the operation of spiritual forces. This is particularly evident in the case of Brigham Young. Mary Ann, years after the event, confided in a grandson, Seldon Y. Clawson, that while her husband was struggling with the issue, she, by chance, overheard a conversation in which Brigham informed Joseph Smith that the Lord had "revealed" the divinity of the principle to him. Brigham confirmed this once in an address to the Saints, implying that the first intimation of the doctrine came to him by spiritual means while he was in Great Britain, months before Joseph broached the subject to him: "While we were in England, I think, the Lord manifested to me by visions and his Spirit, things that I did not then understand. I never opened my mouth to any person concerning them, until I returned to Nauvoo. . . . When I returned home and Joseph revealed these things to me, I then understood the reflections that were upon my mind while in England." Then, he related details that coincide with the story Mary Ann shared with her grandson: "When I told Joseph what I understood, which was right in front of my house in the street, as he was shaking hands and leaving me, he turned round and looked me in the eyes, and says he—'Brother Brigham, are you speaking what you understand,—are you in earnest?' Says I—'I speak just as the Spirit manifests to me.' Says he—'God bless you, the Lord has opened your mind,' and he turned and went off."[4]

Following these events, and with the full approval and blessing of Mary Ann, Brigham Young married his first plural wife, Lucy Ann Decker, on June 15, 1842. This faithful, energetic woman, who was twenty at the time of her marriage, was to bear seven children and survive her husband by thirteen years.

Within less than a month after his marriage to Lucy Ann, Brigham passed another milestone in his domestic life when his oldest daughter, Elizabeth, married Edmund Ellsworth. Still another family highlight occurred that summer, when, on August 1, Mary Ann gave birth to her fifth child and third daughter, Luna. This increased to seven the number of Brigham Young's children.

With a family this size, including two living wives, and with the probability that other wives and children would be added later, Brigham was under great pressure to earn a living. He labored unceasingly, either in pursuit of his artisan skills or in following other lines of endeavor that his experience and new leadership status opened up to him. He now began to engage in some construction and in handling real estate transactions. An ad that appeared in the *Nauvoo Neighbor* in the spring of 1843 sheds an interesting light on Brigham's financial dealings. It announced that he would leave soon on a mission and had lots and buildings he would sell very cheap.

The mission to which this advertisement referred was one to the eastern United States to collect funds for the Nauvoo House and the temple. A few months earlier, however, there was serious doubt among some of Brigham's family and friends that he would ever fill another mission in mortality. In the latter part of 1842 he was afflicted with an illness at first diagnosed as a light attack of apoplexy. When he began to rally, little attention was paid to his illness, it being looked upon merely as one of the passing maladies to which the residents of Nauvoo had become accustomed. Within a day, however, ominous symptoms began to appear. The most fearsome of these was a burning fever that produced intermittent delirium accompanied by nausea, vomiting, and violent retching.

At Mary Ann's request, the Prophet came, with Willard Richards, to administer to Brigham. Joseph remained for six hours comforting his friend and disciple and giving assurance to Mary Ann and the family that the promise of recovery given in the blessing would be fulfilled.

Had not Mary Ann possessed implicit confidence in that blessing, the eighteen days that followed would have been all but unbearable. During that time, Brigham was racked with a fever of such intensity that the skin peeled off over the entire surface of his body. One story connected with the episode is that Isaac Decker, clad in a greatcoat, boots, and mittens, suffered frostbite on his fingers and toes while fanning Brigham to keep him cool.[5]

At the end of eighteen days the fever broke, leaving Brigham Young near death. Bolstered up in a chair to relieve the tedium of lying for so long, he sat like a corpse, with glazed, staring eyes that would not close. Without warning, his mouth fell open, his jaw slackened, and his breathing stopped. Alarmed, Mary Ann doused his face with cold water to revive him. There was no response. She then threw camphor into his face and eyes with like results. As a last resort she applied a technique of artificial respiration that is now commonly used but in that day was rare. Mary Ann "held my nostrils between her thumb and finger," Brigham later explained, "and placing her mouth directly over mine, blew into my lungs until she filled them with air. This set my lungs in motion, and I again began to breathe."[6]

There can be little doubt that Brigham's life was preserved on this occasion by the quick thinking and resourcefulness of his wife. This woman who gave so much and asked so little was a model of Christian charity. Stoically and uncomplainingly, she bore the burden of the numerous and diverse roles in which she was cast—wife, mother, manager, nurse, confidante. She shifted easily and surely from one role to the other, bestowing on each the same intelligent aptitude and concern. During Brigham's frequent trips away from home, her responsibilities and the demands upon her time were multiplied as she endeavored to fill the void created by his absence. We perceive some special qualities in Mary Ann's character and comprehend better how Brigham's domestic relations contributed powerfully to his success from an incident that occurred during his trip east to collect funds for the temple and the Nauvoo House.

In company with Wilford Woodruff and E. P. Maginn, Brigham left Nauvoo on July 7, 1843, on the steamer *Rapids*, which took them downriver to Saint Louis. From there, by steamer or coach, they made their way eastward via Louisville, Pittsburgh, and Philadelphia. At each stop along the route, the travelers pleaded with the Saints who assembled to hear them that they be liberal in donating for the support of mis-

sionary work. In his pocket Brigham carried a letter
signed by the Prophet, designating him as a "legal
agent" to collect funds for this purpose and containing
words of praise that imbued him with zeal and a special
sense of urgency.

Because of the imperious mandate that had impelled him along since his elevation to the apostleship
seven years before, and because of the new momen-
tum the Prophet's recent call had provided, Brigham
seemed oblivious to all else except the mission at hand.
Yet he did not entirely ignore or neglect his family, as
he wrote newsy, though brief, letters home at regular
intervals. But he did not spend undue time in reflec-
tive concern about his family, as all had been well when
he left home, and he had full confidence in Mary
Ann's judgment and competence. However, a letter
from her dated August 16 had a spirit so foreign to her
usual serene character as to arouse feelings of concern
and foreboding. The letter turned out to be a veritable
compendium of woe: "Our little family is quietly resting in bed," she began, "which has been very seldom
for four weeks past. I was taken with influenza and Colamorbus the first," she confided. Young Brigham
came next. He "was taken with the Scarlot fever." Before he could recover, "the three little girls were
taken." Then Mary, who was young Brigham's twin,
"had the canker so she did not swallow for ten or
eleven days anything but drink except a little fish flesh
once." Finally, it was reported that Vilate "was taken
very sick one week with scarlot fever" and that "the
Colamorbus took hold of her yesterday in a very severe
manner so she appeared nigh unto death." The only
member of the family at home who appears to have
avoided these multiple plagues was nine-year-old
Joseph.

As Mary Ann re-read this letter, she apparently
realized what a black, though factual, picture it painted, and sought to soften it. "I do not want to say things
to you to trouble you," she apologized. "You must excuse me for saying so much about the distress we have
passed through."[7]

But any hint in Mary Ann's letter that the storm was over or was subsiding was premature. In less than two weeks her namesake, Mary Ann, who was a few months less than seven years old, died of what was diagnosed as "dropsy of the heart." The inefficient postal service of the day, coupled with Brigham's erratic travel schedule, delayed the notification of his daughter's death, so that he did not learn about it until some time after her burial. This shifted the full burden of the funeral arrangements to the grieving mother.

Within a few months after his fund-raising tour through the eastern states, Brigham was to return there, this time on an errand quite foreign to his experience and personal tastes. He went this time as a political campaigner promoting the presidential candidacy of the Prophet Joseph Smith.

The events that led to the decision for Joseph to run for the presidency were complex and fraught with explosive implications. At the root of the problem were the lingering antagonisms stirred up by the Missouri expulsion and the bitterness engendered by the Nauvoo apostates over the polygamy issue. Abortive attempts had been made by Missouri officials to extradite the Prophet to stand trial on the stale and unsubstantiated charges of treason and murder that had hung over his head when he escaped from the Liberty jail; and to answer to charges of complicity in the assault on ex-Governor Lilburn W. Boggs, who was shot in the head by an unknown assailant in May, 1842. The anxieties created by these difficulties were intensified when the Nauvoo apostates, including John C. Bennett and William Law, linked hands with the Missourians in an attempt to destroy Joseph Smith.

In the meantime the Prophet and his followers had not been idle in this controversy. With the aid of legal counsel, frequently relying upon the vast powers of the Nauvoo courts, Joseph was able to fight off every attempt at extradition. And, with the assistance of the Twelve and other leaders, repeated attempts were made to obtain federal reparations for the injuries and damages suffered by the Saints at the hands of the Missouri mobs. All these efforts were unavailing, however, being countered on every hand with the advice that any redress must come from the Missouri courts or legislature, bodies that were controlled by the Saints' bitterest enemies.

In an effort to breach the wall of federal indifference to the plight of their people, the Mormon leaders polled presidential hopefuls in the latter part of 1843 to ascertain their attitudes toward reparations for the Saints. The results were disheartening. Indeed, only two of them, Henry Clay and John C. Calhoun, had the courtesy to reply. And they held out no hope whatsoever.

It was against this dreary background that, in January, 1844, the Church leadership decided that "Joseph Smith be a candidate for the next Presidency" and that "all honorable means" be used to secure his election.[8] Having been rebuffed by both federal and state officials, the obvious intention of the Saints was to take their case to the people.

As President of the Twelve, Brigham Young had the responsibility to assign and supervise the speakers who would campaign. At the April general conference, 344 brethren volunteered to go on the stump in support of Joseph's candidacy. These speakers were assigned by Brigham Young to conduct forty-seven "general conferences" in the twenty-six existing states between May 4 and September 15. The final conference was scheduled to be held in the nation's capital from September 7 through September 15, where the campaigners expected to reap a publicity bonanza resulting from the interest they hoped to generate during four months of intensive electioneering.

The admonitions Brigham gave to these volunteers, who, according to Joseph Smith, possessed oratorical skill enough to "carry [him] into the presidential chair the first slide"[9] illustrated his precise and forthright qualities of leadership. He said the elders were to "preach the truth in righteousness, and present before the people 'General Smith's Views of the

Powers and Policy of the General Government,' and seek diligently to get up electors who will go for him for the Presidency." Then, giving emphasis to the fact that the campaigners were not to neglect their ecclesiastical duties, he added, "All the Elders will be faithful in preaching the Gospel in its simplicity and beauty, in all meekness, humility, long-suffering and prayerfulness."[10]

The feverish activity of Brigham Young in organizing and directing the Prophet's presidential campaign was conducted against the background of one of the most tense dramas the Church has known. The leading roles in this drama were played by the Prophet on the one hand and by William Law and Robert D. Foster on the other. The points of conflict that lent intrigue and suspense involved nothing less than questions of life and death and the dominance over and control of the Church.

After William Law's breakup with Joseph over the issue of the plurality of wives, he began to grope for a way out of a dilemma: Joseph had more spiritual depth and power than anyone else he had ever known. But Joseph stood between him and his worldly wealth, since William Law, the leading realtor and builder in Nauvoo, was convinced that the doctrine of polygamy would destroy the Mormon foothold in Nauvoo. So, with his business partner Robert D. Foster, several other Nauvoo conspirators, and a group of the Prophet's Missouri enemies, he had plotted Joseph's assassination. This conspiracy came to light shortly after Joseph announced his presidential candidacy. Two weeks after Brigham scheduled the nationwide general conferences and assigned the campaign speakers, Law and Foster and several others were excommunicated from the Church.

With their conspiracy to kill Joseph exposed, Law and the others changed their tack, deciding to destroy the Prophet's reputation and influence. The chief instrument of this destruction was to be a printing press that arrived in Nauvoo on May 7. A few days later

there appeared on the streets of Nauvoo the prospectus of a newspaper the apostates intended to publish,
provocatively named the *Expositor*.

On May 21, 1844, in the midst of the threatening
storm created by the appearance of the *Expositor's*
prospectus, Brigham Young left Nauvoo for his campaigning mission to the East. With him as he boarded
the steamer *Osprey* were his fellow Apostles Heber C.
Kimball and Lyman Wight. As Brigham grasped Joseph's hand to bid him farewell, he seemed not to have
known he would never see his friend again in mortality. Nor did he seem to perceive that when he again set
foot upon Nauvoo's streets, he would do so as the head
of the Church, ultimately responsible for the guidance
and safety of its ever-growing membership.

Were the whole truth known, however, it may be
that when these two powerful men parted on the Nauvoo docks that day, some unspoken intuition conveyed
the idea that their earthly association was near its end.
Given the acuteness of their spiritual perceptions, the
gravity of the conditions at Nauvoo, and the intermittent premonitions of impending death that had come
to Joseph, it is not beyond the realm of reason that they
discerned what lay ahead, even though dimly.

But, there was still much labor and anxiety ahead
for both of them. Brigham and his companions faced
the customary pleasures and inconveniences known by
travelers of that time. When the weather was fair, travel by steamer was enjoyable, with its easy pace and
ever-changing scenery. But in times of inclement
weather or when the steamers were over-crowded and
reeking with body odors and tobacco smoke, to ride
them was a burden rather than a joy. The Brethren
were fortunate to have six pleasant, quiet days on
steamers traveling between Nauvoo and Pittsburgh,
with intermittent stops at St. Louis and Cincinnati.
This afforded an opportunity to plan their itinerary in
more detail and to arrange their thoughts for the
heavy campaigning that lay ahead.

At Pittsburgh Elders Kimball and Wight left
Brigham and traveled directly to Washington, D.C.,

where they had special work to do. Meanwhile, Brigham, assisted by John C. Page (who was in the area), conducted a series of meetings in and around Pittsburgh, always serving the dual purpose of presenting Joseph's qualifications and platform and expounding the doctrines of Mormonism.

From Pittsburgh Brigham backtracked to Kirtland, where he was impressed again by the cold indifference of the residents; traversed Lake Erie by steamer from Fairport to Buffalo; crossed New York from Buffalo to Albany on the newly completed railroad; sailed down the Hudson by steamer to New York City; and thence, by coastal ship, sailed to Boston, where he arrived on June 16.

Boston was to be the hub of Brigham's activities for over a month. From there he ranged out to Lowell, Salem, Petersboro, and other nearby Massachusetts communities. He made several trips to Salem, mainly because his fourteen-year-old daughter Vilate was staying there temporarily with relatives.

On June 27, 1844, Brigham sat with Wilford Woodruff in the Boston depot waiting for a train to take him to see Vilate in Salem. "Spent the day in Boston with brother Woodruff," he wrote in his journal, "who accompanied me to the railway station as I was about to take cars to Salem. In the evening, while sitting in the depot waiting, I felt a heavy depression of Spirit, and so melancholy I could not converse with any degree of pleasure. . . . I could not assign my reasons for my peculiar feelings."[11]

Shortly after 5:00 P.M. that evening, Joseph and Hyrum were murdered in the Carthage jail.

It was July 9, twelve days after the martyrdom, before Brigham received any objective indication that Joseph and Hyrum were dead. On that date, while in Salem, he and Orson Pratt heard a rumor of the killings, but having no solid evidence to verify or disprove the rumor, the two Apostles went on to Petersboro, where a conference was to be held. There, a week later at the home of Brother Bement, Brigham read a letter written by Joseph Powers from Nauvoo that contained details about the murders. "The first thing which I thought of," Brigham recorded, "was, whether Joseph had taken the keys of the kingdom with him from the earth; brother Orson Pratt sat on my left; we were both leaning back on our chairs. Bringing my hand down on my knee, I said the keys of the kingdom are right here with the Church."[12]

It was not until he reached Boston, where several of the Twelve had assembled, that Brigham gave in to the powerful emotions that word of Joseph's death had aroused in him. There, at the home of Sister Vose, he wept openly in the presence of the Brethren and their hostess.

After counseling with Heber C. Kimball, Orson Pratt, Wilford Woodruff, and Orson Hyde, who were with him at the Vose residence, and with Lyman Wight, who joined the others a week later, Brigham decided to return immediately to Nauvoo. Traveling by railroad, stage, and steamboat via Albany, Buffalo, Detroit, Chicago, and Galena, they arrived on August 6 to find a scene of confusion and turmoil agitated by grief for the martyrs and by the pretensions of Sidney Rigdon, who sought to seize control of the Church.

Chapter Thirteen

Order out of Chaos—
Preparation for Exodus

Joseph Smith had but one counselor, Sidney Rigdon, at the time of his death. The vacancy in the First Presidency caused by William Law's fall and excommunication had not been filled by the time the Prophet was shot. But Sidney Rigdon was a counselor in name only, as a schism had opened between him and the Prophet because of personal differences and Sidney's adamant refusal to accept the doctrine of the plurality of wives. The personal relationship between these two longtime associates became so tense that Sidney moved to Pittsburgh several months before the martyrdom, where he built up a considerable following.

An articulate man of commanding presence, Sidney Rigdon's chief role as a Church leader had been as an assistant to Joseph in the laborious task of revising the scriptures, as a participant in many of the impressive spiritual experiences the Prophet enjoyed, and as a "spokesman" for the Church. However, he was almost entirely devoid of administrative skills and was often lacking in judgment.

Sidney Rigdon returned to Nauvoo on Saturday, August 3, 1844, three days before Brigham's arrival, to offer himself as a "guardian" for the Church. The following day, Sunday, in concert with William Marks, the Nauvoo stake president, he addressed a public meeting of the Saints and presented his claims. Had it not been for the influence of William Clayton, the Prophet's personal secretary, who argued that such action was premature and would be improper without the Twelve present, a vote as to whether Sidney was to lead the Church might have been taken at that time. As it was, William Marks scheduled another meeting for Thursday, August 8, in which it was expected the question of who was to lead the Church would be resolved.

Brigham Young and his associates of the Twelve arrived on Tuesday. After greeting his own family and paying his respects to the widows and families of the martyrs, Brigham moved promptly and surely to prepare for the confrontation he expected two days later. Because of the realization that came to him at Petersboro, several weeks before, that the keys of the ministry were vested in the Twelve, Brigham seems to have known precisely what his course of action would be.

The day after his arrival he met first with the other eight members of the Twelve who were then in Nauvoo, Heber C. Kimball, Parley P. Pratt, Orson Pratt, John Taylor, Wilford Woodruff, George A. Smith, Willard Richards, and Lyman Wight. This meeting was held at John Taylor's home. At that time a special meeting was planned for the same evening in the Seventies Hall. The high councilors and high priests in Nauvoo, along with Sidney Rigdon, were invited to attend. What transpired had the effect of heightening the already extreme tension in the city and of clearly drawing the lines between the two opposing camps. Sidney Rigdon repeated the claims he had made the previous Sunday and offered himself as a guardian for the Church. Brigham Young, on the other hand, declared that it was a matter of indifference to him who led the Church, as long as the person had been properly authorized. He then pointed out that before his death Joseph had conferred upon the Twelve the keys of administering the affairs of the Church in all the world.

This debate, heard only by a small, select group of priesthood leaders, set the stage for the general meeting scheduled the next morning. Since William Marks had called the meeting, the Twelve decided not to interfere with it, but to let it run its course.

Following the Wednesday night meeting in the Seventies Hall, word spread rapidly through the city of the confrontation that was building. A huge crowd ga-

thered near the temple at 10:00 A.M. Thursday.
Mounting a wagon box so he could be seen and heard
by all, Sidney Rigdon addressed the vast congregation
for an hour and a half, presenting his claims of leadership in his customary eloquent though florid style. After a lunch break the meeting resumed, this time with
Brigham Young in charge.

Brigham had arranged for the Apostles, the high
priests, the seventies, and the elders to be seated separ-
ately in different parts of the assembly. Visually this
demonstrated to the general membership the basic import of Brigham's position in this sensitive and important matter.

In his speech, Brigham made no pretensions other
than to rely upon the foundation laid by Joseph Smith
of the Apostles and the other priesthood officers in the
Church. He returned to this theme again and again:
"The Twelve are appointed by the finger of God. . . .
an independent body who have the keys of the priesthood—the keys of the kingdom of God to deliver to all
the world: this is true, so help me God. They stand
next to Joseph, and are as the First Presidency of the
Church."

Referring to the claims of Sidney Rigdon, he declared: "You cannot fill the office of a prophet, seer,
and revelator: God must do this. . . . You must not appoint any man at our head; if you should, the Twelve
must ordain him."

Then, to leave no doubt as to the status of those
who might presume to select their own head, he
added, "but if you do want any other man or men to
lead you, take them and we will go our way to build up
the kingdom in all the world."

Brigham refuted the misconception that because
Sidney Rigdon was Joseph's counselor, he had jurisdiction over the Twelve: "Here is President Rigdon,
who was counselor to Joseph. I ask, where are Joseph
and Hyrum? They are gone beyond the veil; and if
Elder Rigdon wants to act as his counselor, he must go
beyond the veil where he is."[1]

It was during this speech that the oft-remarked

transformation occurred—Brigham Young appeared to many present as if he were the Prophet Joseph Smith. The independent and uniform reports of eyewitnesses to this phenomenon attest to its authenticity. Wilford Woodruff, a trained and careful observer, said that no one could have convinced him "that it was not Joseph Smith." William C. Staines, an emigration agent for the Church, wrote in his journal under the date of August 8, 1844, that Brigham Young's declaration that the Twelve were to lead the Church was with a voice "like the voice of the Prophet Joseph. I thought it was he," wrote Elder Staines, "and so did thousands who heard it." George Q. Cannon, later a counselor in the First Presidency, declared: "If Joseph had arisen from the dead and again spoken in their hearing, the effect could not have been more startling than it was to many present at that meeting; it was the voice of Joseph . . . which was heard, but it seemed in the eyes of the people as if it were the very person of Joseph which stood before them."[2] Edward Hunter, who was then a mature fifty-one-year-old man, and who was later the Presiding Bishop of the Church, recorded that while he sat at this meeting, with his head in his hands, he heard a voice, "the Prophet's voice as natural and true" as he had ever heard it. "I raised up quickly," he wrote, "fully expecting to see the Prophet, and I did. There he stood and gradually changed to that of Brother Brigham, but the voice was not Brother Brigham's. It was still the Prophet's." Then Edward Hunter recorded a phenomenon not mentioned by other eyewitnesses: "Beside Brother Brigham I saw the Prophet, who turned toward the speaker and smiled."[3]

Following Brigham Young's powerful address, Amasa Lyman delivered brief remarks, saying he never understood his unofficial role as a counselor to Joseph Smith gave him any "precedence to go before the Twelve."

Sidney Rigdon was surprised when W. W. Phelps, whom Sidney had designated to speak for him, advised the audience: "If you want to do right, uphold the Twelve."

W. W. Phelps's remarks, coming as they did from a prominent man who had known Sidney Rigdon in the early days in Mentor and Kirtland before Sidney joined the Church, removed any lingering doubts about the outcome of the confrontation. In concluding remarks that followed brief comments by Parley P. Pratt, Brigham Young put this proposition to the audience: "If the church want the Twelve to stand as the head, the First Presidency of the Church, . . . manifest it by holding up the right hand." According to the minutes of the meeting, "There was a universal vote" in favor of this proposition. When a contrary vote was called for, there were "no hands up."[4]

While the effect of the action taken was to vest control of the Church in the Twelve as a body, no one acquainted with the personality and skills of Brigham Young and with the cohesive nature of the Mormon priesthood structure entertained any doubt that Brigham Young was the man in charge. He was the President of the Twelve, serving without counselors; and because of his diligence and ability, the members of the quorum uniformly respected him.

Yet not all the Twelve sustained him unreservedly, as later events were to prove; and there were factions in the city whose opposition did not surface at the August 8 meeting. These would later evolve into centers of dissent, creating schisms and fragmenting.

Sidney Rigdon continued to assert the right of dominance in Church affairs, despite the vote at the August 8 meeting. This inevitably brought him into collision with Brigham Young. So irreconcilable were these differences, that Sidney Rigdon was excommunicated for insubordination on September 8, 1844, just a month after the Twelve were sustained to lead the Church. He returned east, where he lived for over thirty years, leading a small and ever-dwindling group.

Lyman Wight, who rose to early prominence in Kirtland and who ordained Sidney Rigdon a high priest only fourteen months after the Church was organized, could never reconcile himself to Brigham's leadership. Being five years older than Brigham Young and having preceded him into the Church, Lyman Wight assumed a superior, condescending air toward his leader and was unwilling to follow his direction. His recalcitrance caused him to leave the main body of the Church and to lead a group to Texas that, like Sidney Rigdon's group, dwindled away. He was excommunicated in 1848.

William B. Smith, Joseph's brother, and John E. Page, both members of the Twelve, dissented to Brigham's leadership and were excommunicated in 1845 and 1846 respectively.

Emma Smith, Joseph's wife, refused to have anything to do with Brigham Young, looking upon him as being incapable of succeeding her husband. A group of dissenters, including William Marks, the Nauvoo Stake president, shared her views. Years later some of these people, with the remnant of another small group that followed James J. Strang to Beaver Island in Lake Michigan, joined to form the Reorganized Church of Jesus Christ of Latter Day Saints.

But Brigham Young was not deterred, indeed, was not unduly troubled by these dissensions in the Church. The fact is that the great majority of the Saints supported him and the Twelve without qualification. Now that the prophetic mantle had descended upon him, the faithful members of the Church would be expected to show toward him the same loyalty they had shown toward Joseph.

So, after the August 8 meeting, Brigham's chief concern related neither to his authority to act nor to the support he might expect from his followers. The principal issue he faced was precisely what to do with the vast authority that had been suddenly thrust upon him.

After prayerful reflection and lengthy counseling with the Twelve and others, he took a course that in retrospect appears to have been the wisest and most astute one available. Instead of showing bitterness and a spirit of retaliation toward the enemies who had killed Joseph and Hyrum, he took an affirmative, peaceful course. He stated his fixed purpose to go forward without delay, to complete the temple and the Nauvoo House, the projects that had been most important to Joseph before he was killed. Recognizing that these tasks would not be easy, Brigham sought to strengthen the Saints' resolve with his own positive words and actions. "We want to build the Temple in this place," he declared, "if we have to build it as the Jews built the walls of the Temple in Jerusalem, with a sword in one hand and the trowel in the other."[5]

Nor did he intend to neglect the spiritual duties of his office while this exhausting work was being carried forward. Within a week after the confrontation with Sidney Rigdon, the Twelve, at Brigham's instigation, resolved "to bear off the kingdom of God in all the world, in truth, honesty, virtue and holiness, and to continue to set their faces as a flint against every species of wickedness, vice and dishonesty in all its forms."[6]

In furtherance of these goals, Brigham took occasion at the October general conference to appoint eighty-five men to preside over mission districts in the United States and to assign Wilford Woodruff to return to the fertile proselyting fields in Great Britain. He admonished the Saints to work diligently to complete or to improve their Nauvoo holdings, to paint and fix their homes and outbuildings, and to fence and cultivate their garden plots. Furthermore, they were not to neglect their religious studies and devotions nor to fail to develop their intellectual gifts and social graces.

These initiatives made it clear beyond doubt to member and nonmember alike that the change in Mormon leadership had effected no significant change in the doctrines, procedures, aims, lifestyle, or competence of the Latter-day Saint community. We can only surmise with what shock and consternation the mobbers and Mormon-haters faced this reality. It dawned upon them that their assumptions and calculations had been grossly in error. Their basic assumption appears to have been that the vitality of

Mormonism had its roots in the charismatic leadership of Joseph Smith and his brother Hyrum. Beginning with that premise, the answer to their problem seemed obvious enough—merely sever the root from the vine. With this object in view, the conspirators had managed the arrest of the Smiths, separated them from the protection of the Nauvoo Legion and courts, isolated them in a jail to which they had easy access, and placed them in the custody of a company of hostile militia whose members had openly threatened the death of the prisoners.

To see their plans thwarted was a source of deep annoyance and consternation to the mobbers in Illinois. Once it became apparent that Mormonism would survive the death of the Smiths, indeed, when it was seen that their martyrdom would only serve to fan the flames of enthusiasm and dedication among the Saints, the enemies of the Church began to plot anew the expulsion of the Mormons from their midst, or, if necessary, their extermination.

Not long after the martyrdom, an anti-Mormon committee in Warsaw adopted a resolution calling for the complete evacuation of the Saints from Illinois. When this produced no results, a Warsaw group under the direction of Colonel Levi Williams organized a military campaign whose object was either to drive the Mormons from the state or to destroy them. Advertised as a wolf hunt, this effort at extermination or expulsion failed when Governor Thomas Ford sent General John J. Hardin to intervene. In early September, 1845, the continuing demand for the Mormons to leave was punctuated by the burning of twenty-nine homes in the small community of Morley; and later that same month an anti-Mormon mass meeting was held in Quincy, Illinois, to discuss plans for the expulsion of the Latter-day Saints. The following month delegates from nine counties near Hancock County met in convention and adopted a resolution declaring, "It is now too late to attempt the settlement of the difficulties in Hancock county upon any other basis than that of the removal of the Mormons from the state."[7]

The intensified pressure upon the Saints to leave Nauvoo propelled Brigham Young toward two main objectives: first, to complete the temple and other unfinished projects in Nauvoo; and second, to find and prepare to depart for a new place of settlement.

Part of the motivation to attain the first objective is to be found in the words of Parley P. Pratt delivered to the general conference in October, 1845: "We do not want to leave a desolate place, to be a reproach to us, but something that will be a monument to those who may visit the place of our industry, diligence and virtue."[8] Beyond that, however, President Brigham Young was anxious that the Saints have the spiritual blessings from the temple ordinances. Toward that end the workmen labored indefatigably upon the temple night and day.

While to the anxious onlookers outside Nauvoo it may have appeared that the Mormons intended to remain forever, behind the scenes, keeping pace with the feverish activity to complete the temple and to build up the city, went forward a quiet, consistent effort to prepare for exodus. At the threshold of this effort Brigham and his associates were faced with the hard questions: Exodus to where? And when?

While Joseph was alive, consideration had been given to a westward move. A few months after the martyrdom, discussions of such a move revived. Both California and Oregon were discussed as possibilities. In April, 1845, Brigham Young wrote to President James K. Polk, asking for help in the Saints' plans to migrate to "Oregon, the northwestern territory, or some location remote from the states."[9] In addition, Brigham directed letters to the governors of all the states in the union except Missouri and Illinois asking whether asylum could be offered to his people. Judge Stephen A. Douglas, an off-and-on friend of the Saints, urged Brigham to take his people to Vancouver Island, while Governor Ford, anxious to rid himself of the nagging, ever-recurring trouble the Mormon presence in Illinois had caused him, suggested that it would be "a pretty operation for [the Saints] to go out there [to California], take possession of and conquer a portion of the vacant country, and establish an independent government of [their] own subject only to the laws of nations."[10]

By the end of the summer, 1845, Brigham Young, in consultation with the Twelve and others, had practically excluded all areas as places of likely settlement except the "Great Salt Lake Valley." He had assembled all available written materials about it and adjacent areas, as well as taking into account the verbal reports and rumors circulated by explorers, military personnel, and trappers who had been to the mountainous West. Especially helpful were the report and maps prepared by John C. Fremont.

Indicative of the focus being concentrated upon the Salt Lake area was a decision reached on September 9 that a company of 1,500 men be selected to go there. Events unforeseen at the time of this meeting prohibited these plans from being brought to fruition.

Toward the end of September, Governor Ford sent General John J. Hardin to assume military control of Nauvoo. The governor considered this extreme action necessary because of the increased threats and depredations directed at the Saints by the local mobs and by frequent though usually unfounded rumors of retaliatory action taken by Nauvoo's defenders. It was just such a rumor that had triggered the governor's order to General Hardin. The rumor was that the Mormons had killed two missing men and hidden the bodies. Apparently convinced that the rumor was grounded in fact, the general's troops, on his orders, ransacked the city for the two bodies, going to the extent of combing manure piles in a stable where the searchers had been led by yet another false rumor. The general began to understand the extent to which he had been misled when Brigham asked whether, if the general thought him to be a murderer, he also thought him to be so imbecilic as to hide the bodies rather than to bury them or to weight them and throw them in the river.

It was the yoke of General Hardin's military rule

that called forth from Brigham Young and his brethren of the Twelve a definitive statement of the plans for exodus. In a communication the first week in October, addressed to General Hardin and others, the Mormon leaders advised they had "commenced making arrangements to remove from this county previous to the recent disturbances." These "arrangements" entailed the organization of a thousand families into ten companies comprising five to six thousand people. These Saints, with others yet to be organized, were "fully determined to remove in the spring." After providing other details of the Mormon plan for exodus, the letter continued, "if all these testimonies are not sufficient to satisfy any people that we are in earnest, we will soon give them a sign that cannot be mistaken; *we will leave them!*"[11]

From this point on, the plans and preparations for the westward trek were openly and aggressively discussed and prosecuted. The *Nauvoo Neighbor* carried lists of supplies and equipment that each family making the trek should procure. This included everything from cayenne pepper to fish hooks and nets. It was not long before Nauvoo was little else than a gigantic workshop, with everyone involved in what Governor Ford characterized as "the most prodigious preparations for removal." He wrote, "The people from all parts of the country flocked to Nauvoo to purchase houses and farms, which were sold extremely low, lower than the prices at a sheriff's sale, for money, wagons, horses, oxen, cattle, and other articles of personal property which might be needed by the Mormons in their exodus into the wilderness."[12]

In the midst of these heavy exertions, during late November and early December, 1845, the upper rooms of the temple were sufficiently completed to enable Brigham Young and the Twelve to administer the endowment and the sealings for which the faithful Latter-day Saints had waited so long and so patiently. Assisted by other members of the Twelve Brigham worked almost around the clock, often spending the night in the temple in a special room on the top floor fitted out for his use. In the meantime, he continued to direct the preparations for exodus that were going forward throughout the city with undiminished vigor. Troops and officials were seen on every hand, some being in Nauvoo ostensibly to protect the Saints, and some to serve warrants on the Brethren in connection with the harassing litigation brought against them.

Although it was obvious the scheduling would be exceedingly tight when the original decision was made to leave in the spring of 1846, Brigham seemed confident that the enormous problems of the move would be solved by then. Such confidence was based on the assumption that all would cooperate and work to full capacity. The Saints had done this, and as time went on there appeared to be little doubt they would be ready to leave on schedule. When, however, it was made known that the exodus would be accelerated by several months, that the weather would be wintry at the time of departure, all plans were thrown into disarray. An air of improvisation and uncertainty settled upon the Saints, replacing the relatively deliberate, methodical attitude that had prevailed before. Also, mobs and hostile officials pressing from behind and sharp-dealing land-grabbers conniving to drive prices down to the lowest possible level added a psychological burden difficult for some to bear.

Despite the agony and turmoil adverse circumstances had thrust upon his people, Brigham was stoically self-confident as he completed the plans for a premature departure from Nauvoo. He admonished his followers "not to be self-important" and to "walk humbly before the Lord." He counseled his people to "realize that we are engaged in a great and important movement."[13]

On Monday, February 2, 1846, Brigham "counselled the brethren to procure boats and hold them in readiness to convey our wagons and teams over the river, and let everything for the journey be in readiness."[14] Two days later, he was found "loading up [his] wagons, preparatory to starting west."[15] On the ninth, "the roof of the temple was discovered to be on fire" as the result of an over-heated stovepipe in an upper room where clothing was being dried. After half an hour of feverish activity, a hastily organized bucket brigade directed by Willard Richards brought the fire under control. Viewing the fire impassively, Brigham observed, "If it is the will of the Lord that the Temple be burned, instead of being defiled by the Gentiles, Amen to it."[16]

A contingent of the Nauvoo police under Hosea Stout, directed by Brigham Young, had assembled a motley collection of old flatboats, lighters, and skiffs, which were used to transport the Saints and their belongings across the river.

The crews worked around the clock for days to move the beleaguered Saints across the broad Mississippi. Later, as winter's grip tightened on Nauvoo, the river froze over, making it possible for some of the wagons to cross on the ice.

By Sunday, February 15, 1846, Brigham Young was ready to depart, and crossed the river with his family, accompanied by Willard Richards and his family, and by George A. Smith.

Chapter Fourteen

On the Prairie

At the first encampment on Sugar Creek, life went on as usual, although under more difficult and stressful conditions than the Saints had ever before encountered. The first night nine babies were born.

Brigham used Sugar Creek as a temporary base camp to complete plans for a leapfrogging move across the prairies of Iowa. Here he was comparatively immune from danger, yet near enough to Nauvoo to give effective direction to the evacuation of the remainder of his people and to supervise the liquidation of the Saints' assets through a number of agents headed by Almon Babbitt.

The general plan for the move across Iowa had been sketched by Brigham Young before he forded the Mississippi. Indeed, it had been a matter of such wide discussion that even the hostile anti-Mormon press was privy to it. Two days before Brigham departed from Nauvoo, an item in the *Daily Missouri Republican* accurately outlined how the Mormon Apostles intended to shepherd Israel's camp across the prairie: "It is said to be the plan of the leaders to send this company forward as a pioneer corps. They are to proceed about five hundred miles westward, where they are to halt, build a village, and put in a spring crop. They are to remain there until those who follow in the spring reach them—when another pioneer company will start for a point five hundred miles still further west, where they will stop, build a village, and put in a fall crop. The company remaining behind will, in the spring, move on to this second station; and in this manner they hope to accomplish the long journey which is in contempla-

tion. Many of those who now go as pioneers, are to return, so soon as their crop is in, for their families."

Herein we see, in dimly sketched outline, the blue-
print from which the temporary communities of
Garden Grove and Mount Pisgah came into being.
These waystations, lying between Nauvoo and the Missouri River, were to provide needed succor and respite
for the new travelers. And the experience gained in establishing them was to build self-confidence in the pioneers' ability to survive under adverse conditions, and
to provide training for the more difficult tasks of pioneering and community-building that lay ahead.

By the first of March everything was ready to move
out from Sugar Creek. Having suffered a painful
attack of rheumatism the day before, Brigham was
unable to attend a 10:00 A.M. meeting that Sunday
morning and found it necessary to appoint Heber C.
Kimball to represent him there and to explain to the
Saints the necessity of moving to the next camp.

The companies began struggling up out of the
creek bottom onto the high ground at noon following
Heber's final instructions, and aligned themselves
along a road laid out six days before by Bishop George
Miller, who had gone ahead with sixteen wagons. Four
days behind Bishop Miller was Colonel Stephen Mark-
ham with a crew of a hundred men whose job it was to
build bridges and otherwise prepare the road marked
by the bishop. Acting as outriders to protect the flanks
of the serpentine caravan were a hundred men armed
with rifles who worked in shifts under the direction of
Hosea Stout. Another hundred men were assigned to
Colonel John Scott's artillery brigade.

Tied to the end-gates of the wagons or herded
across the snow-covered prairies on either side of the
slow-moving column were the hundreds of animals
the Saints had accumulated for the trek—cows, goats,
and extra teams of horses and oxen. One student of
the Mormon exodus has painted this interesting word
picture of Israel's Camp as it moved deliberately across
Iowa: "In good weather or in foul, unimaginative men
seeing that people in movement, hundreds of wagons,

thousands of animals, two or three thousand men, women and children, will catch their breath with the momentary feeling that they have looked back through more than two thousand years at the veritable Children of Israel."[1]

Included in the company was a brass band that summoned Israel's Camp from sleep each morning and set its members on the trail toward another day of travel and toil. At night the band played accompaniment to the vigorous dances, French fours, Copenhagen jigs, and Virginia reels that helped the pioneers relax. A witness of one of these nocturnal entertainments was touched by the vocal rendition of a young Latter-day Saint woman sung to the accompaniment of a quartet ensemble from the band. "Silence was then called," he wrote reflectively, "and a well cultivated mezzo-soprano voice, belonging to a young lady with fair face and dark eyes [sang] . . . a little song, the notes of which I have been unsuccessful in repeated efforts to obtain since—a version of the text, touching to all earthly wanderers:

> 'By the rivers of Babylon we sat down and wept
> We wept when we remembered Zion.' "[2]

Owing to the penurious condition of the Saints as they moved slowly across Iowa, Brigham Young encouraged the brethren to earn extra money whenever possible by hiring out to the settlers they encountered along their line of march, splitting rails, husking corn, and shoeing horses. Here again the band was of assistance, playing for a fee at dances or concerts in the scattered communities near the camp's line of march.

Brigham Young and his followers negotiated the journey from Sugar Creek to Council Bluffs on the east bank of the Missouri River in three and a half months. In between, stops of varying duration were made at Richardson Point, near a branch of Chequest Creek, some 55 miles west of Nauvoo, which was reached March 7; at the Chariton River, where the camp arrived March 22; at Locust River, reached on April 6; at Garden Grove, about 150 miles west of

Nauvoo, on April 25; at Mount Pisgah on May 25; and, finally, at Council Bluffs on June 14.

While this summary of the trip accurately states the essential facts, it contains no hint of the struggle, the adversity, and the heartache it entailed. At the root of much of the difficulty lay the almost impassable trails, whose condition varied from bad to deplorable, due in large part to the vagaries of the weather. A day out from Sugar Creek some wagons were damaged by the rough and rutted roads. The very next morning the temperature was a frigid twenty-three degrees, but shot up during the day, causing an unseasonable thaw that slowed the caravan because of the sticky mud. A week later, the rain poured down in torrents. With great exertion a part of the camp traveled about six miles. Many wagons were stuck fast in the deep mud. Two days later during the night the mud froze hard.

As discontent and irritability became more widespread among the less stable elements in the camp, Brigham Young's task of leadership became progressively more difficult and distasteful. Thus, only a few days out of Sugar Creek, we find him declaring that he "did not want a man along who was not willing to help in every place. . . . We want every man to quit this Camp who cannot quit swearing. You had better go now, if you do not the law will be put in force by and bye."[3] Within a few days some of the Saints came to see that they were not physically or emotionally equipped for pioneering, and began drifting back toward Nauvoo. This attrition in Israel's Camp continued throughout the difficult move across Iowa as first one and then another wagon turned back.

But the worst attrition in the camp came from death. Weakened by fatigue, malnutrition, and a whole compendium of bodily ills, the Saints died in such numbers that the trail across the prairie was literally marked by graves.

But, those who survived the physical hazards of the prairie and were not intimidated into turning back developed a toughness and resiliency that equipped them admirably for the next stages of the exodus across the plains and badlands of Nebraska and Wyoming and into the valley of the Great Salt Lake. "By spring, they . . . were a hard core, tested and tempered by tribulation and shared hope, as tough and durable a people as this republic has ever produced."[4]

Chapter Fifteen

At the Missouri

Some of the leaders had entertained the hope of going far beyond the Missouri in 1846, but the move across Iowa had been much slower than expected. After reaching the river, and after an advance party had pushed as far west as Grand Island and the Pawnee villages, it became apparent it would be necessary to regroup at the Missouri and plan for the last and longest part of the trip the following year.

Brigham Young wasted no time once he had arrived at Council Bluffs. At 5:00 P.M. on Sunday, June 14, 1846, the day of arrival, all the companies joined to form a hollow square on the east bank of the river. At 8:00 P.M. the horn sounded and a general meeting convened. The camp was informed that it was illegal to trade with the Indians (the peaceful Pottawatomies occupied the east bank and the Omahas the west bank of the river), rules governing movements in and out of the camp and the feeding and herding of the stock were decided upon, guards and sentinels were designated, a committee was appointed to confer with the Indian traders, a fishing party was organized, and a large body of brethren was assigned to build a ferry.

The next day Brigham Young found it necessary to repeat the instructions because misunderstandings had arisen. It was also decided at that time to move the camp from the riverside back to the bluffs, where good spring water was available and where conflicts with the Indians could be avoided.

Here Brigham Young set up his first temporary command post. It consisted of a simple tent whose floor was covered with a buffalo skin. From here

Brigham gave direction to modern Israel, scattered
across Iowa from Sugar Creek to Council Bluffs and
westward to the Elkhorn, where he was soon to send
George Miller and his vanguard of trailblazers. It was
initially intended that Bishop Miller would cross the
Elkhorn and then press onward, with the pioneer company to follow close behind. These plans were altered,
however, chiefly because of the arrival at Mount Pisgah on June 26 of Captain James Allen, a recruiter for
the U.S. Army, who had a commission from General
Stephen F. Kearney, Commander of the Army of the
West at Fort Leavenworth, to recruit 500 Mormon volunteers to serve in the war with Mexico. This recruitment sprang from the diplomatic efforts of Jesse C.
Little, president of the Eastern States Mission, whom
Brigham Young had assigned to contact President
James K. Polk to seek aid for the Church. The fruits of
Jesse Little's diplomacy hardly coincided with Brigham's expectations. Brigham had understood the government planned to construct a series of blockhouses
and forts along the Oregon Trail. He envisioned that
his people could easily accomplish this work during
their westward flight, thereby generating funds to fuel
the exodus. However, during Jesse Little's negotiations hostilities between the United States and Mexico
flared anew, which changed Uncle Sam's focus from
forts to troops. Although Brigham viewed this alternative with far less enthusiasm than the first, he soon
endorsed it, both out of a sense of patriotism and as a
means of defraying the cost of the Mormon migration.
In fact, Brigham Young became Captain Allen's chief
aide in his recruitment efforts. Shuttling between
Council Bluffs and Mount Pisgah and sending mes-
sages backward and forward along the trail to Garden
Grove and the Elkhorn, the leader of the Saints
exhorted his young men to come to the aid of their
country in its time of need and, in the process, to bless
their people in the quest for religious asylum.

Few things attest more convincingly to the leadership ability of Brigham Young than the willingness
and speed with which the young Latter-day Saint men

responded to his call to enlist. Within a matter of weeks after Captain Allen first appeared at Mount Pisgah with his commission, the five hundred men had enlisted, arranged their private affairs, bid emotional farewells to their families and friends, and were on their way downriver to Fort Leavenworth, where they were to be mustered in, equipped, and trained for their historic march to San Diego.

With the departure of the Mormon Battalion, which included much of the youthful brawn and energy needed to propel Israel's Camp along the trail west, any thought of pressing forward in 1846 had to be abandoned.

In negotiating with Captain Allen to assist in his recruitment effort, Brigham Young sought permission for the Saints to remain in the Council Bluffs area for a season or more to enable them to prepare for the move to the mountains. Although he lacked authority to do so, the captain agreed to the request. In this he ignored the autonomy of the Pottawatomies and the Omahas who controlled both sides of the river except for tracts occupied by the Indian agent and the traders. Recognizing the need to obtain consent from the tribal leaders to remain on Indian lands, Brigham entered into negotiations with them. In a parley with the Omahas held on August 28, the Mormon leader, who arose from a sickbed to attend the meeting, secured approval from Chief Big Elk for his people to remain on tribal lands for two years or more.

In accordance with this arrangement, Brigham selected a townsite, later given the name "Winter Quarters," located several miles north of the future city of Omaha, Nebraska. There the dispossessed and wandering Saints proceeded to lay out, subdivide, and build a new city in the wilderness. By December 1, within two months after taking possession of the Omaha grant, the industrious Mormons had constructed 621 residential buildings housing 3,483 shivering, sick, but undaunted members of Israel's Camp.

To meet his people's spiritual needs, Brigham divided Winter Quarters into twenty-two wards, with a bishop over each one. The work of these shepherds, who were expected to care for the temporal as well as the spiritual needs of those under their charge, was overseen by a high council that, according to directions received from Brigham Young and the Twelve, coordinated the work of the Church throughout the settlement.

Most of the homes at Winter Quarters were log cabins fashioned from the trees that grew profusely in the river bottom. A few were built of sod. Brigham Young's home was typical, with doors but no windows, and chimneys built of brick obtained from the ruins of the old fort at Council Bluffs.

In drafty, insubstantial buildings of this kind, during a winter noted for its severity (the temperature plummeted to a bone-chilling twenty degrees below zero), we can understand how illness and death ravaged a people whose physical and emotional strength had already been drained by the expulsion from Illinois and by the agonizing journey across the prairies of Iowa. Plagued with fevers and dysentery, with colds, pneumonia, whooping cough, measles, pleurisy, and numerous other ailments, the Latter-day Saints died in frightening numbers during their first winter on the Missouri. There was hardly a family that escaped the cold hand of death. Many believe that in all the adversity and heartache through which the Mormons have passed in their turbulent history, few incidents equal, and none exceed, in magnitude the anguish generated during that awful winter.

Yet, throughout the ordeal, Brigham Young and his followers maintained an unusually high level of morale and esprit de corps, typified by the now-famous hymn "Come, Come Ye Saints," composed during this period by William Clayton, whose optimistic refrain, "all is well," became the watchword of the exodus.

We may gauge the depth of Brigham Young's resolve during this period from a letter written in January at the height of that frigid winter to Charles C. Rich, who presided at Mount Pisgah. After informing him of the plans to send a pioneer company to the mountains in the spring and of the desire that he join it, Brigham, writing from the cramped and frosty confines of his Winter Quarters home, aroused the enthusiasm of his friend with words that one finds compelling even today: "Gird up your loins," the Mormon Prophet admonished, ". . . put on your armor, cheer up your heart, and being filled with Almighty faith, prepare for the battle as fast as possible. If you are sick, be made well. If you are weak, be made strong. Shake yourself like a mighty man, make the forest to echo the sound of your voice and the prairies move at your presence."[1]

These sentences only hint at the driving energy of the Mormon leader as he waited restlessly for spring to break on Nebraska's broad plains.

In the meantime things were astir in Winter Quarters. During the short intervals between nursing the sick, burying the dead, and caring for the needs of those who could move about, Brigham perfected his plan for the final push to the mountains. It included the formation of a pioneer company of mostly young, vigorous men possessing every skill necessary to open and mark the trail, prepare maps and traveling instructions, and plant a summer crop in the mountains preparatory to the mass leap of modern Israel, strung out now from Nauvoo to Winter Quarters.

Chapter Sixteen

On to the Mountains

As the stocky, muscular, forty-five-year-old leader of the Mormon Church perfected his plan for the final push toward the mountains, he was conscious not only of the obvious analogies between his own flight and that of his illustrious predecessor, Moses, but of being the instrument by which the predictions of two other deceased prophetic leaders would be fulfilled. An avid student of the scriptures, Brigham was well acquainted with the writings of Isaiah, the study of which had been specifically enjoined upon the Saints by the Book of Mormon. Thus, he was acquainted with that biblical prophet's allusion to the establishment in the last days of "the mountain of the Lord's house . . . in the top of the mountains." (Isa. 2:2.) And Brigham's mentor, Joseph Smith, had predicted that the Latter-day Saints would be driven west, where they would become a mighty people in the midst of the Rocky Mountains. The ultimate destination of the wandering Mormons was not, therefore, a matter of conjecture or uncertainty, to this spiritual man. Yet, pragmatist that he was, Brigham used study and objective analysis to confirm the spiritual indications and to demonstrate that the environment satisfied the criteria he and the Twelve had established: favorable climate and soil, adequate water and building materials, and, most importantly, isolation.

But while the Brethren knew they were headed for the mountains, there was still an element of uncertainty as to the exact place the main body of the Saints would settle. That decision was to await an on-site inspection.

As Brigham prepared to lead his people from Winter Quarters westward, he felt the need for divine guidance. The spiritual enlightenment he fervently sought came in the form of a revelation. Later identified as section 136 of the Doctrine and Covenants, it became the only revelation received by Brigham Young to be included in the standard works of the Church.

It prescribed the organization of the "companies" into which Israel's Camp was to be divided, each of which was to be directed by a president and two counselors, with captains of hundreds, fifties, and tens to serve under the presidency. Judging from the terminology used, these companies were to be both ecclesiastical and military. The presidency was to provide spiritual direction, while the captains would furnish discipline and protection.

Each company was to be wholly self-sufficient, with "teams, wagons, provisions, clothing, and other necessaries for the journey." Moreover, each was to help care for "the poor, the widows, the fatherless, and the families of those who have gone into the army," according to the "dividend" of their property. From each company were to be selected "a sufficient number of able-bodied and expert men, to take teams, seeds, and farming utensils, to go as pioneers to prepare for putting in spring crops." (See D&C 136:5, 7-8.)

As it prepared to hit the trail the pioneer company included 144 "able-bodied and expert men." In addition to the original plan, however, it also included three women: Clara and Harriet Young, the wives of Brigham and his brother, Lorenzo Dow; and Ellen Kimball, one of Heber C. Kimball's wives. With the addition of two of Harriet Young's children, the total number in the company was 149.

The members of the pioneer company did not leave Winter Quarters simultaneously. They began drifting out of the settlement as early as April 5, 1847, when six wagons under the direction of Heber C. Kimball traveled three miles west onto the Nebraska plains following a well-marked trail. Other small groups followed later, moving slowly toward the Elkhorn River, twenty miles west. The river was the main staging area from which the trek would begin in earnest. Later, at Brigham's direction, the location of the staging area was changed to a point on the north side of the Platte River some thirty-five miles west of Winter Quarters.

A main reason for the delay in getting the caravan fully organized and in motion was news on April 8 that Parley P. Pratt had returned from his mission to England and that John Taylor was not far behind on the trail east of Council Bluffs. Brigham was anxious for news of the emigration and the condition of the Church in Great Britain that Parley P. Pratt could provide, and perhaps more important, he wanted the surveying and other scientific instruments John Taylor was reported to have purchased in England.

By Thursday, April 15, the entire company had gathered at the Platte River staging area. Judged by almost any standard it is doubtful that any pioneering expedition up to that point in history was better organized, equipped, and administered than this one. The company included teamsters, blacksmiths, road and bridge builders, carpenters, masons, farmers, cattlemen, coopers, and hunters. Moreover, there were those skilled in negotiation, whose expertise would be helpful in dealing with Indians and others to be encountered along the trail; there were historians and muscians; there was a doctor, Willard Richards; and a scientist, Orson Pratt, whose celestial sightings and mathematical computations along the trail were to keep the company apprised of its exact location. At the apex of this impressive organization, of course, stood Brigham Young, whose grasp of administrative techniques had already been demonstrated in the flight across Iowa.

The night before the departure from the Platte River staging ground, Brigham called the company together to impart advice and to announce the rules that would govern the camp during the thousand-mile journey that lay ahead. He admonished the brethren to be almost as assiduous in caring for their teams as

themselves, and to avoid light-mindedness. He warned
that persecution of the Latter-day Saints was not over,
and that reports had revealed that enemies intended
to inflame the Indian tribes along the line of march to
attack the Mormon company and to steal their animals
and supplies. He cautioned the company to be prayerful and diligent, promising that obedience would
bring them safely to their journey's end.

He then laid down a number of rules that were to
govern the camp. All were to arise at 5:00 A.M. at the
sound of the bugle. Prayer, breakfast, and chores were
to be completed within two hours, with the camp ready
to move out by 7:00 A.M. Each man was to remain near
his own team with guns loaded and within easy reach.
All were to start and remain together, with no more
than twenty rods separating the wagons. Noon meals
were to be precooked to avoid delay. Where possible,
the wagons were to be arrayed in a circle at night, with
the animals protected within the circle. Following a
bugle call at 8:30 P.M., fires were to be banked and
prayers offered. Everyone was to be in bed by 9:00 P.M.
As a precaution against attack, each man was to main-
tain his rifle and pistol in perfect working order with a
piece of leather placed over the firing mechanism to
protect it against moisture. A guard was to attend the
cannon in the rear and to see that nothing was left behind.

Convinced of the need for repetition for the
benefit of those who may have been inattentive,
Brigham Young called the camp together again the
following morning, Friday, April 16, and reviewed the
organization and rules of the camp. By 3:00 P.M. everything was ready, and the pioneer company moved out
along the lonesome Platte River.

For many years before the exodus, wagon trains
rattling their way toward or from the Pacific Northwest had used the Platte River as a guide along six
hundred miles of what became known as the Oregon
Trail. These trains followed either the north or the
south bank of the river, the choice frequently depending on whether the grazing was better on one side or

the other. More often, however, the travelers used the south side because the point of departure or arrival on the Missouri river was customarily Independence, whose location made necessary two extra crossings of the Platte for those opting to follow the north side.

Brigham, therefore, decided to follow the north bank of the river because there was less traffic there. On the south side were many trains that included belligerent Missourians or those whose minds had been poisoned against the Saints by Missourian lies or exaggeration. Typical of these was a train headed by former Missouri governor Lilburn W. Boggs, who had issued the notorious extermination order against the Mormons. When Brigham's pioneer company reached Fort Laramie, they discovered that the Boggs wagon train had preceded them there and had left their customary untruths about Mormon conduct and intentions.

On the north side of the Platte, therefore, Brigham and his cadre of expert men marked the route that was later to be identified as the Mormon Trail and would be followed in the years ahead by tens of thousands of dispossessed Mormons as they struggled toward the promised land.

For the first few days the pioneers made good time across the plains of Nebraska. The weather was fair, the terrain flat, and the surface neither muddy, dusty, nor rocky. Everyone was fresh and eager, with little to occupy their thoughts other than the excitement of high adventure and the optimistic prospects of helping to found a new civilization in the wilderness.

Two days after leaving the Platte River staging area, Ellis Eames, one of the pioneers, turned back because of ill health. This reduced the size of the company to 148, the number usually associated with it.

After five days on the trail, the immigrants had their first encounter with the Pawnee tribe, a people noted for its friendliness, but among whom thievery was looked upon as a virtue and almost an art. It was, therefore, with a feeling of suspicion mingled with wry amusement that the pioneers greeted the first Pawnee they met, who rode toward them at breakneck speed, pulled his horse to a snorting, frothing halt, and vaulted from his mount only to shake hands all around! This ambassador of good will was accompanied by eight braves, who seemed to act as a somewhat shy and reticent staff. Later the same day, the train passed a Pawnee village consisting of more than a hundred lodges constructed of skins. The pioneers feared attack when they discovered that an estimated two hundred Pawnees were trailing after them. However, their fear dissipated when a group of leaders came to parley. Brigham Young was wholly unprepared for the ritual that followed. He was not offered a peace pipe, a popular misconception, nor castigated for trespassing on Indian lands. Instead, he was ceremoniously handed a sheath of official-looking documents executed by others who had passed through the Pawnee lands, all attesting to the friendliness and hospitality of these Indians of the plains. Yet the documents also contained a veiled implication of possible harm to the train by noting that *some* of their predecessors had made gifts to their hosts. The pioneers responded to these less than subtle hints by giving out flour, tobacco, fishhooks, and other commodities. The Pawnee chief grumbled at the meager quantity of the gifts and, according to William Clayton, said with "no appearance of hostility" that he "didn't like us to go west through their country." His stated fear was that the Mormons would "kill their buffalo and drive them off." When the chief saw that he had exacted all the tribute the traffic would bear, he pressed no further. As a testimonial to the good intentions of the Pawnee, those who accompanied the chief to the parley insisted on shaking hands with everyone in the camp, running "from one side to the other so as not to miss one." The pioneers may have wondered later whether this almost comedic show of friendship was merely a front to mask Pawnee thievery, as a later inventory showed that two horse bridles and a copper wash pan were missing.[1]

The comparative ease of the journey ended abruptly when the travelers reached the Loup River, a

tributary of the Platte that angles in from the northwest. Quicksand and a swift, waist-high current made
crossing the four-hundred-yard-wide stream a dangerous and tricky operation. Efforts at raft-building
were abandoned when a more favorable crossing was
found upstream where, by lightening the loads and
doubling or tripling the teams, the party was able to
cross safely.

After the crossing, the soil became hard and somewhat crusty. To protect the tender feet of the oxen,
Brigham moved the horse teams to the head of the
column to break up the turf. Also about this time cold
spring winds began to sweep the Nebraska plains,
blowing dust into the eyes of the travelers and sending
them to dig deep in their trunks for the heavy macki-
naws and wool or fur caps and gloves they had had the
foresight to bring.

As if the elements had conspired with diabolic perversity to make this part of the trip as unpleasant as
possible, the pioneers had difficulty on these treeless
plains in finding fuel to cook their meals and to provide warmth at their nightly campsites. That lack was
soon filled, however, when they entered buffalo country and discovered that the droppings of the huge,
shaggy animals served admirably in lieu of firewood or
coal. These "buffalo chips" were looked upon by the
more levitous segment of the camp as an earthy shad-
ow of the manna that sustained the children of Israel.

The pioneers encountered their first buffalo on
May 1, when a comparatively small herd of seventy was
sighted. In need of meat to replenish their dwindling
stores, several of the brethren, mounting their horses
and pursuing the spooked herd in pell-mell fashion,
were able to kill a bull, three cows, and six calves "far
exceeding our expectations and best hopes," William
Clayton noted. Later, after having sampled his first
buffalo steak, he pronounced it "very sweet and tender
as veal."[2]

During the following week, the size and frequency
of the herds increased until, on May 8, Wilford Wood-

ruff recorded, "the face of the earth was alive and moving like the waves of the sea."[3] William Clayton wrote, "The prairie on both sides of the river is literally black with buffalo," and "No pen nor tongue can give an idea of the multitude now in sight continually."[4]

Given what seemed to be an infinite number of buffalo running wild, many white men on the Oregon Trail slaughtered them with indiscriminate abandon. The Mormons saw evidence of this profligate waste in the bleached bones of countless buffalo that littered the plains through which they passed. Realizing that this senseless killing of the buffalo herds was the chief irritant in the deteriorating relationships between whites and Indians, and remembering the concern expressed earlier by the Pawnee chief, Brigham Young adopted a strict policy as to killing these animals. "Multitudes would have been killed," wrote William Clayton, "if the president did not prohibit the brethren from shooting them only as we need the meat."[5]

However, the abundance of buffalo during this segment of the trek was not an unmixed blessing. The animals were voracious eaters, and the giant herds denuded the land of grass and other forage by heavy grazing and trampling. So, in passing through areas recently occupied by large herds of buffalo, the travelers often found it almost impossible to obtain enough feed for their livestock. This problem was intensified by occasional prairie fires ignited by lightning or human hands. Because of the warning Brigham had received of possible Indian harassment, he suspected some of these fires were intentionally set as an impediment or an intimidation.

During this hazardous adventure, Brigham was especially attentive to the need for both public and private devotions. A day did not pass during the pioneer journey but that vocal, group prayers were offered, either by the entire company or by the smaller units of fifties or tens. A Sabbath never passed without some kind of general worship service. Frequently, Brigham, alone or with selected associates, would leave the train to go to a solitary place where special prayers could be offered for guidance, inspiration, or to express thanks for blessings already received.

Brigham's spirituality led him to be concerned about a spirit of levity and carelessness beginning to creep into the camp. Some of the pioneers were indulging in card playing, general coarseness in speech and manner, and, in some rare instances, vulgarity and profanity.

On Saturday, May 29, only a few days after the company had passed Chimney Rock, the half-way point of the trek from Winter Quarters, Brigham summoned the entire camp and mounted a platform within the circle so he could be easily seen and heard by all.

He declared bluntly that he refused to travel further with the company unless there was a change in its spirit and demeanor. "I go no further," he declared with finality. "I am in no hurry. . . . When I wake up in the morning, the first thing I hear is some of the brethren jawing at each other and quarreling because a horse has got loose in the night." He then condemned their gambling, their checkers, and their dominoes, and their "joking, nonsense, profane language, trifling conversation and loud laughter." He then called upon each one to "repent of his weakness, of his follies, of his meanness, and every kind of wickedness, and stop your swearing and profane language." Satisfied that his blunt words had produced the desired effect, the Mormon leader moved to reinforce and solidify his position. He arranged the camp according to rank in the priesthood, whereupon, at his direction, they all covenanted to repent "with uplifted hands without a dissenting vote."

William Clayton recorded the effect of Brigham's rebuke upon the company: "No loud laughter was heard, no swearing, no quarreling, no profane language, no hard speeches to man or beast. It truly seemed as though . . . we had emerged into a new element, a new atmosphere and a new society."[6]

Many members of the company held an impromptu testimony meeting Sunday morning that was devoted chiefly to acknowledgments of imperfection and resolves to improve. Later in the day Brigham and several other leaders retired to a nearby bluff, where, dressed in their temple robes, they offered prayers "for ourselves, this camp and all pertaining to it, the brethren in the army, our families and all the saints."

Within days after Brigham's speech, the welcome sight of Fort John loomed up on the opposite side of the river. Later renamed Fort Laramie for a nearby stream, this rustic stockade, presided over by a friendly and well-liked Frenchman, James Bordeaux, served as a trading post for the Sioux and the Crow Indians who roamed the surrounding plains and for the numerous travelers on the Oregon Trail.

Brigham found an unexpected group of seventeen Latter-day Saints waiting for him at Fort Laramie. They were from Mississippi and had been led west in 1846 by John Brown and others whom Brigham had sent south about the time of the Illinois expulsion. The group had traveled as far west as Fort Laramie in 1846 and, finding that the pioneer company had not passed through, turned south to winter at Pueblo. There they were joined by sick and disabled members of the Mormon Battalion who had left their outfit at Santa Fe and traveled north to the winter camp.

These Mississippians were added to the pioneer company, and Brigham dispatched four brethren, led by Amasa Lyman, to bring along the others from Pueblo as soon as arrangements could be made to travel.

In the meantime the pioneers forded the Platte near Fort Laramie and laid up for several days to regroup and prepare for the last arduous leg of the trek. Here the blacksmiths were kept busy making the wagons shipshape and seeing that the horses were properly shod. During this interlude some shopping was done at the trading post, but high prices kept purchases to a minimum. Also, Brigham used the time profitably to question trader Bordeaux and others about likely places of settlement in the Great Basin. He was interested in a favorable report of the Bear River

Valley, located in what is now southern Idaho, said to
have ample timber and forage, rich soil, a wide variety
of fish and game, and a comparatively moderate climate. While Brigham seemed confident that the initial
Mormon settlement would be south of the Bear River
Valley, he likely made a mental note of this as a future
site for expansion, recognizing that as the existing
members of the Church moved to the mountains, and
as the Mormon population was swelled by new converts from abroad and the children born to members,
there would be a need for numerous valleys to accommodate modern Israel.

It pleased Brigham to hear Bordeaux, whose con-
glomerate organization included French, half-breeds,
and Sioux, observe that he had "never before had such
a company" as the Mormons pass Fort Laramie. His
reaction was all the more favorable because of the distorted portrait of the Saints painted by ex-governor
Boggs. Brigham better understood the significance of
his compliment when he overheard three men with
packhorses, who arrived at the fort on the morning of
June 3, say they had passed more than two thousand
wagons on the trail between Fort Laramie and the Missouri. Even allowing for some exaggeration, Brigham
realized that in the view of the amiable French trader,
his pioneer company was the best among many, not
just a few. And the comments of the three men also
confirmed the wisdom of traveling on the north side of
the Platte, thereby avoiding unnecessary conflict with
the ever-increasing number of emigrants that
thronged the Oregon Trail to the south.

However, any feelings of elation Brigham may
have entertained as he reflected upon the trek
between Winter Quarters and Fort Laramie were les-
sened by the realization that most of the balance of his
journey would be spent on the Oregon Trail. For five
weeks the Mormons would be jostling and jockeying
with many other companies, most of which would
include Missourians, for good campsites, watering
places, and grazing for livestock.

Within two days after leaving Fort Laramie,

Brigham was given an insight into what the next few weeks held in store. Early in the morning of June 6 a group of eleven wagons of Missouri emigrants passed the Mormon train that had halted for the Sabbath. A tense and strained silence prevailed as the two groups eyed each other suspiciously. The Mormons had no way of knowing whether these travelers were of the same cut as those who had mercilessly driven them into Illinois, and the Missourians may have been intimidated by the size of Brigham's company and by false tales of Mormon Danites. Whatever the reason, this encounter in an isolated wilderness was, strangely enough, entirely wordless. Indeed, the only human sounds heard were the gee-haws of the wagoneers and the cry of a baby from one of the passing wagons.

Later in the day, just as the pioneers had completed a worship service, four horsemen appeared, announcing themselves as part of a nineteen-wagon Missouri company on the trail behind. According to William Clayton, some of these riders were recognized by the brethren. "They seem a little afraid and not fond of our company," he wrote. "I feel to wish that their fears may follow them even to Oregon."[7]

When the train appeared, it was found to be under the charge of a garrulous and friendly professional guide, who volunteered helpful information about the location of watering holes and campsites up ahead. The information he provided caused Brigham to break camp later in the day, despite the fact that it was Sunday, and before nightfall they passed the other company, which had reined up early.

Thus, in one day, the pioneers had had three encounters with Missouri companies on the Oregon Trail. This far exceeded their contact with gentiles during six weeks of traveling north of the Platte. And this was only a sample of what they would experience until they would reach Fort Bridger on July 7, a month away, where they would veer off southwesterly from the Oregon Trail.

During the long trek across what is now the state of Wyoming, Brigham and his pioneers were introduced to the twin plagues of crickets and dust. At a noon stop on June 9, they found the ground so thickly covered with crickets that they could hardly walk without stepping on them. The dust filled the air around them, impregnated their clothes and bedding, and found its way into their food stores.

Near the site of the present city of Casper, Wyoming, the pioneers prepared to make their last crossing of the Platte. Brigham Young had sent a party ahead to the river with a large leather boat the pioneers had brought along to help in fording streams. There they found a group of Missourians waiting to cross the river, who, on seeing the boat, offered to pay $1.50 a load for ferrying their supplies. While waiting for the rest of the pioneer company to arrive, this offer was accepted, and by the time Brigham Young reached the river, his enterprising boatmen had earned $34.00 paid in flour, corn, and bacon. According to William Clayton, this was a great "blessing" to the camp, "as a number of the brethren have had no breadstuff for some days."[8]

Taking into account the large number of companies on the trail and their lack of equipment to negotiate a crossing of this kind, Brigham saw an opportunity to capitalize on the circumstances and at the same time provide an easy means of crossing the river for the thousands of Saints who would come later. So he directed the construction of a large raft to be used in ferrying wagons across the swift, deep stream and left ten men there to operate it after the company had moved on. This proved to be a profitable enterprise as well as a great convenience for the Saints who followed, and was operated successfully by the Mormons for many years.

On the third day after leaving the Platte, the pioneers passed Independence Rock, a tall monolith almost eighty yards wide and four hundred yards long that loomed up on the plains and was visible for miles. Here the pioneers set up a wooden marker showing the distance to Fort Laramie to be 175 miles. This was but one of numerous similar signs they left along the

route for the guidance of the hosts of Israel who would
follow. The distances were computed by means of the
ingenious Mormon "roadometer" that was conceived,
designed, and constructed on the trail.

Wilford Woodruff and John Brown scaled Independence Rock and on its highest point prayed in behalf of Brigham Young.

Beyond Independence Rock Brigham began to encounter numerous traders and trappers who were going east. Invariably he stopped to pass the time of day
and to seek information about likely places of settlement in the Great Basin. On June 26, near the South
Pass, he met Major Moses Harris, a grizzled old moun-
taineer who had roamed the western wilds for almost a
quarter of a century. With the possible exception of
Jim Bridger, it is doubtful there was another man then
living who had a more exact knowledge of the Great
Basin than did this friendly, talkative stranger. "His report like that of Captain Fremont's," wrote Orson
Pratt, "is rather unfavorable to the formation of a colony in this basin, principally on account of the scarcity
of timber."[9]

At the same encampment Brigham met and conferred with another noted mountain man, Thomas L.
Smith, who operated a trading post on the Bear River
near Soda Springs. He spoke discouragingly of the Salt
Lake Valley and, according to Erastus Snow, "earnest-
ly advised us to direct our course northwestward from
Bridger, and make our way into Cache valley." So per-
suasive was this man, and so optimistic were his
reports, that the Mormon leaders were "induced to enter into an engagement with him to meet . . . at a certain
time and place some two weeks afterwards to pilot
[the] company into that country." For some unexplained reason Smith failed to make this rendezvous, a
failure that Erastus Snow attributed to the "providence of . . . God. The impressions of the Spirit signified that we should bear rather to the south of west
from Bridger than to the north of west."[10]

Two days later, on June 28, Brigham Young met
Jim Bridger, whose legendary exploits as a trader and

trapper had invested him with a certain aura of unreality. Yet, here he was in the flesh, urging Brigham to make camp early to afford ample time to expound his views on the Mormon plans for settlement. This seasoned frontiersman, a respected member of the American Fur Company, spoke highly of the Salt Lake Valley. Yet, he considered it "imprudent" to settle a large population there without proof that grain could be raised. "He did not know but the frost would kill the corn," noted Wilford Woodruff, and Brigham wrote that "he said he would give $1,000 for a bushel of corn raised in that basin." Brigham's response was typical: "Wait a little, and we will show you."[11]

On June 30, at the Green River, Brigham Young met Samuel Brannan, a member of the Church who had led a group of Saints from New York to San Francisco by ship. Although he had been in California for only a few months, this energetic and imaginative man had already begun to make his mark there, having acquired extensive business interests, including a newspaper, the *California Star,* which he had founded. Indeed, his fame and notoriety had spread so rapidly in the West that Major Moses Harris, whom the pioneers had met earlier, had had several issues of the *California Star* with him!

Knowing that the pioneers would be on the move westward, Samuel Brannan and two companions had left California in April; had crossed the Sierra Nevadas, following, in part, the trail of the unlucky Donner Party; had traversed the monotonous deserts east of the Sierras; had negotiated the high ranges of the Wasatch Mountains; and had found the way to the Green River crossing of the Oregon Trail, a distance of more than eight hundred weary miles.

After the unexpected but joyful reunion with this likeable man, it soon became apparent he had not traveled so far merely to say hello. His object was to persuade Brigham not to settle the Latter-day Saints in the harsh, unforgiving environment of the mountains, but to go onward to the benign climate of the Pacific Coast.

Samuel Brannan proceeded to describe California, a land where, he said, oats grew wild; the barley was without hulls; the clover grew naturally to the height of a horse's belly; and the waters abounded with fish, the air with game birds, and the land with wild horses waiting to be tamed. He extolled the mild weather and the ample rainfall that would obviate the need for irrigation. In fine, he pictured California as a veritable Garden of Eden, where the living would be pleasant and modest effort would yield bounteous rewards.

So little did Samuel Brannan understand the objectives and motivations of Brigham Young, that he failed to see that the aspects of California that attracted him were the ones that repelled his leader. The conditions he described would attract settlers in great numbers. The Mormon leader had seen the immense wagon traffic to the West Coast, and his acquaintance with the railways at Liverpool and Manchester and with the B&O in the eastern United States, which even then was pushing its line toward the Ohio, could not have helped but convince him that within a few years the North American continent would be girdled with iron rails. With the inevitable influx of vast numbers of gentiles into California, he saw nothing but a repetition of the sad experiences the Mormons had endured in Ohio, Missouri, and Illinois were he to follow Samuel Brannan's advice. Beyond this, however, Brigham believed that his people would prosper and be blessed more abundantly if they had to struggle alone in the mountains.

These considerations caused him to reject his enthusiastic friend's proposal. The overriding question he faced at the time was not the choice between California and the mountains, but between one valley and another.

At the Green River Brigham's company was also augmented by the addition of thirteen men of the Mormon Battalion who had caught them from behind, and was diminished by the assignment of five men to go back on the trail to guide the other emigrant companies that were following. From there the company pushed on to Fort Bridger, its last contact with organized outposts on the Oregon Trail.

On July 9, after a day's stopover at Fort Bridger, Brigham led his company, seasoned now by three months of travel on the pioneer trail, southwesterly along what became known as the Hastings track, or cut-off. No longer would they have the river or a well-defined wagon road to guide them—only a set of crude maps and descriptions; the faint, often indiscernible, trail left by the Donner party; and Orson Pratt and his sextant.

As the pioneers pushed forward, the terrain became progressively more rugged and the rate of travel more slow and deliberate.

On July 12 Brigham Young was stricken with mountain fever, a disease that had afflicted other members of the camp earlier. When their leader was stricken, however, and especially when he became delirious, the company stopped.

Brigham's illness caused the pioneers to mark time for almost three days. While waiting they became restive and filled with apprehension. Their concern was rooted not only in Brigham's illness, but in the ever-increasing ruggedness of the terrain, in the intermittent loss of the faint trail left by the Donner party, and in the fleeting passage of time. They were aware of the urgent need to reach their destination, plant a crop, and send a contingent back along the trail to shepherd Modern Israel to the mountains. Their concern was intensified by the realization that the numerous Latter-day Saints behind them would require food when they arrived at their destination, and by the gloomy predictions of those who knew the country best that crops would not mature in the harsh mountain climate.

These and other pressures influenced Heber C. Kimball, second in command, to ignore the basic rule against separating the company, and to send an advance party under the direction of Orson Pratt ahead to open the trail. In the meantime Wilford Woodruff made a bed for Brigham in his carriage and brought him along toward the trail's end.

The first Mormon penetration into the Salt Lake Valley occurred on July 21, 1847, when Orson Pratt and Erastus Snow entered it together. Except for Brigham and his small party that lingered several miles behind, the remainder of the pioneer company arrived the following day, and on July 23, an assembly was held under the direction of Orson Pratt and Willard Richards. They offered prayers of thanksgiving and consecrated the land to the Lord. Immediately thereafter the pioneers began plowing a tract lying northwest of the present site of the city and county building in Salt Lake City.

On the following day, July 24, Brigham Young first saw the valley that was to be his mountain home. As Wilford Woodruff's carriage bumped its tortuous way down Emigration Canyon, fording the creek no less than eighteen times, its languid passenger, still showing the debilitating effect of the mountain fever, had ample opportunity to reflect upon the significance of his journey and upon what lay ahead. Whether his thoughts were sufficiently concentrated to enable him to grasp the full significance of the event that immediately faced him is, of course, a matter of conjecture. Certain it is, however, that from the beginning of the trek, when he designated his people as the Camp of Israel, and later when he bestowed the name Mount Pisgah upon one of the temporary Mormon settlements in Iowa, he was keenly aware of the historic analogies between his trek and that of Moses. This being true, it is a fair assumption that at some time, perhaps during his delirium or his rough ride down Emigration Canyon, Brigham speculated about whether his trek would end as Moses' did, just short of the promised land. "Get thee up into the top of Pisgah," the Lord told Moses, "and lift up thine eyes . . . and behold it with thine eyes: for thou shalt not go over this Jordan." (Deut. 3:27.)

As Wilford Woodruff guided his team out of the

mouth of the canyon and onto the shoulder of ancient
Lake Bonneville, he swung the carriage around so
Brigham could see what has been called "one of the
great views of the continent." The scene has been described by Wallace Stegner: "From where they stood
above the alluvial fan of Emigration Creek, the
Wasatch ran in an abrupt wall southward, but on the
north it swung an arm around to half enclose the valley. Beginning nearly straight west of them, perhaps
twenty-five airline miles away, the high smooth crest-
line of the Oquirrhs also ran southward until it all but
met the Wasatch at a low notch on the southern sky.
And northward and westward from the northernmost
foot of the Oquirrhs, fabulous, dark blue, floating its
pale islands, lapping the world's rim, went the Great
Salt Lake."[12]

After absorbing the scene laid out before him,
Brigham "expressed his full satisfaction in the appearance of the valley as a resting-place for the Saints,"
wrote Wilford Woodruff, "and said he was amply
repaid for his journey." Years later Wilford Woodruff
added that Brigham had seen the valley in an earlier
vision and that upon viewing it from his carriage
declared, "It is enough. This is the right place, drive
on."[13]

At 2:00 P.M. Brigham's party reached the pioneer
encampment. Pioneers were already plowing and
planting a five-acre potato patch and digging ditches
to convey water from a nearby creek to the parched
land.

Here was the trail's end, where the dispossessed
and unwanted Saints would sink their roots deep into
the mountain soil. Here was the isolation for which
Brigham had been seeking.

But having arrived at his destination, Brigham had
many important matters yet to resolve: obtaining the
approval of the pioneer camp, scouting the environment, laying the foundations of a new city, and preparing for the return to Winter Quarters.

Chapter Seventeen

In the Valley

The pioneers held a meeting on July 27, 1847. The first and most important item on the agenda of that meeting was whether the Salt Lake Valley should be the principal place of Mormon settlement in the mountains. Although Brigham and others in the company knew by spiritual means that the valley was the right place, Brigham was anxious that a decision of such magnitude be based upon agreement rather than command. The issue, therefore, was presented for general discussion, and all had the opportunity to freely express their views. Then on motion, seconded by Norton Jacob, who left a careful record of the meeting, the decision was made to settle in the valley. As if to underscore the democratic process, there was one dissenting vote, registered by William Vance.

Norton Jacob noted: "The President then said, 'We shall have a committee to lay out the city, and also to apportion the inheritances, and who shall it be?' It was unanimously resolved that the Twelve should be that committee. Says the President, 'We propose to have the temple lot contain 40 acres, to include the ground we are now on—what do you say to that?' " Then followed discussion and decision about the width of the streets and sidewalks, the size and the position of homes on the city lots, and animal control and zoning for business.

With these matters out of the way, Brigham delivered a memorable sermon. First, he declared that religious freedom would predominate in the promised land on condition that there be no blasphemy and no derision of Joseph Smith. Second, he called upon the

Saints to become wholly self-sufficient and independent "of the gentile nations," producing and manufacturing "every article of use, convenience or necessity."

Brigham was to remain in the valley a month and two days. During that period he spent his time recuperating from his illness, exploring, instructing, and preparing a shelter complex. With some of the brethren he rode on horseback to Ensign Peak and to the lake, where they took a swim in its buoyant waters. He designated the temple site, located between the forks of City Creek, and directed that the streets be laid out in true alignment with the points of the compass, beginning at that place. He selected his homesite just east of the temple, and with the aid of others built a crude adobe stockade.

Brigham discovered that the mountain fever was a hardy and resistant disease. Intermittently he suffered a recurrence of the miseries that attended it. He spent all day Sunday, August 1, in his wagon, unable to move about. He usually took advantage of such periods to catch up on his journals and correspondence, to pray, and to plan ahead.

On August 2 he directed a letter to Charles C. Rich, who was leading a company on the trail. "Let all the brethren and Sisters cheer up their hearts," he wrote, "and know assuredly that God has heard and answered their prayers and ours, and led us to a goodly land."[1] The couriers for such letters sent east were groups of pioneers who now began to return to Winter Quarters for their families. Brigham always had words of counsel for these brethren as they left the valley. Occasionally these were phrased in almost jocular language, as when he told Shadrach Roundy, "Do not give way to an overanxious spirit so that your spirits arrive at Winter Quarters before the time that your bodies can possibly arrive there."[2]

On August 8 Brigham directed a letter to the members of the Mormon Battalion in California. He gave the letter to Samuel Brannan and James Brown, who were preparing to leave for the San Francisco Bay area. In it he urged the brethren there to come to the

Salt Lake Valley as soon as possible, closing with words of fatherly affection: "We want to see you, even all of you, and talk with you, and throw our arms around you and kill the fatted calf and make merry. Yes, brethren, we want to rejoice with you once more."[3]

Two days before he dispatched the letter to California, "President Young went down into the water and baptized all his brethren of the Twelve present," wrote Wilford Woodruff. "He then confirmed us and sealed upon us our apostleship, and all the keys, powers and blessings belonging to that office." Later, most of the other members of the pioneer company followed their leaders into the small reservoir created by damming up the waters of City Creek, where they too were rebaptized, symbolizing their new start in a new land.[4]

As the end of August drew near, Brigham made hurried preparations to leave for Winter Quarters.

He called the pioneers together the Sunday before his departure to give them final words of instruction. He cautioned about the dangers that surrounded them, the untamed environment, hostile Indians, and wild animals. He admonished them to enclose the entire stockade "so that Indians cannot get in." He gave specific instructions about the height of the stockade walls and counsel about the homes to be constructed later.

Satisfied that nothing had been left undone, Brigham mounted his horse on Thursday, August 26, 1847, and reined up in front of the stockade, where he called "good-bye to all who tarry. I feel well"; and rode eastward through the mouth of Emigration Canyon toward a rendezvous on the Bear River with others who had left the valley earlier. There the returning company of one hundred and three men was organized for the trip back to Winter Quarters.[5]

Chapter Eighteen

Return to Winter Quarters

Brigham's party broke camp and departed from the Bear River rendezvous on August 31. Because of word brought to him by Ezra T. Benson, his faithful associate in the Twelve, Brigham knew that soon he would begin to meet the succeeding waves of Israel's Camp, almost fifteen hundred strong, traveling steadily toward their mountain destination.

Two days later, on the Big Sandy, the first of four large companies was encountered, this one, led by Daniel Spencer, consisting of about fifty wagons. The travelers halted, shared news from either end of the trail, broke bread, and counseled together. Invariably Brigham or others assigned by him gave instructions to the newcomers on how to proceed along the trail and what to do upon arriving in the valley.

The second company, led by Parley P. Pratt, was encountered on September 4. Brigham severely chastised Parley for deviating from the rules of travel laid down before the Pioneer company left Winter Quarters. He had apparently organized differently and brought too large a group. The burden of responsibility he carried doubtless explains in part the harshness of his rebuke.

A day behind Parley followed a large company led by John Taylor, and twelve miles beyond his company, Brigham met Jedediah M. Grant, who led the last of the four companies that would arrive in the Salt Lake Valley in September, 1847.

One night Brigham allowed a lapse in guarding procedures. The results were almost catastrophic. The wily Sioux, taking advantage of the Mormons' negligence, rustled twenty-eight of their best horses. This critical loss made it necessary for some of the brethren to walk or hitch rides on the wagons. Putting the incident in the most optimistic light, Brigham "called upon all the returning brethren, except the teamsters, to take a walk with me to Winter Quarters."[1] The fact that their destination lay roughly seven hundred miles to the east seemed to make little difference to the man who, in years past, had logged thousands of miles on foot.

Notwithstanding its loss, the returning party averaged from fifteen to twenty-five miles a day. Pushing at this speed for over a month, however, with no respite for the remaining horses, had a debilitating effect upon the animals and produced no little anxiety among the brethren. Brigham wrote in his journal on October 13: "Each morning of late the brethren have had to assist five of the horses to rise to their feet. Several others are obliged to be driven loose and most of the rest are very weak." Four days later the brethren decided to leave their wagons near the Platte, prepare a supply of dried buffalo meat, and, in Brigham's words, "continue our journey to Winter Quarters as best we could."[2]

Thirteen days later the travelers reached their destination. "We drove into the town in order about an hour before sunset," Brigham recorded. "We were truly rejoiced to once more behold our wives, children and friends after an absence of over six months, having traveled more than two thousand miles, sought out a location for the Saints to dwell in peace, and accomplished the most interesting mission in this last dispensation. Not a soul of our camp died, and no serious accident happened to any, for which we praise the Lord."[3]

Chapter Nineteen

President of the Church—
The Last Trip West

Brigham Young had now led the Church for over three years as the President of the Twelve. That leadership, spanning one of the most crucial periods of Church history, had been both bold and efficient. Yet it was cumbersome to direct the affairs of an international organization through the medium of twelve men who, because of their mandate to teach all nations, seldom were all assembled in the same place at the same time. The deficiencies of this arrangement had been especially evident during the exodus, as Brigham often found it necessary to make decisions unilaterally or with the counsel of one or two of the Twelve because of the exigencies of the moment. Despite the justification for such expediency, Brigham began to reflect and pray about the propriety of reconstituting the First Presidency of the Church. It was apparent from the revelations that the First Presidency, like the Twelve, was a permanent fixture of Church organization. If vacancies in the Twelve were filled when they occurred, as they had been for many years, why should not the same practice be followed as to the First Presidency?

It is unclear exactly when Brigham decided upon the reorganization of the First Presidency. Nor is it known whether his determination was based upon a new revelation or upon his inspired application of the revelations previously received. It is plain, however, that by October 12, 1847, he had begun to take steps leading to the reestablishment of the First Presidency. On that date Wilford Woodruff recorded in his journal, "I had a question put to me by President Young, what my opinion was concerning one of the twelve apostles being appointed as the president of the church with his two counselors. I answered that a quorum like the twelve who had been appointed by revelation, confirmed by revelation from time to time—I thought it would require a revelation to change the order of that quorum. *Whatever the Lord inspires you to do in this matter, I am with you."*[1]

In discussing the matter with other members of his quorum then on the Missouri, Brigham found that they shared Wilford Woodruff's views. A meeting was held on December 5, 1847, at the home of Orson Hyde in the Mormon community on the east bank of the river, later to be identified as Kanesville but now known as Council Bluffs. Present at the meeting were nine of the Twelve, Brigham Young, Heber C. Kimball, Orson Hyde, Orson Pratt, Wilford Woodruff, George A. Smith, Willard Richards, Amasa M. Lyman, and Ezra T. Benson. Parley P. Pratt and John Taylor were in the Salt Lake Valley, and Lyman Wight had gone to Texas instead of accompanying the other members of his quorum and the main body of the Saints to the West.

Each member of the Twelve in attendance, in order of seniority, freely discussed the reorganization of the First Presidency and the identity of the President, who, it was understood, would have the prerogative of selecting his counselors. On motion of Orson Hyde, seconded by Wilford Woodruff and unanimously carried, Brigham Young was sustained as the President of the Church. He then nominated Heber C. Kimball as first counselor and Willard Richards as second counselor, both nominations being duly seconded and unanimously approved.[2]

These actions of the Twelve were sustained in a special conference of the Saints in Council Bluffs on December 27 in the "log tabernacle," a 65 x 40-foot building constructed especially for the occasion.

The action of this conference in sustaining the new First Presidency was confirmed at the annual conference of the Church held in Council Bluffs on April 6, 1848 and was ratified at a conference held in the Salt

Lake Valley on October 8, 1848, and at a general conference of the Saints in the British Isles held in Manchester, England, on August 14, 1848.

In December, 1847, Brigham Young and the Twelve published a "General Epistle" addressed to the members of the Church "dispersed throughout the earth." In addition to chronicling the history of the Church from the beginning of the exodus, it gave notice of the intention to reorganize the First Presidency, apprised the Church of future plans, and instructed the Saints to gather to the Salt Lake Valley. All were enjoined to keep the commandments, spread the gospel, and educate their children. The Brethren asked the Saints to secure "at least a copy of every valuable treatise on education," and to bring "all kinds of choice seeds, of grain, vegetables, fruits, shrubbery, trees, and vines." Moreover, they counseled them to bring "the best stock of beasts, bird, and fowl of every kind," and "the best tools of every description."[3]

With the First Presidency reorganized and the members of the Church throughout the world properly instructed, there remained one important step to unify the Church—to fill the four vacancies in the Council of the Twelve Apostles caused by the excommunication of Lyman Wight and the reorganization of the First Presidency. While consideration was given to this step at Kanesville, it was not taken for over a year. On February 12, 1849, several months after Brigham reached the Salt Lake Valley the second time, Charles C. Rich, Lorenzo Snow, Erastus Snow, and Franklin D. Richards were ordained to the apostleship and set apart as members of the Council of the Twelve. The delay was probably to give Parley P. Pratt and John Taylor a voice in the selection and to permit additional seasoning of the four candidates.

Although these dramatic organizational changes during the winter of 1847-48 claimed the spotlight, there were many other important events that deserve attention. Chief among these was the movement of the Saints from the west to the east side of the river. The Indian agent was concerned about a restiveness among the Omahas and urged the Saints to move to the bluffs on the east side to avoid conflict. Although the Mormon stay at Winter Quarters had not been as long as Brigham had understood it would be, he was agreeable to the move; indeed, he favored it, as he preferred to oversee the operation rather than to have it occur after he had gone to the valley. Without undue murmuring, the pioneers abandoned the hundreds of temporary shelters they had thrown up on the Omaha lands and, at Brigham's direction, began to build anew at Council Bluffs.

In the meantime, preparations went forward for the mass migration west scheduled for the spring and summer. In many ways this presented more complexities than existed with the pioneer company the year before. While the trail and the exact destination were clear now, the differences in personnel and equipment made the operation nebulous and risky. Instead of a small handful of expert men, well equipped and disciplined, Brigham's entourage in 1848 would include hundreds of Saints of both sexes and all ages, some infirm, some destitute, and all, except for the few pioneers sprinkled among them, inexperienced and unskilled in wilderness travel.

The decision was made to divide the 1848 migration into three companies, each to be directed by a member of the First Presidency. The first two of these, under Brigham Young and Heber C. Kimball, geared up for a rendezvous at the Elkhorn crossing on June 1. Combined, these two encampments that included 623 wagons and 1,891 "souls" probably represent the largest migratory body ever to ply the Mormon Trail or the Oregon Trail. It included 2,012 oxen, 131 horses, 44 mules, 983 cows, 334 "loose cattle," 654 sheep, 237 pigs, 904 chickens, 134 dogs, 54 cats, 3 goats, 10 geese, 11 doves, 5 ducks, and a squirrel. Nor must we forget the five beehives, brought along to make sure that the Promised Land would flow with honey.[3]

Notwithstanding the congestion and disorder such a melange of people, vehicles, and animals must have produced, all was gaiety and optimism at the Elk Horn crossing as the Camp of Israel began to move west. Thomas Bullock wrote to a friend in England that if anyone believed Mormonism were defeated, "he ought to have been in the neighbourhood of the Elk Horn this day." There, he assured, "he would have seen such a host of wagons that would have satisfied him in an instant, that it lives and flourishes like a tree by a fountain of waters; he would have seen merry faces, and heard the songs of rejoicing, that the day of deliverance had surely come."[5]

Once on the trail Brigham saw the same metamorphosis take place among the members of his encampment as had occurred with the pioneer company. The feelings of joviality and lightheartedness slowly gave way to the grim realization that the journey upon which they had embarked would be long and arduous. Day after day they ate up the miles in bumping, jolting, rattling travel.

The monotony of the trip was intermittently relieved by the fording of streams; the sight of buffalo herds; the occasional, tense visits of Indian parties; and the appearance of noted landmarks that stood along the route. Two days beyond the most famous of these, Chimney Rock, Brigham, having reaching about the half-way point of the trip, dictated a letter to Parley P. Pratt and John Taylor in the Salt Lake Valley. Dispatched by messengers who traveled speedily ahead of the slow-moving camp, the letter pleaded for the brethren in the valley to send wagons, one laden with salt for livestock, to rendezvous with the camp at the crossing of the Green River. The plan was to send some of the wagons back to the Missouri from the Green River, transferring to the wagons to be sent from the valley some of the destitute Saints Brigham had brought along. Of these he wrote, "But we have the poor with us; their cry was urgent to go to the mountains, and I could neither close my ears nor harden my heart against their earnest appeals."[6]

As Brigham reached the Sweetwater River in what is now western Wyoming, a sense of discouragement and discontent seemed to have taken hold of the camp,

causing many of its members to look to their selfish
interests and to have a sullen, uncommunicative attitude. The Saints were not to be treated to a scalding
lecture on this occasion. Brigham merely hitched up
his team and left! He said he was "going to the valley; if
anybody wants to follow, the road is open." Having so
spoken, the Mormon leader clucked at his animals and
hit the trail, leaving his astonished followers to watch
in disbelief as his wagon disappeared over the horizon
to the west.[7]

When Brigham did not return, the Saints had only
one logical thing left to do. They hitched up their own
teams, amidst grumblings of surprise and annoyance,
and sheepishly followed their leader along the trail.

Two days later Brigham met two families of Saints
headed east. These were the Shockleys, James and
Richard and their wives and children, who had wea-
ried of life in the rugged mountains and yearned for
an easier existence in a more congenial land. What aggravated the situation in Brigham's view was that they
were headed for Missouri. He proceeded to deliver a
"very severe lecture on their going to serve the Devil,
among our enemies," and instructed them never to
return to the valley "until they knew they were Saints
indeed." But he told them to go in peace and gave
them twenty-five pounds of meat.[8]

The requested relief train from the valley met
Brigham Young's camp on August 28 at the last crossing of the Sweetwater. Led by Lorenzo D. Young,
Brigham's brother, and Abraham O. Smoot, this train
included forty-seven empty wagons and one hundred
and twenty-four extra yoke of oxen to assist the camp
in crossing the mountains. This enabled Brigham to
release an equal number of borrowed teams and wagons to return to the Missouri River for the use of other
companies that would follow.

The news from the end of the trail, brought by
Lorenzo, was good, indicating that the Saints were
making headway against their rigorous mountain environment. And the bounteous harvest at Winter
Quarters and Council Bluffs the past season had vastly

improved the conditions of the Saints on the Missouri as they planned for later migrations. With everything running smoothly and with the spirits of his company lifted as they looked forward expectantly to the end of their journey, Brigham was able to relax somewhat. He and Daniel H. Wells spent all day in Brigham's carriage on September 8 listening to the camp historian, Thomas Bullock, read three newspapers that had fallen into their hands.

Jim Bridger's pessimistic views about early frost and a short growing season may have risen to haunt Brigham when, at the crossing of the Bear River on September 14, the weather suddenly turned cold and snow fell in sufficient quantities to blanket the ground.

Six days later the valley came into view at the summit of Big Mountain. As Brigham descended into the valley through Emigration Canyon, he was much stronger and observant than he had been the year before. No longer afflicted with the mountain fever, he felt alert and vigorous. He seemed fit in every way to begin the herculean task of establishing the Saints in the mountains.

Chapter Twenty

Beginnings in the Promised Land

T wo major problems faced Brigham Young after his arrival in the Salt Lake Valley on September 20, 1848: first, how to provide for his large and ever-growing family, and second, how to direct, simultaneously, the colonization of the new land and the flood of immigration over the Mormon Trail that, in the two following decades, would channel almost seventy thousand newcomers into the Latter-day Saint mountain communities.

Because the main public focus on Brigham Young's life is the extraordinary colonizing effort he directed, there is an unfortunate tendency to overlook his remarkable domestic achievements. Actually, the latter took precedence in his order of priorities, recognizing as he did that in the eternal scheme of things his role as husband, father, and family patriarch stood above all others.

As Brigham assayed his family situation after arriving in the valley in the autumn of 1848, he began to comprehend the enormity of his task more fully. By this time he had several wives and roughly a dozen children, ranging in age from one to twenty-three. The two eldest children, Elizabeth and Vilate, were married by this time, however, Elizabeth having married Edmund Ellsworth in 1842, and Vilate having married Charles F. Decker at Winter Quarters in 1847. This still left Brigham with more than twenty mouths to feed.

In the discharge of this heavy responsibility, however, he did not act alone. Except for the very young children, John W., four; Brigham Heber and Edward P., three; Oscar Brigham, two; and Mary Eliza and Ella

Elizabeth, one; all of the wives and children worked productively. The oldest son, Joseph A., was now a robust fourteen-year-old, while Brigham, Jr., was twelve. Trained from their childhood to work, these boys were almost able to keep pace with their energetic father. Alice and Luna, who were now respectively nine and six, were able to care for themselves and in many ways were able to help with the domestic chores and to tend the younger children. In considering the domestic load Brigham carried at the time, we must not forget that his wives, for the most part, were young and vigorous women capable of great physical exertion. Lucy Ann (Decker) was twenty-six; Harriet (Cook) and Emily (Partridge) twenty-four; Clarissa (Decker) twenty; Margaret (Alley) twenty-three; Emmeline (Free) twenty-two; Margaret (Pierce) twenty-five; Zina (Huntington) twenty-seven; and Lucy (Bigelow) eighteen. The older wives, Mary Ann (Angell), Eliza (Snow), Louisa (Beaman), and Clarissa (Ross), were wise and able managers who made up in experience and judgment what they may have lacked in youthful energy.

Given his administrative skills, energetic drive, and inspired leadership, Brigham was able to organize and direct his family in a way that spread the authority and responsibility among all who were able to work and produced the maximum results under the circumstances. Later, as Brigham became more affluent, many of the menial tasks that at this time were performed by the family were taken over by a corps of workmen employed not only to free the family for other tasks, but to help provide gainful work for some of the numerous converts who flooded into Salt Lake Valley from the mission fields abroad.

Under the harsh conditions of the day, the family was made painfully aware of their vulnerability when, in 1848, Louisa Beaman Young lost twin boys, Alvah and Alma. She had previously lost infants Moroni, Joseph, and Hyrum. This brought to six the number of children Brigham had lost in a period of five years. Brigham was not to lose another child until 1856, when Jedediah Grant Young, the infant child of Clarissa Decker Young would pass away.

While Brigham was grappling with the difficult problem of providing for his own in the wilderness, he also carried the heavy burden of overseeing the work of settlement of the Saints who had already arrived in the valley.

When the Saints first arrived in the Salt Lake Valley in 1847, the area was under the jurisdiction of Mexico. It did not become part of the United States until the treaty of Guadalupe Hidalgo in 1848. And when the United States acquired jurisdiction, there was no effective way to administer it because of the remoteness of the area and the lack of effective communications. In these circumstances Brigham Young and his associates in Church leadership took the only practical stance available to them—they acted as if they owned the land by reason of preemptive settlement. They rightly judged that their government would later ratify the ownership they now assumed on the basis of possession.

Working on this premise, one of Brigham's first acts in the fall of 1848 was to allot "inheritances" to the Saints. This was done in line with a mandate he had issued the year before that no one could "buy" land in the valley, but each would have his land "measured out" to him for city or farming purposes. By way of implementing this policy, the city was divided into ten-acre blocks with eight lots to the block. Adopting a plan devised by Joseph Smith years before his martyrdom, the streets were to be wide and uniform, and zoning was to segregate the business and industrial sections from the residential areas.

Following the allotment of inheritances came a whole spate of official acts necessary to control and direct the development of a new city: building codes were adopted; the construction of a council house and clerk's office was decided upon; arrangements were made to construct a canal to bring water directly into the city; and plans were laid to take the first steps toward constructing a temple by building a wall around the temple block. Since mud would be the main building material for years to come, adobe yards were established to fuel the feverish construction boom that now began. And plans were projected for a foundry and tannery.

The severe winter of 1848-49 put a damper on Brigham's enthusiastic plans for expansion and development. In early December heavy snows began to fall, ultimately drifting to a depth of up to five feet. As the inclement weather worsened, the Saints were severely restricted in their movement and ability to work. Pinned down in crude, drafty buildings, with their food supplies dwindling, many Saints became discouraged. A stifling pall of discontent settled on the community. Many began to talk of returning east, while others approvingly discussed following Sam Brannan to balmy California. Conscious of the deteriorating morale of his people and the danger this created to the success of his enterprise, Brigham, on February 25, 1849, assembled the Saints in the bowery, constructed within the Old Fort, to deliver another of his spine-stiffening discourses. "We have been kicked out of the frying-pan into the fire," he cried, "out of the fire into the middle of the floor, and here we are and here we will stay." He then emphasized that God had revealed to him "that this is the spot to locate His people, and here is where they will prosper," and prophesied that God would temper the elements and rebuke the frost and the sterility of the soil.[1]

The spring that dawned a few weeks later, coupled with the stimulus of Brigham's discourse, implanted new hope and enthusiasm in the Mormon pilgrims. By April the settlers had begun to move their houses from the temporary forts onto their city lots. An eight-thousand-acre field south of the settlement was surveyed and divided into five- and ten-acre tracts, which were distributed by casting lots. Also, a Church farm of about eight hundred acres was set aside.

A "general epistle" of the new First Presidency that issued from the valley on April 9 revealed the rapid expansion of the new community through the construction of roads and bridges, including a major bridge across the Jordan River to the west and six or seven bridges across minor streams—all to be financed by a one percent property tax. The settlers also built three grist mills, six or seven sawmills, and a bathhouse at the warm springs. All things considered, Brigham, the principal author of this general epistle, concluded that Salt Lake City was "already assuming the appearance of years, for an ordinary country."

With the physical development of the new land moving forward satisfactorily, the Mormon leader turned his attention to a mechanism suitable to govern the growing city and the neighboring communities he envisioned. The establishment in February of the Salt Lake Stake, governed by a stake presidency, and the creation of nineteen wards, presided over by bishops, provided the necessary ecclesiastical control that for some time to come would exert a dominating influence in many purely civil matters.

But Brigham correctly foresaw that the promised land would not long remain the exclusive domain of the Latter-day Saints. Soon there would be numerous gentile neighbors, whose rights and duties could not, indeed, should not, be adjudicated or defined through channels of the Mormon priesthood. So in early March a constitution of the Provisional State of Deseret was adopted, and Brigham was promptly elected governor. The next month he and his associates made a strategic error by memorializing Congress to create a territorial government. On the advice of Colonel Kane, this action was later rescinded and a plea made to create a state instead. This availed nothing, however, and on September 9, 1850, an act creating a territorial government for Utah became law. Eleven days later Brigham Young was appointed governor of Utah Territory by President Millard Fillmore. The new governor was to serve in this capacity for almost eight years, during which time the Latter-day Saints enjoyed comparative freedom from the civil abuse that had been routinely inflicted upon them in the East.

Later, however, under other governors, Brigham

and his people would become painfully aware of the hazards of territorial government and of the blunder in not working initially and aggressively in favor of statehood.

In the meantime, the Mormon leader, in his dual role as President of the Church and Governor of the Provisional State of Deseret, or the Territory of Utah, wielded such broad ecclesiastical and civil authority that he was able to control effectively the rate of growth, the scope, and the quality of economic development in a vast area of the Intermountain West. It was this set of unusual circumstances that enabled Brigham Young to leave the imprint of his own character and that of the Church he headed upon so many communities and individuals within the area he dominated.

With the reins of authority firmly in his grasp, Brigham moved forward confidently and effectively to consolidate the Mormon foothold in the mountains and to fuel the fires of conversion and migration.

The multiplying quality of Brigham's colonization efforts became apparent soon after Salt Lake City was firmly established. The common reservoir of manpower and resources was divided and then divided again and again to create other Latter-day Saint communities north and south along the Wasatch front and elsewhere.

As early as 1847, small groups led by Perrigrine Sessions and Hector C. Haight gained a tenuous foothold to the north on lands now included within the Utah cities of Bountiful and Farmington. Later, Captain James Brown of the Mormon Battalion acquired the interests of Miles Goodyear in the Ogden Basin, and on September 3, 1849, Brigham selected the Ogden townsite, lying between the Weber and Ogden rivers. Earlier that year, on March 17, 1849, he had selected a townsite in Utah Valley on the Provo River. Typically, the group sent there to colonize (which included 150 settlers) possessed the varied skills necessary to establish a permanent community.

In the autumn of that year, Brigham also sent a

group of colonists into Tooele Valley to the west under the leadership of John Rowberry and Cyrus Tolman. At about the same time, a colony under the leadership of Isaac Morley was sent to settle in the San Pete Valley (sometimes called San Pitch Valley), a hundred miles south of Salt Lake. This colonization was made in response to the request of Ute Indian Chief Walker, who earlier in the year had gone to the Mormon leader to ask him to send colonists among his people so they could learn "the white man's ways."

Correctly deciding that the areas already explored and settled would be insufficient to accommodate the thousands of Saints yet to gather to the new land, Brigham commissioned an exploring party. Led by Parley P. Pratt of the Twelve with W. W. Phelps and David Fullmer as counselors, this party of fifty men, traveling in twelve wagons and a carriage, left Salt Lake Valley in the latter part of November, 1849. Equipped with an odometer to measure distances, scientific equipment to take sightings for map-making, and skilled observers and clerks, this expedition had the capability of preparing a reliable guide for future colonization. Traveling through Utah, Juab, Sanpete, Sevier, and Little Salt Lake Valleys, the party worked its way into the southern part of the territory to what is now called Utah's Dixie, roughly three hundred miles from the Salt Lake Valley. On the return trip, the party followed the valleys to the west of and parallel to the valleys they had traveled going south. In the years ahead, Brigham would direct the establishment of many communities along the line of travel of this expedition, Gunnison, Richfield, Marysvale, Parowan, Cedar City, St. George, Beaver, and Fillmore, just to name a few.

Also in late 1849, two missionaries, Addison Pratt and Hiram H. Blackwell, accompanied a group of immigrants guided by Jefferson Hunt en route to California. Showing the predominant interest of the day, Addison Pratt, a faithful journalist, commented on the likely places for settlement he observed along the trail: "Saturday, October 13, . . . camped on a fine stream

[Chalk Creek, near Fillmore, Utah] . . . [that] would sustain a small settlement." "October 18 . . . camped on Beaver Creek [near Beaver, Utah]. . . . I think this creek would support a settlement of some thousands." "October 27 . . . camped on the first creek in Little Salt Lake Valley [near Parowan, Utah] . . . it ought to sustain a large settlement."

Elder Pratt and his companions were following a route later to be identified as the "Mormon Corridor," which connected Salt Lake with a Latter-day Saint community at San Bernardino, California, whose settlement Brigham Young was to reluctantly approve a few years later. The frequent use of the Mormon Corridor in the years ahead caused Brigham to direct the establishment of several Latter-day Saint communities in southern Utah and Nevada, including those at Las Vegas Springs and St. Thomas on the Muddy River, the latter now being inundated by Lake Mead.

Some who study Brigham Young's achievements and methods are astonished to discover that at the very moment he was struggling to gain a foothold for his people in the mountains, when the help and leadership of experienced and trusted men were sorely needed at home, he began a missionary initiative that sent many of his ablest associates abroad. At the general conference held in October, 1849, Brigham, using the leadership devices of surprise and suspense that he often employed, announced without prior warning that some of the brethren would be sent into the world to help fulfill the divine mandate to preach the gospel to every creature. He then reeled off a list of assignments that many, especially the families of those involved, heard with a sense of amazed disbelief. Addison Pratt and Hiram Blackwell, already mentioned, were called to the Society Islands. Indeed, they were en route there when they joined Jefferson Hunt's wagon train.

Calls were also extended to Lorenzo Snow and Joseph Toronto to go to Italy; to Erastus Snow, Peter O. Hansen, and John Forsgren to go to the Scandinavian countries; to John Taylor, Curtis E. Bolton, and

John Pack to go to France and Germany; and to Franklin D. Richards and several other elders to join Orson Pratt, who was already in England.

This bold action, much more than a symbolic gesture, served notice on all, members and gentiles alike, that the Mormon proselyters meant business. The talk about gathering scattered Israel from the four corners of the earth to their new mountain home in "Zion" was not mere chatter. Moreover, they were deadly serious about plans to create a community of believers fit for the society of Jesus upon his return. They anticipated that their stay in the mountains would be of short though indefinite duration, and that ultimately, in God's own due time, they would return to the land of Missouri, given to them as an everlasting "inheritance," from which they expected all earthly affairs would be governed during Christ's millennial reign. Meanwhile, they intended to make their stay in the mountains as comfortable and pleasant as possible and, from outward appearances, as permanent as man could make it.

Two decades of experience in proselyting had demonstrated to Brigham Young that most converts would come from the lower economic strata of society. Since 1837, for example, a steady stream of new members had flowed from the factories, mines, and workshops of Great Britain, men and women of intelligence and integrity who, because of a static economic, political, and social system, had remained poor and deprived. These would need financial help if they were to heed the call to migrate to Zion. Yet the Mormon leaders lacked the means to subsidize the moving costs of such large numbers, and even if they had had the means, they did not want to establish a precedent of doling out money without compensatory service or repayment. In these circumstances, Brigham established what later became known as the Perpetual Emigration Fund Company. In doing so, he adopted the practice he had followed in bringing Saints from Great Britain. The contract embodying the plan was executed October 6, 1849. The company acquired a

legal existence on September 14, 1850, under the provisional government of the State of Deseret, which was
affirmed October 14, 1851 by the Utah territorial
government.

The key to the plan was the provision that required
those who received aid to be subject to the "appropria-
tion" of the company until the full cost of the emigration had been repaid "with interest if required."[2] During the almost forty years of its existence this fund
financed the emigration of thousands of converts
from many parts of the world, offering them a chance
to prosper in the new land and providing a vast reservoir of talents and skills to help expand and accelerate
Brigham Young's ambitious plan to fill up the valleys
of the mountains with Latter-day Saints.

Chapter Twenty-one

A Mixed Blessing

No community on the continent was more exposed to the effects, good and bad, of gold fever than was Salt Lake City. Its founding in 1847 and its rapid evolution into the only substantial community between the Missouri and the West Coast caused most of the forty-niner traffic on the Oregon Trail to take the Hastings Cutoff through the Mormon capital. This proved to be a mixed blessing to Brigham and his people. It heightened the unrest of those Saints who had contracted gold fever, and it often taxed the scanty resources of the struggling community, as migrants who got a late start on the trail had to winter in the valley to avoid the same fate as the Donner Party. The Mormon settlers would not allow these unexpected guests to suffer, and so shared their meager food stores with them.

But the heavy gold-rush traffic also produced an unexpected benefit. Many of the trekkers had loaded their wagons with miscellaneous supplies and commodities that they expected either to use or sell in California. Upon reaching Salt Lake City, however, many were anxious to dispose of their surplus stores in order to spare their animals, already weakened by the long trek from the Missouri and still facing the exhausting journey across the western desert and over the rugged Sierra Nevadas. This made Salt Lake City the literal dumping grounds of the excess goods the gold-seekers wanted to dispose of before heading toward the salt flats to the west. So heavy did the volume of these commodities become and so wide was the selection available that Salt Lake shoppers were almost as favored in terms of price and choice as were the residents of the populous cities in the East.

This unusual condition was anticipated by Brigham Young's counselor, Heber C. Kimball, who, in a public meeting in Salt Lake City, long before the gold rush began, prophesied that goods would sell as cheaply on the streets of Salt Lake City as in New York. At the time, the idea seemed so ludicrous that when he sat down after finishing the talk, Elder Kimball said he probably had "missed it this time," and Charles C. Rich was heard to mutter, "I don't believe a word of it."[1]

The frantic rush to the gold fields of California that afflicted the entire country to one degree or another had a special impact upon the Mormon settlers. Not only was there the lure of instant, easy wealth, but there was the prospect of trading the harsh climate of the mountains and the years of back-breaking toil Brigham's ambitious colonization plan entailed for the balmy verdure and easy living that California offered.

The depth of the Mormon leader's concern about the magnetic pull of California's gold was shown by the frequency and intensity of his attacks upon it. He never missed an opportunity to elaborate the evils and the vulgarities of wealth acquired without honest effort. He expressed again and again his deeply held conviction that those who remained to toil on the land would reap more of the earth's substance than would those who scurried off to California.

Nor was he reluctant to chastise those who refused to heed his counsel. They were branded as gold diggers, gold seekers, or fair-weather Saints blinded by the allurements of the world, who, in their shortsightedness and venality, would forfeit their eternal birthright for a mess of pottage.

Dramatist and mimic that he was, Brigham Young drove home his point in meetings and private conversations all over the territory. His letters were filled with blunt criticism of those who turned from farming to gold. And, whenever he learned of one who had been spectacularly unsuccessful in his quest for wealth, he used the example as a theme in his rousing sermons and exhortations to the people.

There can be little doubt that the oratory, vigor, persistence, and unbending will of Brigham Young were the major reasons the Mormon communities in the mountains did not disintegrate under the combined weight of the gold rush and the discontent caused by the harsh Utah climate.

As the flow of humanity toward the gold fields accelerated, carrying with it some of the Saints, Brigham became more vigorous in his opposition, whether the object in going was to mine or for any other reason. There came a time, however, when his frustration over the issue reached the point that he was rendered speechless. In the spring of 1851 he gave approval for Amasa Lyman, Charles C. Rich, and about twenty others to go to southern California to locate way stations between Iron County and California for a mail route and for necessary travel to and from the coast. Brigham went to Utah Valley on March 23 to give final instructions to the party. To his consternation, he found not a small group of twenty or so prepared to leave, but a company of 570 in 152 wagons. Most of them, Brigham said later, "had become so enamored of the California 'paradise' that they had determined to try their fortunes there." When the time came for the usual instruction meeting before the party left, Brigham called on Heber C. Kimball and others to speak while he sat silent. "I was sick," he reminisced later, "at the sight of so many of the saints running to California, chiefly after the God of this world, and was unable to address them."[2]

It was not long after Brigham's disheartening experience in Utah Valley that the flood of migration to the California gold fields crested. While the flow continued for some time thereafter, it was in an ever-diminishing volume. With its subsidence, the problems Brigham had experienced because of it correspondingly slackened, only to be replaced by other problems of equal if not greater immensity.

Chapter Twenty-two

Carpetbaggers and Indians

The problems that supplanted gold fever as the main object of Brigham Young's oratorical and administrative genius were carpetbaggers and Indians. Between the two, the Mormon leader seemed less troubled by the Indians, whose motives and tactics were usually predictable and whose conduct ultimately was amenable to his control. It was not so with the territorial officials from the east who began to swarm upon the Saints in 1851.

The main body of President Millard Fillmore's federal appointees arrived in August. Later events demonstrated that most, if not all, of them came with distorted views about the Mormons and with fixed, though erroneous, ideas about how they should be dealt with. These misconceptions had been nourished by twenty years of falsehoods that had poured from the bitterly anti-Mormon press, the most recent specimen being a libelous piece that appeared in the *Buffalo Courier* in the early summer branding Brigham Young as an "abuser of democracy," and as a conspirator with the Indians to harass and intimidate migrants en route to California.

Apparently believing all this and more about the Mormon leader and his people, the newcomers arrived in Salt Lake City filled with a zeal for reform. The self-anointed spokesman for the group was Judge Perry E. Brocchus, a man characterized by the historian Bancroft as "vain and ambitious . . . full of self-importance, fond of intrigue, corrupt, revengeful, hypocritical."[1]

Brigham, who bore an official relation to these presidential appointees as territorial governor, welcomed them warmly, introduced them to the leading men and women of the Church, and saw to it that they were as comfortably situated as the spartan accommodations of the new community would allow.

Within a few weeks after Judge Brocchus had arrived, after he had become settled and had had the opportunity to appraise his new surroundings and the people among whom he was to live, he asked Brigham Young for an opportunity to address the Latter-day Saints. This request was granted during the semiannual conference of the Church held during the early part of September. The judge mounted the stand of the Bowery on Temple Square on Monday morning, September 8, and began a two-hour speech that dropped a bombshell in the midst of the Saints, destroying any hope of his being able to work harmoniously with them.

The speech began mildly enough. He expressed thanks for the hospitality shown by his hosts, especially for thoughtful care given to him during a brief illness after his arrival. He then turned to themes that a wise man would not have dared to approach under the circumstances, theology, polygamy, and the federal government's conduct during the Missouri and Illinois persecutions. As to the latter, he adhered to the legalistic views of President Martin Van Buren that the federal government was powerless to act in the matter and that any redress must be sought at the hands of those who had driven and persecuted them. The mild-mannered Wilford Woodruff recorded that this part of the judge's speech "stirred the blood of the whole congregation."[2] Addressing the polygamous women in the congregation, the judge "strongly recommended them to become virtuous."[3]

Having carefully absorbed all the judge had to say, Brigham rose and began his reply. He got to the point immediately. Said he, "Judge Brocchus is either profoundly ignorant, or wilfully wicked, one of the two." Following this attention-getting opener, Brigham proceeded to lecture the judge with keen oratorical skill sharpened during two decades of incessant preaching and counseling. He at once recognized and rejected the narrow legalism on which Judge Brocchus had justified the federal government's failure to intervene in the savage persecutions inflicted on the Saints. "It is well known to every man in this community," he declared, "and has become a matter of history throughout the enlightened world, that the government of the United States looked on the scenes of robbing, driving, and murdering of this people and said nothing about the matter, but by silence gave sanction to the lawless proceedings. Hundreds of women and children have been laid in the tomb prematurely in consequence thereof, and their blood cries to the Father for vengeance against those who have caused or consented to their death."

Brigham saved some of his most direct and pungent comments for last. In retaliation for the judge's attack upon the Church's doctrines, and upon the sisters present who had entered into polygamy, he said: "I am indignant at such corrupt fellows as Judge Brocchus coming here to lecture us on morality and virtue. I could buy a thousand of such men and put them into a bandbox. Ladies and gentlemen, here we learn principle and good manners. It is an insult to this congregation to throw out such insinuations. I say it is an insult, and I will say no more."[4]

It would have required no prescience to predict that Judge Brocchus's days in the Salt Lake Valley were numbered after his ill-conceived speech and Brigham's scalding response. In fact, he lasted less than three weeks, departing in haste on September 28 in company with Chief Justice Lemuel H. Brandebury; Broughton D. Harris, territorial secretary; and Henry R. Day, sub-Indian agent. In the meantime, some interesting legal shenanigans took place when Judge Brandebury called the territorial supreme court into session, the one and only session at which he presided, to grant an injunction sought by secretary Harris that prevented the U. S. marshall from taking charge of the territorial funds, documents, and other official paraphernalia in the secretary's possession.

The territorial legislature had authorized the marshall to seize these items when it became apparent that Mr. Harris intended to leave the valley and take them with him.

This half-comic, half-tragic episode became known as the case of the "run-a-way officers." It acquired almost instant notoriety as the news spread with a speed that belied the existing primitive communication system. When the story hit the populous centers east of the Missouri, it was spread by the newspapers and word of mouth until it became a matter of common knowledge and a theme for public jest or outrage, depending on one's point of view. Even the hard-core Mormon haters had difficulty suppressing a chuckle over the sight of Judge Brocchus and his friends—they who had gone west with such high hopes of taming Brigham and rescuing the Mormons from their benighted condition—leaving the territory in hurried confusion after less than a two-month stay. The essential humor of the scene was captured by Mormon poetess, Eliza R. Snow, who composed an eight-verse song based on the incident. The first verse and chorus convey the good-natured humor with which the Saints viewed the episode:

> All hail the day Columbia first
> The iron chains of bondage burst;
> Lo, Utah's valleys now resound
> With freedom's tread on western ground.

> *Chorus*

> Tho' Brocchus, Day and Brandebury,
> And Harris, too, the secretary,
> Have gone,—they went—but when they left us,
> They only of themselves bereft us.[5]

But not everybody was laughing. Once the "run-a-ways" arrived in the East, they published a scathing report of their short stay in Utah that focused on the alleged defection of the Mormons from the federal

government, on the rumored squandering of federal
funds by Governor Young, and on alleged irregularities of the governor in his administration of territorial
affairs.

There is no doubt that Brigham and his people
were outspoken and extreme in their criticism of the
federal government for its negligence in the Missouri
and Illinois persecutions. But there was nothing seditious or disloyal in these complaints and grumblings.
They were merely exercising the acknowledged
American prerogative of dissent and opposition.

The charge of squandering public funds lacked
solid foundation. It arose from a grant of $20,000 in
the territorial enabling act for "the erection of public
buildings." The money was used, instead, to purchase
the State House of Deseret, often called the Council
House, that consisted of two halls and four offices, initially erected at a reported cost of $45,000.

The alleged irregularities in administration had
their root in differences of style and emphasis and in
the complexities that grew from Brigham's dual role as
ecclesiastical and civil head. Often it was impossible to
unravel the threads of his official acts, to determine accurately which hat he had worn at which time. This
puzzle became even more perplexing for the visitors
because of their ignorance of the elaborate system of
Mormon theology and procedure. These elements,
added to the mutual distrust with which the gentiles
and Brigham regarded each other, precluded visitors
from making an accurate appraisal of the conditions in
Utah.

What emerged before the eyes of official Washington and, indeed, the whole nation, was a distorted view
of Brigham and his people. The Saints were made to
appear as an intractable, even arrogant, people, dishonest, unreliable, and seditious, whose aim was to
take advantage of Uncle Sam's liberality and wealth
while going their own obdurate way. This public view
of the Latter-day Saints was to remain for decades to
pollute relationships with the federal government, un-

duly delay the admission of Utah into the union as a state, complicate the proselyting efforts of the Church, and help sow the seeds of dissension that ultimately grew into the so-called Utah War.

But while the agony and distress of the Utah War lay in the somewhat distant future, Brigham Young was faced with a more imminent and potentially more dangerous conflict with the Indians, whose lands the Mormons had begun to occupy ever more extensively.

Ironically, the first point of significant conflict occurred in San Pete County, to which the Mormon colonists had been specifically invited by Chief Walker in 1849. Soon after, however, the Indians began to see that the presence of the settlers was not an unmixed blessing. Although they were peaceful and taught the Indians many useful things, the fences they began to erect to protect their cultivated fields infringed upon the complete freedom of movement the Indians had previously enjoyed. So almost from the beginning there were frictions and controversy that put the Mormon settlers constantly on guard against thievery and the danger of attack.

Another source of friction was Brigham's opposition to Chief Walker's policy of selling Indian women and children into slavery. The chief had carried on a brisk business with slavers from Mexico, who had lined his pockets with top-dollar prices. The Saints had such repugnance for this practice, they were able to push a bill through the 1852 territorial legislature authorizing probate judges to purchase Indians who had been sold into slavery and place them in homes where they could be educated and civilized. This interference with Walker's lucrative slave trade antagonized the Indian chief, who retaliated by periodic intimidations and cattle rustling.

By the summer of 1853, Indian relationships had become exceedingly tenuous and volatile. The spark that ignited open warfare was the murder of Alexander Keele by Aropeen, Chief Walker's brother. The victim, who had been posted to guard the Mormon

herd near Payson, Utah, was gunned down when Aropeen learned that his movements were under surveillance.

This homicide, coupled with Walker's threat of a
massacre at Manti, sent a shiver of apprehension
throughout the Mormon community. On Brigham's
order, the brethren immediately tightened up their
security and became nervously wary of any suspicious
moves made by the Indians. In this atmosphere of tension and mistrust, armed conflict was inevitable. Soon
Indians attacked the guard at Mount Pleasant and
raided the Mormon herd at Manti. This was followed
by attacks on the herds at Nephi and Springville and a
pitched battle at Mount Pleasant, where several Utes
were killed. The settlers then withdrew into the fort at
nearby Spring City, which was attacked again and
again. From this refuge the men cautiously ventured
forth to harvest their crops. Part of this yield was
milled, under guard, at a grist mill in Manti Canyon,
and part was shipped to the Salt Lake City markets in
an ox-team wagon train that left San Pete Valley shortly before the October general conference. While
camped at Uinta Springs, site of the present community of Fountain Green, the wagon train was attacked by
Walker's braves, who killed the Mormon teamsters
and afterward, in a rage, mutilated their bodies. It is
believed this brutal act was in retaliation for the killings
at Mount Pleasant. Rather than to intimidate the Mormon settlers, as Walker may have expected, the
incident only served to escalate the tension and hostilities.

A few weeks later Captain J. W. Gunnison, a government surveyor, and his party were massacred at an
encampment on the Sevier River, east of the Sevier
Lake, by a band of enraged Indians who sought
revenge for the murder of their chief, Moshoquop,
who had been killed by Missouri emigrants en route to
California. It was of no concern to the Indians that
those upon whom they heaped revenge were innocent
of the murder of their chief. It was sufficient that they

were white and were intruding upon their land, fishing their streams, and killing their game.

The unrestrained passion and fury of the Indians, revealed by the Uinta Springs and Sevier River massacres, erupted again and again during the winter that followed. Allred's Fort at Spring City was incinerated, and numerous acts of depredation were reported in both San Pete and Sevier valleys. The mountain communities of peaceful refuge had suddenly become places of uneasy terror for the Mormon settlers, who never knew when or from what quarter the next attack would come.

Brigham was deeply troubled by the reports of violence and death that reached him from the battlefields of the Walker War. It grieved him that blood had been shed, it worred him that the hostilities might escalate beyond the point of reason and negotiation, and it concerned him that the policy of helpful friendliness he had always applied to Indian relations had, for some reason, gone awry. With these thoughts weighing heavily on his mind, Brigham organized a southern expedition to parley with the Indians and to inspect the growing Mormon communities that were springing up in the valleys to the south. Brigham invited a large group to accompany him, including Heber C. Kimball and six members of the Twelve. Also accompanying Brigham was Dimmick Huntington, a man fluent in the Indian dialects spoken in the area.

Although spring had been ushered in more than a month before, it was cold and crisp when Brigham and his party left Salt Lake City on May 4, 1854, amidst the bustle, the noise, and the seeming confusion that always accompanied the departure of a wagon train. The company consisted of eighty-two men, fourteen women, and five children traveling in thirty-four carriages.

The party spent the first night in Union. Here, for lack of public accommodations or an invitation to lodge with a resident, Brigham slept in his carriage. The next day was spent breasting a "boisterous" and

ice-cold south wind that knifed through the travelers'
light clothing and wrapped the wagon column with a
blanket of choking, grimy dust. After staying overnight at American Fork, where it rained heavily, they
were harassed with muddy roads the next morning on
their journey to Pleasant Grove, which was characterized by the camp's scribe as "the cleanest, neatest and
prettiest fort" they had yet seen.

Pushing their animals during the afternoon, they
forded the Provo river, whose swift waters flowed over
the wagon beds, and reached Provo Fort, where
Brigham Young was the welcome guest of Harvey
Redfield and his family.

At Provo Brigham laid the groundwork for his
diplomatic mission. Through Daniel H. Wells he sent
word to Chief Walker, who had camped on Chicken
Creek, west of Nephi, that he wanted to parley. He
then directed the brethren at Provo to send four beef
cattle ahead to the chief, correctly gauging that this
might open the door to dialogue and negotiation that
would never be opened by mere words.

Traveling through Spanish Fork, Springville, and
Payson, Brigham and his party arrived at Nephi three
days later and, after spending the night there, made
final preparations to confront the Indian chief. These
consisted of gathering a herd of cattle, trinkets, arms,
ammunition, blankets, and clothing, all to be offered
as gifts, symbols of peace and goodwill. When word
came that the chief refused to meet Brigham except in
Walker's own camp, Brigham good-naturedly said, "If
the mountain will not come to Mahomet, Mahomet
must go to the mountain," and left for Chicken Creek
with an entourage of fifty mounted men and his peace
offerings.

With some feeling of apprehension Brigham approached the camp of the man whose mercurial
temper and hair-trigger responses had aroused terror
and foreboding throughout the Mormon communities in the San Pete and Sevier valleys. There was no
guarantee he would not give Brigham the same kind of
treatment meted out by his brother Aropeen at Payson

or by his braves at Uinta Springs. It would have been fresh in Brigham's mind that there had been no massive blood-letting by Walker in retaliation for the executions at Nephi, nor could he have forgotten how Captain Gunnison's party had been brutally massacred just a few miles to the south.

Entering Walker's village at noon on May 11, 1854, picturesque with bright splotches of paint on the wicki-ups, smoke curling up from the smoldering fires, and the incessant yapping of the Indian dogs, Brigham presented himself at the chief's tipi with the request that they talk. Walker refused because he said he was "sick" and had "lost his spirit." The Mormon Leader returned to counsel with his brethren and later sent the chief a gift of some flour and wheat.

Presenting himself at Walker's tipi again the next morning, Brigham learned that the chief's daughter was ill, whereupon he sought out the girl and, laying his hands on her head, blessed her in the authority of the priesthood. So overwrought was the chief at his daughter's illness that he struck his wife, warning that if the girl died someone else must die with her.

It was against this background of domestic strife and sorrow that Brigham was finally able to bring the volatile Chief Walker to the bargaining table. The setting was in the tribal lodge, where Walker was attended by a coterie of grim-faced, sullen chiefs. Among these were Ammon, Squash Head, Grosepine, Petenit, Kanosh, and Sanpete, all well-known to Brigham, and all reserved and proud.

With Dimmick Huntington acting as interpreter, there began two days of tense, often emotional, discussion, during which each chief in turn aired his complaints and criticisms. Two of them, with almost uncontrollable emotion, told of the cold-blooded shooting of Indians by "Americats." As the discussion progressed during the first day, however, doubt arose in Chief Walker's mind whether the blame for these cruel murders could be laid upon the Saints. There was, after all, an increasing volume of wagon traffic toward Southern California, and the murders could easily have been committed by members of these companies. Toward the end of the day, Walker announced he wanted to talk to the "Great Spirit" that night about the issue of peace or war. A calumet was passed to all in the circle, which boded well for the proceedings the next day.

In the morning before the council reconvened, Brigham Young moved promptly to take advantage of the favorable turn of events of the previous evening, and made Chief Walker a gift of sixteen oxen in addition to some clothing and colorful trinkets. Chief Walker was pleased.

With such an auspicious beginning, negotiations moved smoothly toward a successful conclusion on the second day. The highlight was a rambling speech delivered by Chief Walker in which he traced the history of his dealings with the Mormons and the Americats, painting a picture of dissension and bloodshed intermingled with brief intervals of peace and amity. He flatly denied any responsibility for the death of Captain Gunnison, while, by implication, admitting that some of his braves were impetuous and hard to control. As to them, he declared, "If Indian kill white man again, Wahara make Indian howl." Turning to Brigham Young, he called him a "good man" who had given him "bread and oxen and clothes to cover his wife and children." Finally he said that during the previous night he had talked with the "Great Spirit," who had said to him, "Make peace." The other chiefs concurring in this, a peace was declared, as evidence of which Walker and some of his braves escorted Brigham Young and his party as far as Fillmore.

Chief Walker died only a few months after the parley on Chicken Creek, and Aropeen, his successor, then entered into a written treaty with the Saints under which he purported to convey all of San Pete County to the Church "together with all material and timber on the same."

Except for minor skirmishes that occurred intermittently over the years, this terminated hostilities with the Indians until the outbreak of the so-called

Black Hawk War a decade later. A genuine fondness developed between the two peoples, reflected in this story related by the author's grandmother who was born in the small Mormon community of Kanosh, Utah, named in honor of the chief who participated in the council that ended the Walker War: Observing the unusual activity of a Mormon family in sprucing up their yard, a friendly Ute Indian paused at the gate to inquire, "Bligum coming?"

Chapter Twenty-three

New Initiatives

Duscapering the Walker War, while beset by many complex and aggravating problems, Brigham Young began some initiatives that had vast and important consequences. One was to commence the systematic and detailed reporting of all the sermons of the leading brethren. Another was to build a temple.

Convening in what is now called the "Old Tabernacle" on Temple Square, which had been completed just six months before, the Saints unanimously and enthusiastically approved the construction of a temple to "be built of the best materials that can be obtained in the mountains of North America." Four months later, on Februry 14, 1853, Brigham called a meeting on Temple Square, where, in the presence of several thousand Saints and civil and military leaders, he broke ground for the new edifice. The proceedings were enlivened by the music of several snappy bands and by the half-comical difficulty the Mormon leader had in digging out the symbolic first shovelful of dirt. The ground was frozen solid to a depth of six inches. Workmen hacked away the icy surface while the spectators pressed in closer and closer to watch. At length Brigham was able to dislodge a shovelful of dirt. Entering into the hilarity of the occasion, with people crowding in on all sides so he could hardly move, he lifted the shovel high and said, *"Get out of my way for I am going to throw this."* The *Deseret News* writer who reported the event observed, "He held it, about one minute, before he could get room to lay it down, from off the Temple site; so dense were the multitude around."[1]

Less than two months later, in connection with the general conference of the Church, the cornerstones of the temple were laid. Showing his flair for pageantry, with bands playing and civil, military, and religious leaders in attendance, Brigham and his counselors laid the southeast cornerstone. Then the Presiding Bishopric, the Salt Lake Stake leaders, and the other General Authorities in turn laid the southwest, northwest, and northeast cornerstones. Thus was begun a mammoth project that was to take forty years to complete. Brigham would die before it was finished.

Three other Utah temples were commenced, finished, and dedicated years before the capstone was laid on the Salt Lake Temple. And many people were born, lived out their lives, and died seeing it only in a formative, unfinished state. So long was this uncompleted structure a symbol of downtown Salt Lake City that it became the butt of many crude jokes by local enemies of the Church and by insensitive visitors. Many chided Brigham for beginning something beyond his capacity to complete. Others criticized him for planning a temple too grand and ornate for such a raw and undeveloped country. There was nothing, however, that could dissuade him from his course, for he declared he had seen the temple in vision long before it was started. He was determined that the building be of such massive proportions and its materials so durable that it would stand throughout the Millennium, not only as a holy sanctuary but as a monument to the faith, devotion, and perseverance of those who built it.

A third initiative was to set up a program of public education applicable to the entire territory. Brigham led out in the enactment of legislation that established the University of Deseret (February 28, 1850), provided for the formation of a uniform system of public instruction (October 4, 1851), authorized the division of counties into school districts to be directed by trustees empowered to levy and collect taxes (March 4, 1852), and created county boards of examiners who were empowered to determine the qualifications of teachers and to compile statistical data for the territorial superintendent (December 10, 1854).

Not only did Brigham advance the cause of education among the Latter-day Saints by establishing necessary organizations and procedures, but he also did so by his incessant preaching and his own good example. Repeatedly in his public discourses he gave strong emphasis to the need for education. "This is our labour, our business, and our calling," he declared at a special conference in 1859, "to grow in grace and in knowledge from day to day and from year to year."[2] It is clear that learning was not to be limited strictly to theological subjects nor to students of a particular age, group, or sex. Said he at the annual general conference in 1867: "I will now urge it upon the people—the young men and the middle-aged—to get up schools and study. If they are disposed to study physic or surgery, all right; they will know then what to do if a person is sickly. . . . I would like very much to urge upon our young people, the sisters as well as the brethren, to pay more attention to arithmetic. . . . I would also like our school teachers to introduce phonography into every school. . . . Introduce every kind of useful studies into our schools."[3]

By way of example to the Church, Brigham established a private school for his own large family. It was across the street east from the Beehive House on South Temple Street. Built solidly of brick, it resembled one of the ward meetinghouses of the day, with a small vestibule in front atop which stood the belfry. At 8:45 A.M. each weekday during the school year, the loud but friendly bell summoned the studentbody, which included Brigham Young's children and, later, some of his grandchildren. Occasionally students outside the family were invited to attend. Heber J. Grant, for example, often nostalgically related his experiences in attending the school. The bell sounded again at 9:00 A.M., signaling the commencement of studies. These included grammar, arithmetic, spelling, and history. Friday afternoons were ordinarily devoted to spelling matches, declamations, and musical numbers. Also, the school paper was read and distributed. Its contributors were drawn from the studentbody.

An interested visitor from the East attended a session of this unique school and found thirty-four registered students. "There were 28 present from 4 to 17 years of age," he wrote, "on the whole looking brighter and more intelligent than the children of any other school I ever visited."[4]

After they had acquired the necessary rudiments of learning, Brigham never pushed his children beyond the limits of their desire or capacity. He held out the offer of a higher education to all his sons, but never pressed it upon them. Don Carlos, for instance, decided he wanted to be a teamster before he had completed all the courses at the family and the local public schools. Brigham promptly honored his wish and put him to work hauling lumber from the sawmill in City Creek Canyon, driving a pair of blind mules. It did not take the boy long to discover which employment he disliked the most, and soon returned to school, studying with a vengeance to avoid ever having to drive a team of blind mules again.

Coincident with the push for expanded education was a move to broaden the Church's propaganda base. As early as 1850 Brigham had established the *Deseret News* as a weekly periodical under the editorship of Willard Richards. Two years later an aggressive step was taken to extend the influence of the Mormon press far beyond the boundaries of Utah. In 1852 Orson Pratt, by assignment from Brigham Young, began to publish the *Seer* in the nation's capital. The prospectus, issued in December 1852, declared the new monthly to be "in commemoration of Joseph Smith, the Seer of the last days." While this doubtless was an underlying purpose of the newspaper that burst unexpectedly upon the Washington scene, a more immediate and cogent reason for its birth could be traced to an incident that occurred in Salt Lake City during the last week of the previous August.

At that time, in connection with the semiannual

conference of the Church, the first public announcement was made that the Church was teaching and
practicing polygamy. While the reality of this fact was
dimly suspected by the gentile community and by
some Latter-day Saints who had not been required to
live the principle, it had never until that moment been
openly acknowledged.

The repurcussions were more violent and widespread than Brigham and his associates had expected.
These, added to the tempest caused by the Brocchus
affair, made them conscious of the need for a counter-
offensive in the news media.

The establishment of the *Seer* at the seat of government, where national political opinions were formed,
was merely the opening gun in a media blitz of gigantic
proportions. Brigham next turned his attention to
New York, the seat of economic power, where less than
a year later he established the *Mormon,* a weekly under
the editorship of John Taylor. As if to demonstrate its
aggressive independence and its intention to be heard
on issues vital to the Church's welfare, the *Mormon*
established its offices on the corner of Nassau and Ann
streets with the *New York Herald* on one side and the
Tribune on the other. The forceful editorials that
crackled in the pages of this upstart publication immediately drew the attention and abusive calumny of the
media barons in New York.

In the meantime Brigham was planning to establish still other Mormon publications in different parts
of the country. This resulted in the later founding of
the *St. Louis Luminary,* edited by Erastus Snow, and the
Western Standard in San Francisco, edited by George Q.
Cannon.

All things considered, this herculean effort by the
Mormon leader to alter the attitudes of America toward his people was largely unavailing. If anything,
the abuse and denunciation increased in proportion to
the efforts to abate it. This was commented on by the
Women's Advocate, which was appalled at the lack of
public sympathy toward the beleagured Mormons,
who, in addition to their other woes, were battling

another cricket invasion. "But not one word is spoken anywhere of regret or sympathy," chided the *Advocate*. "On the contrary there are frequent manifestations of satisfaction that the problem of Mormonism and its destiny is likely to be settled by the grasshoppers. What little comment we have noticed here and there has a tone of delighted chuckle that chills the blood. *There is a spirit of murder in it,* a suppressed shout of triumph of the persecutor over his victim, that is suppressed only because the triumph is not yet sure."[5]

Chapter Twenty-four

The Reformation

As the decade of the fifties wore on, as Brigham Young contested with Indians, carpetbaggers, and a biased press, he became aware of another menace that threatened to overshadow all the others. What he saw (and what a religious leader fears as much as anything else) was a deterioration in the will and moral fiber of his people.

The Church had always been afflicted with its malcontents, grumblers, and apostates. The list of erstwhile Saints turned excommunicants and enemies extended from Philastus Hurlburt to the Law brothers and included such well-known names as Warren Parrish, William E. McLellin, George M. Hinkle, John C. Bennett, Robert Foster, William Marks, and the Higbee brothers. Brigham was well acquainted, therefore, with the problems of dissent, controversy, and disobedience within the Church.

What emerged now, however, was not a few isolated cases of virulent transgression followed by apostasy and an embittered reaction against the Church. Instead, there occurred a general weakening of the people, a blurring of goals, and a loss of incentive. What faced the Mormon community was widespread moral apathy that threatened to undermine and destroy the group that had originally aspired to be worthy of and to enjoy the society of Jesus.

It is not difficult to understand the reasons behind this new crisis. At this time the Saints had been in their wilderness home for many years and had been preoccupied with establishing a new civilization in a harsh land. There were farms to be rescued from the desert and cultivated, streams to be harnessed, forests to be cut, roads to be built, and villages to be raised on the desert floor. And the words "necessity" and "expediency" best describe the methods the settlers employed to subdue their rough environment. Whatever it took to survive, they did, or were prepared to do. So pervasive and demanding were their physical wants, that in time these came to dominate their thoughts, often to the exclusion of spiritual things. Over a period of several years this change in focus radically altered the general climate of the Mormon communities. Instead of aiming toward moral perfection, too many of the Saints had fixed their sights on temporal goals.

With these changes came an alarming relaxation of Church standards. Profanity, stealing, Sabbath-breaking, and sexual sins occurred with increasing frequency. Also, a divisive spirit of faultfinding and destructive criticism crept into the Church, replacing the attitude of love and cooperation that had existed before. Viewing this spiritual retrogression with concern, Brigham was determined to alter his people's attitudes and conduct.

Thus was introduced among the Latter-day Saints what was later called the "reformation." In effect, it was a call to repentance, an insistence by Brigham and his associates that the Saints return to the basics of their religion: love for God and man, faith, repentance, moral cleanliness, and reliance upon the Holy Ghost in the conduct of life.

Near the dawn of this crisis Brigham lost his trusted counselor and kinsman Willard Richards. The Mormon leader's cousin (through the Howe line) died March 11, 1854, from a combination of internal ailments conveniently lumped under the generic term *dropsy*. His successor in the First Presidency was the young, vigorous Jedediah M. Grant.

The "reformation" was compressed into a few short months. Beginning on September 13, 1856, Jedediah M. Grant touched off the movement with a series of powerful and stirring sermons delivered at Kaysville, Utah, the text for which, "Saints, live your religion," was supplied by Brigham Young. As a result of the Kaysville meetings, over five hundred Saints renewed their religious convenants through rebaptism. Beginning from that point, the spirit of the reformation extended to all parts of the territory.

Even those who were relatively blameless felt pangs of guilt and unworthiness. Wilford Woodruff and Lorenzo Snow, for instance, men of unquestioned character and probity, were moved to tell Brigham Young they would willingly step down from the Twelve if there were others more qualified to take their places. We may wonder how men of such high moral character could have been moved to such an extent, until we read a passage like this one taken from one of Jedediah M. Grant's reformation sermons: "When you are right we will cease to chastise, we will cease to rebuke; we will cease throwing the arrows of the Almighty through you, we will cease telling you to surrender, to repent of all your sins. But until you do this, we will continue to throw the arrows of God through you, to hurl the darts of heaven upon you and the power of God in your midst; and we will storm the bulwarks of hell, and we will march against you in the strength of the God of Israel. And by the power of the Priesthood restored by the Prophet Joseph, by the light of heaven shed forth by brother Brigham and his associates, we expect to triumph; and in the name of Jesus Christ, we do not mean to surrender to evil."[1]

Although Jedediah M. Grant filled the role of an Aaron to Brigham during this crisis, it is not to be inferred that the Mormon leader had lost his tongue. Indeed, this member had always served him well and would continue to do so throughout his life. Brigham contributed to the reformation as the occasion demanded it with his usual candor. This excerpt from a talk delivered on September 21, 1856, in the Bowery in Salt Lake City is typical: "As for living here, as I have done for a length of time, hid up in the chambers of the Lord, with a people that are full of contention, full of covetousness, full of pride, and full of iniquity, I will not do it. And if the people will not repent, let the sinners and hypocrites look out. . . . I shall not spare the wicked; I shall be like a flaming sword against them. . . . I cannot hold men and women in fellowship that serve the devil and themselves, and give no heed to the Almighty; I cannot do it. . . . Well, I just say, my brethren and sisters, it cannot be suffered any longer, a separation must take place; you must part with your sins, or the righteous must be separated from the ungodly."[2]

Typically, however, Brigham offered a way out. His object was not mere chastisement or retribution; it was reclamation. He wanted to bring his people back into the fold and put them on the right path again. "If you will covenant to live your religion," he assured them, "and be Saints of the Most High, you shall have that privilege, and I will have the honor of baptizing you in that font, or of seeing that it is done." Then, as if to demonstrate that the principles applied uniformly to all, including the head of the Church, he said: "I will repent with you and I will try with my might to get the spirit of my calling; and if I have not that spirit now to a fulness, I will get more of it, so as to enjoy it to its fulness."[3]

Predictably, the reformation produced mixed results. For the large majority of the Saints, it had a cathartic effect, purging out the moral dross that had clogged their spiritual perceptions. These Saints willingly accepted the rebukes of the reformation, repented, were rebaptized, and rededicated themselves to the high ideals of the Church.

Others reacted differently to the rebuke. The headstrong and recalcitrant refused to follow the counsel of their leaders. Without any sense of recrimination, Brigham invited these to leave the territory, both for their own good and for the good of the community. He was wise enough and experienced enough to understand that the pride and self-justification of these people would put them into collision with the Church. He had seen this time and again in the communities in the East the Latter-day Saints had inhabited. And he sought to avoid a repetition of those sad days by frankly urging the dissenters to leave.

Some dissenters followed Brigham's admonition, either returning to their homes in the East or migrating further toward the golden West Coast. Most of those who remained formed pockets of vocal and implacable dissent, opposing bitterly most programs and projects of the Church. Many of them ultimately merged with gentile elements in the community to produce a species of persecution that, in many ways, was more virulent and deadly than anything spawned in the Mormon communities in Ohio, Missouri, and Illinois.

Chapter Twenty-five

Handcarts

Drought and crickets during 1854 and 1855 were the prelude to what has been called the year of calamity. The difficulty came not only from drought and crickets, but from increasing demands upon the Saints' everdiminishing resources by the hundreds of converts who regularly migrated to "Zion" from the mission fields and usually arrived destitute, expecting those in the valley to provide them with food and shelter until they could arrange for their own care. Under ordinary circumstances these newcomers were a welcome addition to the community in providing the mechanical and artisan skills necessary to build up the local economy. But now that rations were in short supply, the arrival of hungry converts was the signal for more belt-tightening.

By 1856 the burgeoning numbers of converts, most of whom came from the poor masses abroad, confronted Brigham Young with a difficult problem: how could he reduce the transportation costs of the penniless converts from the East to the Great Basin?

Money from the Perpetual Emigrating Fund was so limited as to make it necessary to discontinue the expensive outfitting of wagon trains. Only one solution remained: the emigrants could walk, carrying their belongings and provisions in handcarts. This would allow them to travel more inexpensively and faster than the cumbersome wagon trains.

The handcart migration (considered as early as 1851) got under way in 1856 when five companies were launched from Iowa City, the westernmost railway terminus. The first three, which left in June, crossed the plains without undue incident, arriving safely in Salt Lake the latter part of September and the early part of October. These companies were ushered into the valley with a triumphant flourish, being met east of the city by military escorts and lively bands. The population turned out en masse to greet the weary travelers who, although footsore and sunbaked from more than three months on the trail, revelled in the euphoric realization that they had accomplished what some predicted would never be done and, in the process, had demonstrated an Abrahamic willingness to make any sacrifice, to endure any privation, for the sake of their religion.

Had the story ended there, handcart emigration for 1856 would have been declared an unqualified success. But even as the cheers welcoming these first companies subsided, two larger companies, toiling on the trail far to the east, were being shown a glimpse of the terrifying ordeal that lay ahead.

These companies, led by James G. Willie and Edward Martin and comprising over nine hundred converts, were delayed in their departure from Iowa City until middle and late July due to the failure of tent and handcart manufacturers to meet production deadlines. Even with the late start, they decided to make the journey. Once on the trail, however, they were alarmed to find that the handcarts had been shoddily made and required frequent and extensive repairs. Since the entire company had to travel at the pace of its slowest member, each breakdown enforced delay for all.

By the time the three vanguard companies arrived in the valley, the Willie Company had only reached Fort Laramie, five hundred lonely miles from its destination. Already it had encountered heavy frosts. And the Martin company was struggling on the trail two weeks and almost two hundred miles behind.

Heavy snows in October turned a bad dream for these unlucky travelers into a horrifying nightmare. Ill-equipped even for fair-weather travel, they were wholly unable to cope with early winter storms that burdened the prairie with over two feet of snow. In the wake of the snow came howling winds kicking up violent ground blizzards that blinded and stalled the hapless walkers. Already weakened by fatigue and a scanty diet, many were unable to endure the added burden of foul weather. Their trail across the wilderness was littered with their dead buried in shallow, hurriedly dug graves. On one especially black day, fifteen died and were laid to rest in a common grave.

The Willie company straggled into the valley on November 9. Unlike the three vanguard companies, its arrival was solemn and funereal. Gone were the jocular well-wishing and the lively band music. In their place was a quiet sense of melancholy gratitude as survivors contrasted the terror that had overshadowed their tragic journey with the kindness lavished upon them by their hosts.

Three weeks intervened between the arrival of the Willie and Martin companies. During that time Brigham dispatched one hundred and four wagons carrying food, clothing, and bedding for the relief of the exhausted walkers. These vehicles were spacious enough not only to carry the baggage but also some members of the company. At a rendezvous west of Devil's Gate, where the relief train met the struggling column, many were found to be so helpless it was difficult to determine who would be permitted to ride and who would be required to walk. "There was considerable crying of women and children," reported John Jacques, "and perhaps of a few of the men, whom the wagons could not accommodate with a ride." One of the members of the relief party said "that in all the mobbings and drivings of the 'Mormons' he had seen nothing like it."[1]

During a Sunday morning meeting in the "Old Tabernacle" on November 30, 1856, word reached Brigham that the relief train and the Martin company were approaching the valley. He promptly interrupted and dismissed the meeting with this admonition: "When those persons arrive I do not want to see them put into houses by themselves; I want to have them dis-

tributed in this city among the families that have good
and comfortable houses." Then, addressing himself
particularly to the sisters, he instructed them "to nurse
and wait upon the newcomers and prudently administer medicine and food to them. . . . to wash them and
nurse them up." To make it clear that none was
exempt from these Samaritan-like ministrations, he
noted, "I have sent word to Bishop Hunter that I will
take in all that others will not take. . . . I am willing to
take my proportion."[2]

About three hundred, or a third, of those in the
Willie and Martin handcart companies died on the
trail. And many of the survivors carried deep physical
and emotional scars to their graves, constant remind-
ers of the terrible ordeal through which they had
passed. Yet this in no way deterred Brigham in his policy of handcart migration. Indeed, as soon as spring
broke the following year, he dispatched a handcart
company going east consisting of seventy-four missionaries destined for their fields of labor in the eastern United States and Europe. Carrying their belongings in twenty-five handcarts, these missionaries
seemed as much as anything else to be Brigham's affirmation that the misfortune of the Willie and Martin
companies would not end handcart migration. This
trek was followed up later in the year by two west-
bound companies that left Iowa City early enough to
arrive in the valley by mid-September. Thereafter, for
several years, similar companies were organized as the
circumstances required. The last one, led by Oscar O.
Stoddard and consisting of 126 souls whose belongings were pulled in twenty-two handcarts, arrived in
the late summer of 1860.

Chapter Twenty-six

At Home with Brigham Young

Wherever the Mormons had gone, they had carried in their hearts and minds the seeds of a civilization that had its origins in New England, Great Britain, and Europe. When they were allowed to remain in one place for any length of time, these seeds invariably took root, grew, and flowered, producing homes and public buildings remarkably similar to those in the areas where the Saints had been reared. To have walked the streets of Nauvoo, for instance, with its numerous examples of colonial, federal, and tudor architecture, would have reminded one of the many villages to be seen in the New England countryside or across the sea in the old countries. It was inevitable, therefore, that once the Mormons had gained a foothold in their new home, they began to plan and build the kinds of homes carried in memory. Thus, within a few short years after Brigham Young first gazed upon the promised valley, attractive and commodious homes began to rise along Salt Lake City's wide boulevards.

Because of his dual role as head of the Church and governor of the territory, it was expected that Brigham's residence would not be cast in the ordinary mold. And his status as the patriarch of a large and rapidly growing polygamous family dictated that his habitation be built on a giant scale.

By 1854, only seven short years after Brigham first saw the valley, the central structure of his domestic kingdom had been completed. This was the Beehive House, a stately, colonial, two-story home that followed the design of the nineteenth-century Greek revival. Distinguished by white colonial pillars on the

south and east sides, by green shuttered windows, by
gracious porches that served both the first and second
floors, and by a beehive-shaped cupola that sur-
mounted an attic structure on the roof, this house
stood at the entrance of the Mormon leader's estate. Its
thick adobe brick walls, plastered and calcimined in a
pale yellow, imparted a sense of mass and solidity that
matched the character of its owner. The interior,
including numerous bedrooms, kitchen, family store,
and gracious sitting and drawing rooms for entertain-
ing, was furnished tastefully in the style of the period.

Two years later Brigham Young constructed a
second home (the Lion House, west of the Beehive
House) three stories high with a center hallway extending the length of each floor. On the upper floor
were twenty bedrooms, each with a dormer window,
occupied by the childless wives and various sons and
daughters. The center floor was divided into apart-
ments for the wives with smaller children and included
a large parlor often called the prayer room because of
its regular use as a place for family devotionals. The
basement floor included a dining room large enough
to seat fifty at once, butteries, kitchen, laundry, stone-
flagged cellars for storage, weaving room, and a
schoolroom. Later, when a family school was built
across the street east of the Beehive House, the last-
mentioned room became a family recreation room.
Brigham had a platform built in one end of it to accommodate dramatic and musical presentations. A porch
that extended the entire length of the west side of the
Lion House was used as an exercise and play area by
the children. This area, which one daughter called a
gymnasium, was equipped with every imaginable con-
trivance for the entertainment and exercise of children.

Connecting the Beehive and Lion houses was a
roomy suite of offices that accommodated Brigham
Young and his counselors and staff, who served him
either in his role as President of the Church or as governor of the territory. For convenience, a door in the
west wall of Brigham's bedroom opened into a narrow

hallway across which was the side door to his private office. The suite also included three other smaller offices (one of which later became the telegraph communication center) and a large staff office equipped with a balcony, reached by means of a corner, circular stair, where correspondence and supplies were filed and stored.

To the rear of these homes and the office stood a conglomeration of smaller buildings that served the needs of what was really a community within a community. These included a carpenter shop, pigeon house, shoeshop, blacksmith shop, flour mill, barns, sheds, and corrals. Beyond were the family garden and orchard, whose productions supplied the Young table with a wide variety of fresh fruits and vegetables in season, the excess being thriftily bottled and stored for use during the off-season.

To provide adequate security and privacy and, according to some, to provide employment (in its construction) for a few of the many converts who entered the valley in a constant stream, Brigham's estate was surrounded by a high rock wall. Above the entrance to the estate hovered a sculptured eagle with outstretched wings, alighting on a beehive, symbol of industry, thrift, and the Jaredite "deseret," or honeybee. Not only do we find this symbol reproduced at the highest point of Brigham's main dwelling and on the eagle gate, but on his family seal, his doorknobs, and his cuff links.

There could be no more lustrous example of "deseret" than life behind the walls of Brigham's estate. Everything moved according to a well-ordered plan. It was no small matter to feed, clothe, and house a family of such gigantic size, and to do so without undue bickering or dissension. In general, Brigham's wives and children lived together amicably. This attests to the organizational skill and sensitivity of their husband and father and to the character and discipline of the wives and children.

Ordinarily, twelve wives and their children occupied the Lion House. Another family occupied the

Beehive House. Later, other homes were built for different families, including the White House, in the
block east of the Beehive House; Forest Farm, in the
south-central part of the valley; and homes at Provo
and St. George. Changes in living accommodations for
the various families were made according to their
needs. Mary Ann Angell, for example, the matriarch
of the wives, first occupied the Beehive House. In
about 1860, however, when her youngest child, John
W., was sixteen, and when most, if not all, of her other
five children were either married or deceased, she
moved into the newly built White House. She vacated
the Beehive House for the second living wife, Lucy
Ann Decker, and her growing brood of seven (ranging
from fifteen-year-old Brigham Heber to the infant
Clarissa Hamilton) who moved over from the Lion
House. With domino effect these moves created similar shifts in housing arrangements down the line as
other wives and children occupied the quarters newly
vacated by those who had moved elsewhere. Such
changes were never made arbitrarily, but only after
due consultation and with the full agreement of all
concerned.

There existed an unusual friendship and loyalty
among Brigham's wives. They comprised a unique
sisterhood, bound together not only by the ties of their
religious convictions, but by their relationship to the
man whom they unitedly called husband and who was
the father of their children. Inevitably there was some
sense of competition and occasional jealousies and
feelings of slight, but most often these were swallowed
up in the spirit of love that customarily prevailed. And
the children, who were often tended and trained by
others while their mothers were engaged in special
tasks, called the other wives "aunt," denoting the close
family relationship that existed.

The housework was delegated so that all shared the
load equally, and each knew precisely what was expected. Each wife did the washing for herself and her
children at prearranged times from Monday through
Saturday. However, the ironing was usually done on a

communal basis, with several wives being assigned in rotation to this work that was performed at night while the others slept. These ironers also doubled as fire guards, making periodic checks during the night to make certain that a flying spark from one of the many stoves and fireplaces had not set the house afire. The wives who were assigned ironing duty were allowed to sleep during the day, while their children were tended by the aunts.

The kitchen was supervised by one of the wives (an assignment that also was rotated), who was provided with as many of the daughters as necessary to help with dishwashing and other kitchen chores.

Except on special occasions, meals in the Lion House were served twice daily on a communal basis, with all the wives and children joining together in the huge basement dining room. Customarily, Brigham took his meals in the Beehive House. His meals were prepared by, or under the direction of, the wife who occupied that home. This wife also had the responsibility to board the men who worked about the estate and the girls who helped with the housework. It was the rule rather than the exception that as many as eighteen men were employed at once by Brigham to perform the many tasks incident to operating his large, complex household.

We learn from the fascinating account of a daughter, Clarissa H., who was raised in the Beehive House, that Brigham was something of a gourmet. He usually had two squab for breakfast, expertly prepared by Clarissa's mother "into a dainty dish." This meal, actually a mid-morning brunch, would be rounded out with the likes of hot doughnuts and syrup, codfish gravy, and strawberries, or some other delicacy grown by Brother Staines who "was a genius at making things grow under glass." To give his brunch the common touch, it was not unusual for Brigham to add cornmeal mush and milk to the menu. This was not only filling, but served to remind the Mormon leader of his earlier years when the daily fare of the John Young family was hardly more sumptuous than this common dish.

Brigham saw to it that his family was properly instructed and that it engaged in daily devotionals. Ordinarily these were held each evening in the large parlor of the Lion House. The signal to gather was the "prayer bell," always kept on a special shelf in the Lion House and rung by Brigham with sufficient vigor as to be heard throughout the three floors of the building. Once assembled, the family and any relatives or neighbors who happened by would be briefed about affairs of current interest, given any needed admonitions, and kneel while Brigham led in prayer. One who ever heard such a prayer never forgot the incident. Heber J. Grant, who occasionally participated in the Young family prayer circle, once said he was afraid to glance up during Brigham's prayer lest he be frightened by the appearance of the heavenly being with whom the family patriarch was conversing.

At first glance the life of Brigham's wives in this environment might appear to have been unduly restrictive. A closer look, however, reveals that this was far from true. The cellular living arrangements allowed each wife to express her own tastes in decor and arrangement, and the communal eating, laundering, weaving, and spinning arrangements eliminated much of the drudgery of these essential chores through the pooling of effort and ingenuity and through the stimulation that cooperative effort usually produces. The problems of child rearing were simplified by the ready availability of babysitters and playmates. Moreover, a mother vexed by a personal problem could turn to any one of the other wives for sisterly counsel and comfort.

Brigham's wives had a great deal more autonomy and responsibility than did their monogamous sisters by reason of the heavy load their husband carried. Thus, the principal responsibility for the upbringing of her children rested on each wife. Certainly, Brigham was there when help was needed, but, in the main he was consulted only as to matters of monumental importance, the ordinary, day-to-day questions of discipline and training being handled by the mother alone or in consultation with other wives. And the childless wives or those whose children had reached maturity and left home had ample leisure time to extend their knowledge, develop their talents, or render compassionate or public service.

Each wife had an open account at the family store and at ZCMI with discretion to purchase items of apparel or other necessities required by her family. It must be assumed that reasonable limits were set upon the amount any wife might charge on either account, and that these were set in counsel with the wife and in light of expected needs that varied with the number and ages of her children and other factors.

The harmony, order, and efficiency with which this vast domestic enterprise functioned attest to the organizational and diplomatic skills of the man who stood at its head. The members of Brigham's family lauded him for his loving, gentle, and patient leadership. This appraisal by his daughter Clarissa H. is typical: "He could be stern when occasion demanded, but he was the wisest, kindest, and most loving of fathers. His constant thoughtfulness for our happiness and well-being endeared him to all of us. . . . I shall always be grateful that I was born his daughter."[2]

The Brigham Young of this era had grown to fit the prophetic image reflected in the pictures that have come down to us. He was careful about his personal appearance, frequently using the services of a barber, Brother Squires, whose shop was near the Beehive House but who went to Brigham's home when summoned. "Daughter, go tell Brother Squires to come and barber me," Brigham would direct, whereupon the obedient and honored craftsman would go with "his bottles of bay rum and sweet-smelling hair oil, the curling irons, and the big calico cloth." Because of a theory he held that cutting hair made the ends "bleed," Brigham would never permit his hair to be cut, insisting that it be singed instead.

He was always neatly attired in public. During cold weather he usually wore "a rather high hat, a Prince Albert coat, and either a green cape or a grey shawl over his shoulders." During the summer "he wore light cream prunella cloth suits—sack coats and trousers, with white shirt and neck cloth and a panama hat."[3]

Long accustomed by now to wielding vast authority in the realms of both church and state, he carried about him an air of power and supreme self-confidence. A perceptive visitor to the Salt Lake Valley in the early years painted this word picture of the Mormon leader: "I had expected to see a venerable-looking old man," wrote Richard F. Burton, a non-Mormon from England. "Scarcely a grey thread appears in his hair. . . . His manner is at once affable and impressive, simple and courteous. . . . He shows no signs of dogmatism, bigotry, or fanaticism. . . . He impresses a stranger with a certain sense of power: his followers are, of course, wholly fascinated by his superior strength of brain. It is commonly said there is only one chief in Gt. S.L. City, and that is 'Brigham.' His temper is even and placid, . . . and where occasion requires he can use all the weapons of ridicule to direful effect, and 'speak a bit of his mind' in a style which no one forgets. He often reproves his erring followers in purposely violent language, making the terrors of a scolding the punishment in lieu of hanging for a stolen horse or cow. His powers of observation are intuitively strong, and his friends declare him to be gifted with an excellent memory and a perfect judgment of character. If he dislikes a stranger at the first interview, he never sees him again. . . . He assumes no airs of extra sanctimoniousness, and has the plain, simple manners of honesty. His followers deem him an angel of light, his foes, a goblin damned: he is, I presume, neither one nor the other. . . . He has been called hypocrite, swindler, forger, murderer.—No one looks it less. . . . Finally, there is a total absence of pretension in his manner, and he has been so long used to power that he cares nothing for its display. The arts by which he rules the heterogeneous mass of conflicting elements are indomitable will, profound secresy, and uncommon astuteness. Such is His Excellency President Brigham Young, 'painter and glazier,'—his earliest craft—prophet, revelator, translator and seer; the man who is revered as king or kaiser, pope or pontiff never was; who, like the Old Man of the Mountain, by holding up his hand could cause the death of any one within his reach; who, governing as well as reigning, long stood up to fight with the sword of the Lord, and with his few hundred guerillas, against the then mighty power of the United States; who has outwitted all diplomacy opposed to him; and, finally, who made a treaty of peace with the President of the Great Republic as though he had wielded the combined power of France, Russia, and England."[4]

Chapter Twenty-seven

Buchanan's Blunder

Richard F. Burton's extravagant statement about Brigham Young's guerrilla warfare and diplomatic coup refers to the incident historians have called Buchanan's Blunder. The curtain raised on this tragicomical drama in 1857 to reveal the continuing struggle between Brigham and the zealous federal appointees from the East who chafed under the dominating leadership of the Mormon prophet. From the point of view of the Saints, the villains of the piece were three non-Mormon judges, W. W. Drummond, George P. Stiles, and John F. Kinney. This trio fled to Washington in the spring of the year, following President James Buchanan's inauguration, bearing tales about sedition on the part of the Latter-day Saints. Among other things, they charged Brigham and other Mormon leaders with the destruction of court records, an accusation later proven false. This indictment, added to earlier charges by disgruntled carpetbaggers that the Mormons were sabotaging the government survey and inciting the Indians to rebellion, painted a superficially ominous picture. Goaded into action by the frantic charges of these Mormon-haters, augmented by the confusing counsel of politicians struggling with the issues of slavery and states' rights and by an avalanche of anti-Mormon literature, the president of the United States ordered the formation of the largest peacetime military force in the history of the nation. Its mission was to install a new slate of Utah territorial officers, including Governor Alfred Cumming, and, if necessary, to subjugate the Mormons by force of arms. It was the vast difference between the problem and the solution

Mr. Buchanan offered that suggested the accusing title this military fiasco was later given.

The first contingent of the new army left Fort
Leavenworth, Kansas, in mid-July. So convinced was
President Buchanan of the accuracy of the reports
about conditions in Utah, he had not bothered to
communicate with Brigham Young, the territorial
governor. So, as the first soldiers left the Missouri,
their creaking wagons laden with the weapons of war,
Brigham Young was planning a party to celebrate the
tenth anniversary of the arrival of the Saints in Salt
Lake Valley.

In the midst of the celebration at Brighton, word
reached Brigham of the approach of the army.
Twenty-five hundred Saints had assembled at the
popular recreation area to commemorate ten years of
pioneer life in their new home. Several exhausted,
dusty horsemen arrived at the Brighton camp, exactly
on the tenth anniversary, to make the incredible announcement that federal troops were on their way to
invade the territory! Assembling his people, Brigham
reported the shocking news, expressed confidence in
the ultimate triumph of the Saints over these and all
other foes, and urged them to complete their festivities
before returning to the city the following day.

Back at his office, Brigham immediately began
counseling with the Brethren. Out of these discussions
came the decision to consolidate their strength. Thus,
Amasa M. Lyman and Charles C. Rich, who led the
Saints in San Bernardino, California, were instructed
to break up their settlement and return to the valley. A
similar order was given to Orson Hyde, who led a
Mormon colony in Carson Valley, Nevada. At the
same time, instructions were sent to the leaders and
missionaries laboring in the eastern United States and
Europe to come home. Moreover, the Nauvoo legion,
consisting of about five thousand men and organized
into two cohorts, or divisions, was alerted and instructed to prepare to defend against the threatened
invasion. Over a thousand men were deployed to
guard the mountain passes east of the valley, and oth-

ers were ordered to conduct harrassing attacks upon the military train, to burn its wagons and drive off the animals. Explicit instructions were given, however, to avoid any bloodshed. "But save life always," the Mormon troops were admonished. "We do not wish to shed a drop of blood if it can be avoided."[1]

As the army toiled across the wastelands of Wyoming, its leader, General W. S. Harney, became acutely aware of the need for supplies, and desiring to open negotiations with Brigham Young, sent a personable quartermaster officer, Captain Stewart Van Vliet, with a request to purchase forage and lumber. Arriving in Salt Lake on September 8, the captain must have been relieved and pleasantly surprised—relieved because his safe arrival had disproven the malicious prediction that the Mormons would kill him if he attempted to enter their valley, and surprised because instead of finding a seditious and priest-ridden community, as he had been led to believe, a community that could be intimidated and subdued merely by the specter of an armed invasion, he found a group of tough, high-minded patriots who were prepared to confront the armed forces of a powerful nation rather than to yield to its unjustified demands.

It was not until Captain Van Vliet parleyed with Brigham Young the day after he arrived, however, that he glimpsed the implacable will and determination of the Mormon community as revealed through the words and conduct of its leader. When told that his undermanned guerrilla force could not forever withstand the military might of the United States, Brigham responded: "We are aware that such will be the case; but when these troops arrive they will find Utah a desert; every house will be burned to the ground, every tree cut down, and every field laid to waste. We have three years' provisions on hand, which we will cache, and then take to the mountains and bid defiance to all the powers of the government."

Any lingering doubts the captain might have had that these hard words merely represented the puffing of a leader and did not reflect the attitudes of his followers were dispelled in the days that followed. Visiting a Mormon home, where he was impressed by the beauty of a well-tended garden, the young officer asked the woman of the house: "Madam, would you consent to see this beautiful home in ashes and this fruitful orchard destroyed?" "I would not only consent to it," she answered, "but I would set fire to my home with my own hands, and cut down every tree, and root up every plant." Later, in the Tabernacle, Captain Van Vliet sat in amazed disbelief as he saw four thousand hands raised in support of a motion, put by John Taylor, that the Saints raze all the buildings in the valley and waste their fields rather than allow the army to enter. Following up that incredible show of resistance, Brigham added a new dimension to the Mormon resolve with this: "When the time comes to burn and lay waste our improvements, if any man undertakes to shield his he will be treated as a traitor. . . . Now the faint-hearted can go in peace; but should that time come, they must not interfere. Before I will again suffer, as I have in times gone by, there shall not one building, nor one foot of lumber, nor a fence, nor a tree, nor a particle of grass or hay, that will burn, be left in reach of our enemies. I am sworn, if driven to extremity, to utterly lay waste this land in the name of Israel's God, and our enemies shall find it as barren as when we came here."

So astounded was Captain Van Vliet by what he saw and heard in the Salt Lake Valley, and so altered was his opinion of the Mormons and their leader, he is reported to have declared "that if the United States made war on them, he would withdraw from the army."[2]

Apparently sensing the need for prompt and daring action, Brigham, in his role as territorial governor, declared martial law the day after Captain Van Vliet left the valley. Accompanying the captain was J. M. Bernhisel, the territorial congressman, who, with his companion, intended to appeal to the general government to reconsider the rash decision to send troops to Utah.

In the meantime, the Nauvoo Legion, led by a cadre of resourceful and intrepid men, began its bloodless campaign of scorched earth and harassment. Fort Bridger and Fort Supply, both owned by the Church, were burned to deprive the advancing army of needed provisions. Further along the trail, Lot Smith and a small band of guerrillas burned seventy-four supply wagons and stampeded a thousand head of government cattle. Prairie fires were set to reduce forage for the remaining livestock, trees were felled to block the trail, river fords were destroyed to impede water crossings, and impromptu night raids were carried out to interrupt the sleep of the harassed troops. To add to the annoyance and frustration, the military column seldom, if ever, saw its tormentors, who ordinarily worked under cover of night or shielded by vegetation or the smoke from their prairie fires.

Meanwhile, internal confusion and dissension further distracted the camp as Colonel Albert Sidney Johnston replaced General Harney as commander and as Governor Cumming argued with the army officers over goals and procedures, Johnston seeking a political accommodation and Cumming a military victory.

By November, eighteen hundred dispirited federal troops reached the charred remains of Fort Bridger and Fort Supply short on rations and patience. Behind them stretched a tenuous supply line hundreds of miles long, and ahead lay a harsh, unforgiving winter.

Stalled a hundred miles from its destination, Buchanan's invading army spent a miserable winter on the plains of Wyoming, eking out a sparse existence and preparing for the invasion the following spring. In the valley, Brigham busied himself preparing the minds of the people against the consequences to flow from the expected attack. In the face of a possible bloodbath or the dislocation of an entire people, the wheels of mediation and peace began to grind slowly in the nation's capital. The prime movers of this initiative were Congressman Bernhisel and Captain Van Vliet, joined by that great friend of the Mormons, Colonel Thomas L. Kane. This trio succeeded in sharpening President Buchanan's fuzzy view of conditions in Utah to the extent that he dispatched an informal letter to Brigham Young that suggested a negotiated settlement. Colonel Kane acted as the intermediary in this effort at private diplomacy, traveling by way of Panama and California to the Mormon stronghold in the Salt Lake Valley, where he arrived in late February, 1858. After obtaining Brigham's concurrence in the plan, he traveled onward to the military encampment in Wyoming, where, overcoming the army's suspicion and reluctance, he persuaded Mr. Cumming to accompany him and a Mormon detachment to Salt Lake City to confer with Brigham. This decision effectively terminated the so-called Utah War, as the new territorial governor was kindly received by Brigham Young, who willingly relinquished the reins of government to his successor. On April 15 the new governor sent word to both President Buchanan and Colonel Johnston of the transfer of power.

There remained only the entry of the army into Salt Lake Valley to symbolize its authority and dominion and to salve the feelings of the officers and men who had anticipated the spoils of a military victory. At first Brigham vigorously opposed this move, but afterward relented on condition that the army not stop in the city, but only pass through it, moving on to a designated campsite beyond the Jordan River.

June 26, 1858, was the day agreed upon for the army to make its ceremonial march through Salt Lake City. Winding their way down Emigration Canyon past the spot where, eleven years before, Brigham Young had declared "this is the right place," and along the tree-lined streets with their unpretentious but substantial homes and frugal gardens, the troops gazed with intense curiosity.

They found the city's streets empty. Most of the Saints had temporarily gone south to wait until the dust had settled on the controversy. Those who remained were concealed in the buildings, warily watching for any false move by the troops, which would be the signal to incinerate their city.

Any concern about the intentions of the troops proved to be unfounded. Led by Colonel Johnston, they marched in disciplined military order to their campground. And one of the colonel's senior officers, Colonel Cooke, bared his head as he rode through the streets of the city in honor of the valiant men of the Mormon Battalion.

This formally ended the war. But the aftershocks were to reverberate through the territory, indeed, through the entire country, for many years. Not the least of these was the ominous rumbling set in motion by the Mountain Meadows Massacre in September, 1857, that resulted in the murder of 120 wagon-train emigrants by a mixed band of Indians and whites, including some members of the Church. The fact and the folklore connected with this tragic incident have piqued the curiosity and imagination of authors and readers for well over a century. Many have tried without success to lay the blame at the door of Brigham Young. The circumstance to which these accusers point is the following statement of Brigham to Captain Van Vliet at their meeting on September 9: "If the government persists in sending an army to destroy us, in the name of the Lord, we shall conquer them. If they dare to force the issue, I shall not hold the Indians by the wrist any longer, . . . they shall go ahead and do as they please. If the issue comes, you may tell the government to stop all emigration across this continent, for the Indians will kill all who attempt it."[3]

By a fateful coincidence, the massacre occurred at about the same time these words were uttered. Those who infer a tie between the two incidents do so in ignorance of, or in disregard of, explicit instructions Brigham gave to a messenger, James Haslam, who arrived while Captain Van Vliet was in Salt Lake City, after a three-day horseback ride of over two hundred and fifty miles, and who, after briefing Brigham about difficulties with the Fancher party, was told: "Go with all speed, spare no horse-flesh. The emigrants must not be meddled with, if it takes all Iron county to prevent it. They must go free and unmolested."[4]

Those who accuse the Mormon leader of complicity in this bloody affair attribute qualities of stupidity and rashness to a man whose whole career as a leader was marked by the highest traits of astuteness and wisdom. It is beyond reason that a seasoned, intelligent man like Brigham Young, faced with imminent invasion by a powerful army backed by the resources of a great nation, would have ordered an act whose grisly consequences could have no other effect than to arouse the most bitter hatred toward him and his people.

The first eyewitness report of the tragedy to reach Brigham Young came from the lips of John D. Lee, the only person to be convicted and executed for involvement in it. He had been one of the bodyguards for Joseph Smith, a confidant of Brigham's, and an Indian agent in the southern part of the territory. He apparently came with reluctance and only at the strong urging of Isaac C. Haight, the stake president in Cedar City. He reported to Brigham on September 29, when the army of invasion was approaching Fort Bridger.

John D. Lee heaped the full blame upon the Indians, not even hinting that he or any other white man was implicated in the massacre. "The Indians fought them five days," Lee told Brigham, "until they killed all the men, about sixty in number. They then rushed into their corral and cut the throats of the women and children, except some eight or ten children which they brought and sold to the whites. They stripped the men and women naked and left them stinking in the boiling sun." Lee said he did not learn of the tragedy until after it had occurred when "he took some men and went and buried their bodies."[5]

Almost a year later Brigham received a written report prepared by George A. Smith, a member of the Twelve, who had made an investigation of the tragedy, including the questioning of many people in the area. This excerpt revealed that John D. Lee had not made a full disclosure, confirming another report to that effect received in the meantime. "It is reported," Elder Smith wrote, "that John D. Lee, and a few other white men were on the ground during a portion of the combat, but for what purpose, or how they conducted themselves, or whether, indeed, they were there at all, I have not learned."[6]

What was vague and indefinite at that time, shrouded by a cloak of secrecy and conspiracy among those who were involved, later became clear beyond doubt. In 1870, thirteen years after the event, Brigham became convinced of John D. Lee's participation in the massacre. In that year Erastus Snow, a member of the Twelve, and Bishop L. W. Roundy, who had been investigating the affair, laid before Brigham, while he was visiting in St. George, irrefutable evidence that Latter-day Saints had been involved. At the same time it was revealed that stake and settlement leaders, even though not involved in the massacre itself, were culpable for permitting actions that resulted in the massacre. On returning to Salt Lake City Brigham laid the matter before the First Presidency and the Twelve, and, on his own motion, John D. Lee, Isaac C. Haight, and others were excommunicated from the Church.

There can be no doubt there were other white men implicated in this sordid affair. The reason that criminal action was not pressed against them was explained by Sumner Howard, the prosecuting attorney in the second Lee trial, who insisted on prosecuting at least one leading participant. "*He was determined,*" it was reported, "*to clear the calendar of every indictment against any and every actual guilty participator in the massacre, but he did not intend to prosecute any one that had been lured to the Meadows at that time, many of whom were only young boys and knew nothing of the vile plan which Lee [and others] originated and carried out for the destruction of the emigrants.*"[7]

This tragic episode must have filled Brigham with a sense of sorrow, humiliation, and shame. These feelings were elaborated by John Taylor in a letter to the *Deseret News* three years before Brigham Young's death. Wrote he: "There is no excuse for such a relent-less, diabolical, sanguinary deed. That outrageous infamy is looked upon with as much abhorrence by our people as by other parties, in this nation or in the world; and at its first announcement, its loathing reci-tal chilled the marrow and sent a thrill of horror through the breasts of the listeners. It was most cer-tainly a horrible deed; and like many other defenseless tragedies, it is one of those things that cannot be undone."[8]

Chapter Twenty-eight

War's Aftermath

Once the army had paraded through the empty streets of Salt Lake City and established its temporary camp across the river, the Saints, at Brigham Young's direction, began to drift homeward from the south. Although President Buchanan had issued a blanket pardon absolving Brigham and his people of any real or imagined blame, it was with some sense of uneasiness and foreboding that they settled back into their homes. What troubled them most was the military presence that had been introduced into their midst, with its claque of unsavory camp followers. Although the troops were later moved to a permanent camp some thirty miles to the south called Camp Floyd, (adjacent to which sprang up a scruffy community called Frog Town), they were still too close to please the Latter-day Saints.

Frog Town was alive with every imaginable vice and degradation. Gambling, prostitution, thievery, and violence flourished in an atmosphere of idleness lubricated by the free flow of cheap liquor.

The only respite from the deadening boredom that pervaded the camp was to visit the nearby Mormon communities, which were not distinguished for gaiety and diversion. Finding little there to amuse and entertain themselves, the unwelcome guests turned to brawling and crime. Street fighting and drunken brawls became commonplace. There were far more murders and bloodshed in Salt Lake City during the first eighteen months after Johnston's army arrived than there had been during the previous eleven years. In an attempt to combat this, the police force was quadrupled during 1858, burdening the people with costs more than double the total cost of police protection for the years 1847 to 1858.

What galled Brigham was the stated purpose of Buchanan's expedition to tame and civilize a people reported to be in rebellion and living in defiance of the laws of the land and Christianity. Viewing the objectives of the army in the light of its conduct, Brigham said to a federal official as he prepared to return to the East: "No doubt you will be asked many questions about me. I wish you would tell them that I am here, watching the progress of civilization."

The sarcasm in this comment was directed not only at the misconduct of the military but at the misuse of the military by the notorious federal judges who had taken office along with Governor Cumming: Delano R. Eckles, chief justice, and associate justices Charles E. Sinclair and John Cradlebaugh. Following in the tradition of the judges whose false reports had triggered the Utah war, these men were imbued with a crusading spirit whose object soon became apparent.

In the early months of 1859 Judges Cradlebaugh and Sinclair undertook judicial action whose object was to convict and humiliate Brigham Young. Judge Cradlebaugh, who presided in the southern part of the territory, convened a grand jury in Provo to consider certain homicides committed in Springville, alleged to have been committed pursuant to the principle of "blood atonement," and to consider charges arising out of the Mountain Meadows Massacre. In an apparent attempt to intimidate the local residents, the judge induced General Johnston to send a hundred soldiers from nearby Camp Floyd and to place them under his charge, ostensibly to guard prisoners. This was done in disregard of the U. S. Marshal and his staff, who had the duty to perform this function, and despite the fact that there was a jail in Provo. Judge Cradlebaugh's action aroused a public clamor that was answered by the assignment of an additional nine hundred troops, including a company of artillery and one of cavalry. Camped within sight of the courthouse, this military

detachment obviously was intended to frighten the
grand jury into indicting Brigham Young. No one mis-
understood his meaning when the judge lectured the
jury: "The very fact of such a case as that of the Mountain Meadows shows that there was some person high
in the estimation of the people, and it was done by that
authority; and this case of Parrishes [the Springville
homicides] shows the same, and unless you do your
duty, such will be the view that will be taken of it. . . . No
person can commit crimes and say they are authorized
by higher authorities, and if they have any such notions they will have to dispel them."[1]

The gross ineptitude that caused him to believe a
Mormon grand jury would indict their leader because
of his fanciful suspicions doomed Judge Cradlebaugh's crusade to failure from the outset. Indeed, the
judge became something of a national laughingstock
when he was later reprimanded for his extraordinary
judicial conduct.

But the Cradlebaugh charade in Provo was a clear
signal to Brigham that these new carpetbagger judges
would stop at nothing in their determined effort to destroy him. It seemed incredible that in just a few years
after fleeing into a remote wilderness, the Mormon
leader would again be surrounded by armed enemies
and subjected to the jurisdiction of biased and antago-
nistic judges. But it was a reality that had to be faced,
and Brigham did so in his usual thorough and compe-
tent way. He began to live a more secluded life, never
appearing in public unless closely guarded by men
with whom he was intimately acquainted. A sentry was
posted at the door to his residence day and night, and
armed guards patrolled the estate.

Toward the end of March, 1859, Judge Sinclair
took up the crusade from his court in Salt Lake City,
issuing a writ for Brigham's arrest based on the
Mormon leader's alleged complicity in forging notes
on the United States Treasury. We may gauge the
judge's objectivity from the fact that the writ was based
on the testimony of a man who admittedly had made a
counterfeit plate used to forge the treasury notes, and

who, in turning state's evidence, testified that one of
Brigham Young's employees had furnished the paper
used in the forgery. From this shaky premise the judge
leaped to the astonishing conclusion that Brigham was
implicated, and issued the writ. When officers from
Camp Floyd, appointed by the judge to serve the writ,
approached Governor Cumming for aid, he exploded
with indignation on learning of their intent to batter
down the walls of the Young estate with artillery
should any resistance be shown. "Gentlemen, you can't
do it!" he shouted. "When you have a right to take
Brigham Young, gentlemen, you shall have him without creeping through walls. You shall enter by his door
with heads erect as becomes representatives of your
government. But till that time, gentlemen, you can't
touch Brigham Young while I live."[2]

Expectedly, this frivolous writ was later dissolved
for lack of evidence. Undeterred however, Judge
Sinclair went forward with preparations for a May session of court, intending to follow the lead of Judge
Cradlebaugh and use Camp Floyd troops as an instrument of intimidation and coercion. When word was
received on April 17 that two regiments of troops were
on their way to Salt Lake from Camp Floyd, reportedly
to make arrests in connection with Judge Sinclair's
May term of court, Brigham Young and his brethren
moved with alacrity. General Daniel H. Wells, who was
also one of Brigham's counselors, promptly mustered
the Nauvoo Legion, and within a matter of hours five
thousand men were under arms. In an atmosphere of
electric tension, the two military forces faced each other. Fortunately, a direct clash between them was averted by negotiation.

It was this last fiasco that brought about the
summary dismissal of all three judges. A letter of
reprimand from the attorney general, focusing on the
attempted use of the military as an arm of the court,
noted that "Surely it was not intended to clothe each
one of the judges, as well as the marshal and all his dep-
uties, with this tremendous authority."

By way of postscript, arrogant Judge Cradlebaugh

challenged the right of the president to dismiss him, and remained in office for a while afterward. Finally, bending to the inevitable, he stepped down and moved to Nevada, where his combative temperament found a more congenial climate in the rough-and-tumble of local politics. He was twice elected as a congressional delegate from that territory.

This difficult episode marked the watershed in Brigham's relationship with the army of invasion. Intermittent clashes followed, but none as tense and potentially dangerous as this one. Much of the credit for the improved relations that followed belongs to Governor Cumming, who administered the affairs of his office with restraint and wisdom. So popular and well-liked did he become among the Mormons that he became suspect in the East, so much so that a faction in the cabinet pressed hard for his removal.

Most of the troops were transferred from Camp Floyd to Arizona and Mexico in 1860, and the following year the remainder left for the East in apparent anticipation of the Civil War, whose dark clouds were already gathering.

Upon the departure of the army, Brigham and his people reaped an unexpected harvest from the distasteful military occupation. The government stores at Camp Floyd, estimated to have had a value of four million dollars, were sold at liquidation prices. It is estimated that not more than one hundred thousand dollars was realized from the sale, roughly forty thousand dollars of which was paid by Brigham Young through his business agent, H. B. Clawson.

Livestock, wagons, clothing, and foodstuffs were sold at unbelievably low prices. Flour, for instance, that had cost $570.00 a ton was sold for $11.00 a ton or less. It was this windfall that formed the basis of Brigham Young's wealth, as well as the wealth of some of Salt Lake City's merchants. And the populace benefited economically through reduced retail prices, as it had benefited during the occupation by having a ready cash market for its surplus commodities.

So, as with all of the experiences through which

Brigham Young and the Saints passed, the invasion and occupation of Johnston's army produced mixed results. The inconveniences, harassments, intimidations, and terrors were counterbalanced, in part, by the economic benefits, by the new insights into military life and political machinations, and by the enhanced national image of Brigham Young and his people.

Chapter Twenty-nine

Polygamy and the Civil War

From 1852, when it was first acknowledged in public, Brigham Young openly lived and advocated the doctrine of plural wives. There was nothing illegal about the practice at that time, nor was there to be until a decade later when, on July 1, 1862, Congress passed the Morrill Act, which imposed criminal sanctions for bigamy, disincorporated the Church, and restricted the ownership of Church property to $50,000.

Ironically, this act followed close on the heels of another abortive attempt to obtain statehood for Utah. Time and again the Saints had tried to acquire this status, but had been disappointed by the opposition of those in the federal government who were unwilling to relinquish control over what they considered to be a dangerous and seditious sect.

The Morrill Act confronted Brigham with a complex dilemma. On the one hand, he was bound to honor the solemn religious covenants he had made in taking plural wives in acceptance of the revelation given to Joseph Smith. On the other hand, he was obligated to adhere to the principle announced by that same prophet to honor, obey, and sustain the law. He reached an accommodation with these colliding ideas by asserting that the Morrill Act violated the first amendment of the constitution and was void. Since the probate courts that administered criminal justice in the territory were controlled by magistrates elected by the Saints, magistrates who shared Brigham's views, the sanctions provided by the act fell into total disuse.

Understandably, the federal appointees from the East rejected this view and saw in it further evidence of the charge of disloyalty and sedition that had been leveled against Brigham and his followers for many years. Stephen S. Harding, appointed territorial governor in 1862, was incensed at what he considered to be a patent disregard of the law, and began to pressure Congress to limit the jurisdiction of the probate courts and to place the selection of jurors under the control of federal appointees. Had not the Civil War intervened, these efforts likely would have borne fruit, greatly accelerating the steps that led to the ultimate resolution of the polygamy issue. As it was, President Lincoln and his new administration were so preoccupied in trying to control the wild forces unleashed by the war that they gave only scant attention to affairs in Utah except as they related to the conflict. The Great Emancipator's policy was summed up in this terse comment made to a Church representative: "You tell Brigham Young if he will leave me alone, I'll leave him alone."

Not long afterward, Lincoln had to call upon Brigham for help in the war effort. Soon after hostilities began, it became necessary to shift the transcontinental stage lines northward, rerouting them through Salt Lake City in order to put them out of the reach of confederate troops. But since the fratricidal nature of the war often made it impossible to differentiate between friend and foe, the new route, though passing through friendly territory, required military protection. The newly completed telegraph line also had to be guarded. Realizing the vast influence the Mormon prophet exerted in the area, President Lincoln ignored the territorial governor and wired Brigham Young: "Raise, arm and equip a company of cavalry for ninety days service, to protect the property of the telegraph and overland mail companies."

Moving promptly, Brigham gave the assignment to the Nauvoo Legion. Lot Smith, whose guerrilla band had been the nemesis of Johnston's army, led the seasoned Nauvoo Legion, which efficiently performed the duties assigned by President Lincoln.

The promptness with which Brigham Young and his followers responded to the call of President

Lincoln indicates the basic sense of loyalty they felt toward the federal government. In fact, Brigham looked upon himself and his people as guardians and saviors-to-be of the Constitution. He often admonished his people in such terms as "Utah in her rocky fortress is biding her time to step in and rescue the constitution and aid all lovers of freedom . . . irrespective of creed or party."

For the federal government, struggling to preserve the union in a bloody war with the South and conditioned by the frequent charges of disloyalty and sedition leveled at the Mormons, it was not difficult to read a secessionist sentiment into such words. Deciding that the Latter-day Saints had to be kept in check by military surveillance, Washington directed Colonel Patrick Edward Connor of Stockton, California, to enlist a corps of 750 volunteers and move them to Utah, ostensibly to relieve the Nauvoo Legion of the duty to guard the telegraph and stage lines. That Secretary of War Edwin M. Stanton had an ulterior motive was made clear when, instead of occupying Camp Floyd, already established as a military base, Connor's men marched ominously through Salt Lake City streets with fixed bayonets and loaded rifles and camped on the bench to the east where the Mormon capital was in the sights of their cannon. This military camp, the second major one to be established in Utah in a five-year period, was given the name Camp Douglas in honor of the feisty senator from Illinois whom the new president had bested in the famous debates that had thrust Lincoln into the national limelight.

The belligerent and threatening way in which Colonel Connor made his dramatic entry into the Salt Lake Valley set the tone for the relationship that existed between him and Brigham Young throughout his tour of duty in Utah. Almost from the beginning this tough, disciplined warrior considered himself to be an almost heaven-ordained instrument to harass, intimidate, and destroy the influence of Brigham Young and his people. No clearer evidence of the Colonel's true objectives can be found than this excerpt from a letter written to a fellow officer in San Francisco: "My policy in this territory has been to invite hither a large gentile and loyal population, sufficient by peaceful means, and through the ballot box, to overwhelm the Mormons by mere force of numbers, and thus wrest from the church—disloyal and traitorous to the core—the absolute and tyrannical control of temporal and civic affairs, or at least a population numerous enough to put a check on the Mormon authorities and give countenance to those who are striving to loosen the bonds with which they have been so long oppressed."

It was predictable that once he had become established at Camp Douglas, Mr. Connor would form an alliance with the territorial appointees and gentile merchants from the East who entertained similar low views of Brigham Young and the Saints. And this coalition made little, if any, effort to placate or understand the Mormon leader and his people, an attitude that was reciprocated in kind. The result was to polarize the community into two separate camps that looked with suspicion and disdain upon each other. Antagonism on the part of the Saints was quickly elevated to fever pitch when, not long after the troops arrived, Mr. Connor, in concert with the territorial judiciary, attempted to arrest Brigham Young on a bigamy charge under the Morrill Act. A threatened clash between the Colonel's troops and the Nauvoo Legion was averted when Brigham willingly submitted to arrest and was immediately released on bail by a sympathetic probate judge.

If he did not know beforehand, Mr. Connor soon learned where the real power in Salt Lake Valley lay. When Brigham saw the drift of the commander's intention and policy, he began to thunder defiance and opposition from the pulpit in the tabernacle. In a sermon delivered March 8, 1863, after alluding to the speed with which the Saints had responded to the call to arms when the Mormon Battalion was mustered, he cried: "But if the government of the United States should now ask for a battalion of men to fight on the present battle fields of the nation, while there is a camp of soldiers from abroad [California] located within the limits of Salt Lake City, I would not ask one man to go."

The soldiers were shunned like the plague on the streets of Salt Lake City. In requital, the troops, with enthusiastic support from their commanding officer, established the first daily newspaper in the territory, the *Union Vedette,* whose pages simmered with libelous attacks upon the Mormons.

But giving free rein to a literary impulse was not the only outlet for the pent-up energies of the army. The discovery of minerals in the Oquirrh Mountains to the west ignited a feverish prospecting effort among Connor's men, an effort in which the redoubtable Colonel was a prime mover. The canyons and mountains ringing Salt Lake City crawled with soldiers in quest of gold. The allure of sudden wealth drew the soldiers to the prospecting that came to occupy most of their leisure time. Their subtle commander had another object in view. A major gold strike would bring an immediate and large influx of newcomers who would dilute the Mormon influence and help bring about the result this devious man sought. Confiding in his San Francisco correspondent, the Colonel wrote: "With this in view, I have bent every energy and means of which I was possessed, both personal and official, towards the discovery and development of the mining resources of the Territory, using without stint the soldiers at my command, whenever and wherever it could be done, without detriment to the public service."

Remembering the difficulty he had had years before in diverting the attention of the Saints from the allurements of the California gold fields, Brigham mounted the pulpit again and again to denounce those who sought after mineral wealth.

In addition, Brigham admonished his people to charge high prices in dealing with the army. Later, when relationships deteriorated further, any trade with Mr. Connor or his troops was channeled through a Church committee at fixed prices. The commander,

who in the meantime had been brevited a general, retaliated by demanding that all Mormons trading at
Camp Douglas first give an oath of allegiance to the
United States. Viewing this as an insult to their integrity, the Latter-day Saints declined, effectively ending
commercial intercourse between the two groups.
Unable to communicate with each other in a produc-
tive way, Brigham and the general began to bombard
Washington for relief, the former pleading for removal of the troops or at least for officers with greater
competence and judgment; and the latter repeating
the abusive charges against the Mormons that had
been heaped upon them for years and, due to frequent
repetition, had now been accepted by official
Washington as fact.

For the most part these pleas fell on deaf ears because of preoccupation with the Civil War and President Lincoln's inclination to ignore Brigham and his
people as far as possible.

Once the war had ended, the problem dissipated to
a large extent as the military garrison was reduced in
size to a mere skeleton crew. Moreover, Colonel
Connor's dream of attracting overwhelming numbers
of gentiles to the valley evaporated for the moment
when his aggressive prospecting effort failed to uncov-
er the rich gold deposits he had hoped to find. The
minerals that were discovered, mainly the low grade
copper deposits in the Oquirrhs, had to await development until the advent of the transcontinental railroad
a few years later, an event that began the dilution of
the Mormon populace the disappointed general had
so much wanted to accelerate.

In the meantime Brigham Young remained as the
effective, though not the official, head of the territory.
This antagonized most of those who came west in the
mistaken belief they were to govern. Inflated with a
false sense of self-importance and lacking the experience and political skills necessary for success (a
notable exception being Governor Cumming), these
frustrated administrators sought to solve the problem
by attacks upon Brigham Young, who, they thought,

was at the root of their difficulties. In most instances, these appointed officials came to Utah with fixed and erroneous ideas about the Mormons, and some with open hostility.

On the other hand, Brigham often seemed unaware of, or to brush aside as unimportant, his incursions into strictly civil matters. This attitude may be understood, though not necessarily excused, in light of the inherent independence and self-sufficiency of Brigham Young and his followers, the all-encompassing nature of their religion, and the merger of civil and ecclesiastical functions during the Saints' early years in the mountains. Neither did the Mormon leader seem fully to grasp or to attempt effectively to dispel the sense of alienation and exclusion most newcomers felt on first contact with the monolithic and decidedly unorthodox society of the Latter-day Saints. Again, we may understand, though not sanction, these conditions, in view of the long history of persecution the Mormons had endured.

Nor did Brigham seem completely to appreciate the antagonisms and opposition raised by his attitude toward the Morrill Act. While he felt honestly that it was unconstitutional, and while he was amazed by the ill-will of those who were the principal architects and enforcers of the law, he seemed not to appreciate the fact that there were others, men and women of good will, who could not reconcile a deliberate disobedience of the law by one whose faith explicitly enjoined obedience.

Thus, the conditions and attitudes that emerged from the chaos of the Morrill Act and the Civil War formed the seedbed out of which grew many of the trials and difficulties that harassed the Mormon leader in the years that followed.

Chapter Thirty

The Storm Without and the Tempest Within

Brigham Young entertained no illusions that the temporary lull in persecution following the Civil War held any hopes of permanency. Long experience had proven that, like the proverbial bad penny, the virulent opposition with its attendant adversity would return soon.

After a brief respite, Brigham's enemies first turned their attention to legislation thought necessary to shore up the sagging Morrill Act. As already noted, that punitive legislation had failed in its purpose because the enforcement of it lay with the probate courts in Utah, whose judges were elected by popular vote and whose juries were impaneled from among the people, the overwhelming majority of whom were Latter-day Saints. The almost unanimous belief among the Mormons that the Morrill Act was unconstitutional guaranteed that it would lie dormant and useless.

The first stirrings among the anti-Mormon faction in Washington to breathe life into this moribund legislation occurred in 1866 with the drafting of what became known as the Wade Bill. Had it been enacted, this bill's sweeping provisions would have effectively destroyed local self-government in Utah. Under it the local militia, originally a creation of the territorial legislature, was to be placed under the governor; the United States Marshal was to select all juries; the probate judges were to be appointed by the governor; Mormon officials were to be prohibited from solem-

nizing marriages; most of the tax exemptions for
Church properties were to be annulled; the Church
was to be deprived of its power to adopt rules for fellowship; and the trustee in trust was to be required,
under penalty of fine and imprisonment, to make an
annual report, under oath, accounting for all Church
properties, including bank deposits, notes, and so on.
Later, additional proposed acts, including the Cragin
and Cullom bills, were drafted that contained other
creatively vicious provisions.

To the credit of an aggressive lobbying effort and
the prevailing influence of wiser heads in Congress,
these acts were never passed. This failure, however,
did not deter the introduction of other bills aimed at
diluting or destroying the power and influence of the
Church and its president. One of the most imaginative
of these was a bill introduced by James M. Ashley of
Ohio, whose object was to dismember the territory of
Utah, slicing off large segments of it and attaching
them to the neighboring states of Nevada, Colorado,
and Wyoming. What, on its face, appeared to be a
good idea to the Mormon haters turned out to be bad
news when analysis showed the proposed dismember-
ment would strengthen, not weaken, the influence of
the Church. Had Mr. Ashley's brainstorm become law,
the large concentrations of Saints in the area to be am-
putated, then engrafted, would likely have given the
Saints political control in four jurisdictions instead of
one.

Though Brigham's foes suffered defeat in the halls
of Congress, they anticipated a practical victory in the
fulfillment of Colonel Connor's dream of the Saints
being engulfed by an overwhelming tide of gentile
emigration. What aroused these expectations was the
eagerly sought completion of the transcontinental railroad. Even as the legislators plotted strategy in
Washington, two railroad crews, one moving west and
the other east, were working feverishly to fulfill the
great American dream of a continent girdled by iron
rails. The sanguine expectations of Brigham's enemies
as they looked forward to the completion of the rail-

road were expressed by George Q. Cannon in an address delivered in the Salt Lake Tabernacle in October, 1868: "We are told—openly and without disguise, that when the railroad is completed there will be such a flood of so-called 'civilization' brought in here that every vestige of us, our church and institutions shall be completely obliterated."[1] Brigham Young said with obvious scorn that Mormonism must be a "poor religion, if it cannot stand one railroad."[2] Indeed, the Mormon leader had long sought the extension of the railroad into the area and as early as 1852 had been instrumental in the passage of a memorial by the territorial legislature urging the construction of a railroad to the Pacific.

But Brigham was not oblivious to the dangers such an event would pose to the Mormon way of life nor to the defensive measures that would be necessary to protect against them. He launched two initiatives designed to increase cohesion among the Latter-day Saints, to brace them for the moral, social, and economic pressures that completion of the railroad would bring. First, he promoted with almost missionary zeal the organization of cooperatives to stimulate home manufacturing, limit patronization of gentile merchants, and lower prices through group buying. Second, he reinstituted the School of the Prophets to increase the spirituality of the Saints and to provide a convenient forum, comprised of the most powerful men in the Mormon community, for the discussion, analysis, and solution of problems caused by the railroad. This body advised making home manufacturies competitive with the flood of commodities from both the East and West that would come in the wake of the railroad. It was the consensus of the School of the Prophets that production had to be increased by greater mechanization, and costs reduced by lowering wages.

In pursuit of this last goal, representatives from each of the trades were elected to submit to their coworkers a proposal to reduce wages. A group of lukewarm Saints who until now had nurtured only

philosophical and theological differences with
Brigham Young seized upon this issue as a potential
means of altering certain Church policies and dimin-
ishing the authority of the Mormon leader. Led by
W. S. Godbe, this group, which included men of talent
and energy who were also members of the School of
the Prophets, now made a vigorous attack upon Brigham Young, accusing him of an attempt to fix wages.
The chief weapon the dissidents used in their internal
warfare was the *Utah Magazine,* a publication that had
had Brigham Young's approval in the beginning, but
whose pages were now used not only to challenge
Brigham's policies but to demean and berate him. The
subtle approach initially adopted by the magazine's
staff was explained by one of its writers, Edward W.
Tullidge, who planned a series of articles on the "Great
Characters" of the world, "and without once alluding
to Brother Brigham, the contrast was to be to his disad-
vantage." Later, the habitual obedience of Church
members to priesthood direction was attacked and
criticized in the same devious way.

Eventually, the articles became more direct and
outspoken until one entitled "True Development of
the Territory" boldly opposed Brigham Young's
policy against the Saints' involvement in mining development. This incident brought into clear focus an internal rebellion that had been festering for some time.
And with the issue drawn so clearly, an open rupture
between the dissidents and Brigham was inevitable.
Never one to temporize or hesitate in the face of a crisis, Brigham acted decisively on October 16, 1869,
when he took steps that resulted in the disfellowship-
ment of the dissidents for "irregular attendance" at
meetings of the school. At the next session the inquiry
was broadened to consider the meaning and intent of
the critical article in the *Utah Magazine.* This brought
about the request that those who continued to endorse
the sentiments expressed in the article relinquish their
tickets to the school. This was followed by formal disci-
plinary action that resulted in the excommunication of

Godbe, E. L. T. Harrison, Henry W. Lawrence, T. B. H. Stenhouse, William H. Sherman, and Edward W. Tullidge. The coup de grace was administered by Brigham a few days later when he published a notice in the *Deseret News* condemning the *Utah Magazine* as "a periodical that, in its spirit and teachings, is directly opposed to the work of God. Instead of building up Zion, and uniting the people, its teachings . . . would destroy Zion [and] divide the people. . . . We say to our brethren and sisters in every place, the *Utah Magazine* is not a periodical suitable for circulation among or perusal by them, and should not be sustained by Latter-day Saints."[3]

Once out of the Church these excommunicants formed the nucleus of an anti-Mormon faction known as the Godbeites, who, dabbling in spiritualism, made an abortive attempt to organize the "Church of Zion," changed the name of their publication to the *Mormon Tribune*, and later exerted a strong political influence inimical to the interests of the Latter-day Saints.

The manner in which Brigham Young handled these dissenters reveals a facet of his character that has subjected him to much criticism by his enemies and detractors: his refusal to tolerate any deviation from the policies he decreed. Indeed, this was the essence of the charge leveled at him by the Godbeites.

Had he not possessed this characteristic, it would have been impossible for him to achieve what he did. But to attribute his conduct and accomplishments to this quality or to other human qualities alone would be a gross distortion. We will come closer to the truth by understanding how Brigham and his followers viewed his role and by gaining insight into the spiritual impulses that moved him.

Brigham's leadership was never dubious or apologetic. Hear him expound to the Saints in the Tabernacle as the pressures from the Godbeite movement mounted: "You may say it is hard that I should dictate you in your temporal affairs. Is it not my privilege to dictate you? Is it not my privilege to give this people counsel to direct them so that their labors will build up the Kingdom of God instead of the kingdom of the devil?" After citing counsel given by Joseph Smith for the Saints to concentrate on building up the kingdom of God rather than the kingdom of the world or the devil, he continued: "Now, if I were to ask the elders of Israel to abide this, what would be the reply of some amongst us? The language in the hearts of some would be—'It is none of your business where I trade.'" Then came a conclusion that illuminates Brigham's motivations: "I will promise those who feel thus that they will never enter the celestial Kingdom of our Father and God. That is my business. It is my business to preach the truth to the people, and it will be my business by and by to testify for the just and to bear witness against the ungodly." Finally, to negate any idea that his intentions were despotic or tyrannical, Brigham added: "It is your privilege to do as you please. Just please yourselves; but when you do so, will you please bear the results and not whine over them."[4]

Non-Mormons did not understand Brigham's jurisdiction in temporal affairs, but the keystone of their criticism, branding the Mormons as non-Christian, was polygamy. When Brigham Young's polygamous society survived the onslaught of public contempt, invasion, official connivance, and social ostracism, the gentile world made the Latter-day Saints, proselyters almost without equal, the object of a vast evangelical crusade. In the vanguard of this assault marched the representatives of a new sect comprised mostly of the remnants of Mormonism left behind in the wake of the exodus. Headed by Joseph Smith III, son of the Prophet, this sect, the Reorganized Church of Jesus Christ of Latter Day Saints, believed that polygamy was the handiwork of Brigham Young, invented to gratify his passions and desires. Despite overwhelming evidence to the contrary, they blindly and aggressively denied that Joseph Smith had initiated the practice, and set about to redeem the Latter-day Saints, whom they derisively called

"Brighamites," from what they considered to be a depraved and fallen state.

In the mid-sixties several reorganite missionaries had proselyted Utah, gaining a few converts from among the malcontents and excommunicants who had withered under the inexorable demands of Brigham Young's leadership. Now, in 1869, a second wave of reorganite missionaries arrived, led by none other than two of Joseph Smith's sons, Alexander H. and David Hyrum Smith. These earnest and exemplary young men, who, regrettably, had been reared on a diet of false or distorted information about their father and his successor, immediately sought an audience with Brigham Young. Their request was promptly granted.

Brigham Young must have had ambivalent feelings toward the two young men who presented themselves at his office. On the one hand, he saw in them the image of their deceased father, a man for whom Brigham had the deepest veneration, a veneration that bordered on worship. Yet, he could not fail to see in them influences and characteristics from their mother, Emma Hale Smith, whom he both respected and disliked.

Brigham's feelings of ambivalence must have been reciprocated by the Smith brothers. They could not have failed to possess a residual sense of goodwill toward the man who had been such a loyal supporter of their father. Moreover, they claimed blood relationship to some of Brigham's followers, including Joseph F. Smith, recently sustained as a member of the Twelve, whose father, Hyrum, had shared a martyr's crown with the Prophet. Yet, because of the claims of Joseph Smith III to lineal succession to their father's prophetic office, they regarded Brigham Young as an interloper who had not only usurped the authority and prerogatives they believed should descend through Joseph's lineage, but had polluted and distorted the religion founded by their father by the introduction of polygamy.

It is little wonder that the meeting between

Brigham and the Smith brothers was not characterized by feelings of harmony. The former was anxious that the sons of his mentor submit to the teachings of the apostleship that had been transmitted to Brigham Young by ordination. The Smiths were equally zealous to convince the Mormon leader that their brother actually held the priesthood keys. Neither party being persuaded by the arguments of the other, the meeting ended on an inconclusive note, except it was made clear that the visitors would not be permitted to preach in the new tabernacle. Brigham was concerned that permission to speak there might be misconstrued as an endorsement of their message. That he entertained no fear the visitors would be able to convince his people with their message is shown by this counsel he later gave the Saints when Salt Lake was inundated by protestant divines who had flocked west to "reclaim" the Mormons: "If you should have visits here from those professing to be 'Christians,' and they intimate a desire to preach to you, by all means invite them to do so. . . . Of course you have the power to correct whatever false teachings or impressions, if any, your children may hear or receive."[5]

Barred from the Tabernacle, the Smith brothers preached in Independence Hall, a gentile-owned facility, "but the mantle of the prophet had not fallen on his offspring," wrote one historian. "They were men almost without force of character, of lamb-like placidity, and of hopelessly mediocre ability; not shrewd enough to contend with their opponents, and not violent enough to arouse the populace. They accomplished little for the cause of the reorganized church."[6]

The comparatively quiet and ineffective voices of the Smith brothers were submerged in the din of other voices that clamored for public attention in the vain effort to wean the Latter-day Saints away from their beliefs. The first protestant crusaders were the Congregationalists who came to Salt Lake in the early 1860s. Their first spokesman was the Reverend Norman McLeod, who had come with Patrick Connor's volunteers and remained after his discharge to badger Brigham Young. In the late sixties and early seventies came representatives of several other protestant churches who conducted an aggressive campaign to persuade the Latter-day Saints to turn to the brand of "Christianity" they advocated. In 1871 one denomination sponsored the first "camp meeting" in Salt Lake City. It extended over eight days. Its object was to stir up the spiritual fervor of the Saints and open their eyes to what the preachers portrayed as their "benighted" condition. To the Latter-day Saints old enough to remember, these meetings were reminiscent of the fervent gatherings held a half-century before in the so-called "Burned-over District," west of the Catskill and Adirondack mountains, where Joseph Smith's spiritual interests were kindled by the Reverend Lane, whose references to the admonition of James triggered Joseph's determination to resolve his religious dilemma through prayer. If for no other reason than to broaden their understanding and to help prepare them for later service as proselyters for the Church, Brigham Young encouraged the Latter-day Saint youth to attend these camp meetings. Any hope for success that the standing-room-only crowds at these meetings may have engendered was dashed by the singular lack of response to the preachers' appeals. "If they have made a single convert of a Latter-day Saint," wrote a *Deseret News* editorialist, "we have not heard of it."[7]

Chapter Thirty-one

Prosperity and the Jethro Principle

After returning to the valley in 1848, Brigham was never again to leave his mountain home except for comparatively short trips to the Mormon communities that ringed it. This is remarkable in light of the apostolic mandate under which he labored and the almost nomadic life he had lived before ascending to the pinnacle of Mormon leadership.

It is not beyond reason that Brigham's course in this matter was merely imitative of his predecessor, Joseph Smith, who, except for infrequent and usually short trips, confined his ministry to the headquarters of the Church. This was best illustrated when it came time to extend Mormon proselyting abroad. Instead of personally leading this effort, Joseph remained home to keep on top of the rapidly developing issues and problems there. Brigham had observed this practice in his mentor, and, as in so many other aspects of his leadership, he may only have been emulating the example of Joseph Smith when he elected to remain in or near Salt Lake directing the affairs of a fast-growing international church.

Then, too, during much of his tenure as head of the Church, Brigham labored under the threat of prosecution for unlawful cohabitation. While shielded by the benign influence of the local Utah probate courts, he felt comparatively secure. But he could not accurately foresee what might happen were he to venture outside the limits of the territory. He had enemies enough at home, but he was wise and practical enough to know that beyond the reach of his home many more enemies were waiting who would not hesitate to use

any force available, within or without the law, to imprison him or even to kill him.

Finally—and this is likely nearer the truth—
Brigham could hardly afford the time to be away from
his people and his duties for too long. There were too
many things that required his personal attention to
enable him to go abroad again. In the last years of his
life, he did, of course, spend long periods of time in St.
George during the winter months. But by then the
telegraph was available, making it possible to be in daily touch with his Salt Lake City headquarters. Indeed,
he had a telegraph office set up in a small building adjacent to his winter home in St. George, so that he was
only a few steps away from the instrument that
enabled him to give instructions or to receive reports
regarding the numerous enterprises in which he was
involved.

Brigham's activities were marked by a diversity that
seems extraordinary, even when measured by the
complex society in which we now live. Aside from his
strictly ecclesiastical duties, he was involved in an
impressive array of political, social, educational, and
business activities that made heavy and continuing
demands upon his time and energies. He served for
many years, for instance, as a member of the Salt Lake
City Council, whose weekly meetings he attended
faithfully when he was in the city. Nor was his participation in that forum of a merely perfunctory nature.
He was anxious about the quality of life in Salt Lake
City, and he therefore took a keen interest in the ordinances and policies that would preserve the kind of
peaceful and cultural atmosphere for which the
Latter-day Saints yearned. Thus, he was unyielding in
his opposition to saloons and prostitution. He was
adamant in insisting upon strict ordinances to curb
gambling, brawling, thievery, trespass, and every other species of public misconduct. Because of the defer-
ence paid to him by the other city officials, who were
members of the Church subject to his ecclesiastical
control, Brigham's power on the city council was greatly disproportionate to that which his constituency

would have exerted had it been represented by a lesser man.

A variety of business interests claimed much of Brigham's time, including railroading. Brigham first became acquainted with the practical aspects of the railroad business when he entered into contracts to help build segments of both the Union Pacific and the Central Pacific lines. Determined that the Latter-day Saints would not leave this vital field entirely in the hands of the gentiles, he became one of the prime movers in the organization and management of the Utah Central and the Utah Southern railroad companies. The former linked Salt Lake City with Ogden and, later, other Mormon communities in northern Utah and southern Idaho. Unlike any other known railroad, the Utah Central was built almost entirely with volunteer labor and with local financing.

The Utah Southern line extended southward through Utah Valley and beyond, with spur tracks extending eastward to the granite quarry in Little Cottonwood Canyon, from which the stone was taken for the construction of the Salt Lake Temple, and westward to the Oquirrh Mountains to serve the expanding copper mining operations there.

Brigham became involved in the organization of the Salt Lake Gas Works, the Salt Lake Water Works, an insurance company, a bank, and the Zion's Cooperative Mercantile Institution. In addition, he acquired an interest in a patent on a grain sowing machine, promoted the importation of cashmere goats, was one of the organizers of the Empire Mill and the Deseret Factory, and acquired the territorial rights to make and sell the Abel looms. As if to demonstrate that his time outside the family was not devoted entirely to church and business affairs, he took a lively interest in the development of the University of Deseret (later, the University of Utah), serving on its board of regents.

These numerous activities were in addition to the burden of shepherding Church members numbered in the tens of thousands and caring for the needs of many wives, children, relatives, friends, and employees.

But this was not all. He continued to give personal direction to the vast colonizing effort of the Mormons that had been commenced shortly after the founding of their mecca in the Salt Lake Valley. The procedures for organizing, outfitting, and instructing colonizing parties had become well established, almost to the point of routine. But there were still vital and sometimes novel decisions to be made by the Mormon leader, decisions only he could make. Brigham was the final arbiter as to all matters pertaining to the expansion, growth, and welfare of the Latter-day Saints wherever they might reside. Since Church members naturally looked upon Brigham as their shepherd, there was a tendency to make excessive demands upon his time and energies, to look to him not only for guidance in Church matters, but in the most personal and minute aspects of private life. Thus, Brigham's personal record, kept faithfully by a long procession of selfless, almost anonymous scribes, is studded with details concerning those members who came for direction about such things as who or when to marry, where to settle, or what business to pursue. We see from the record, for example, that Brigham responded willingly to the request to dedicate Samuel D. Woolley's home. And, with others, he accepted an annual invitation to have dinner with a Sister Blackhurst. He responded frequently to calls to bless the sick, counsel those in trouble, and comfort those who mourned the death of loved ones, by attending wakes or speaking at funerals.

Such interaction between the prophet and his people created bonds of love, friendship, and loyalty that may be difficult to appraise accurately at this remote time. However, this anecdote related by George Gibbs, one of Brigham's personal secretaries, is an example. Brother Gibbs and the President were in the office one day "going over the day's mail when there was a knock at the outer door. This particular door was seldom used as an entrance, all visitors coming in through the clerk's office to the west. The President arose and said, 'I wonder who that could be.' He stepped to the front of the room, unlocked the door and opened it. There before him stood an elderly little woman, whom the President seemed at once to recognize. 'What is it, Sister_____?' 'Brother Brigham,' she replied, 'I've knit you these socks, and I've come all the way from Draper [a small town about fifteen miles south of Salt Lake City] to bring them to you.' At the same time holding up to him and presenting him with a pair of good woolen knitted socks." Brigham took her in his arms, kissed her, and told her how pleased he was to get the socks and that he would surely wear them.[1]

Brigham was like a father to the Saints, concerned about their welfare and accommodating to a fault, yet stern and demanding when the circumstances required it. Given this kind of relationship, he might well have been led into the kind of administrative morass in which Moses found himself when Jethro rescued him. The Lawgiver's wise father-in-law, noting that the children of Israel queued up from dawn to dusk to receive counsel from their leader, told Moses he would "wear away" unless he shifted some of this heavy burden to others. (See Ex. 18:18.) Moses began to use the tool of delegation to spread the work load, develop the skills and confidence of subordinates, and preserve his life and sanity.

Whether he learned it from his biblical studies or from Joseph Smith, or whether it was an inherent talent, Brigham Young seems always to have understood and applied the Jethro principle. Brigham was a delegator par excellence. He never did anything he could get someone else to do for him. If a new mission was to be opened, a new community to be established, a new wilderness to be explored, he sent someone else to do it. His role was to plan and project, to organize and arrange, leaving to others the responsibility to carry out his designs.

Brigham used the principle of delegation in his dealings with the Twelve. Recognizing them as among the most able and dedicated men in the Church, he used their abilities to the maximum. Rather than allow them to remain permanently in Salt Lake City, where there was a high concentration of leadership skills, he sent them in all directions, not only to preach the gospel, but to lead by example in the vast Mormon colonizing effort. Amasa Lyman and Charles C. Rich were sent to establish the Mormon colony at San Bernardino, California. When the pressures exerted by the Utah War caused Brigham to order the abandonment of that community, these two Apostles were later directed to settle in Fillmore, Utah, and Paris, Idaho, respectively. Orson Hyde was ordered back from Carson City, Nevada at the time of the Utah War and was resettled in San Pete County. George A. Smith and Erastus Snow established permanent homes in St. George, Utah, while both Wilford Woodruff and Orson Pratt lived there on a temporary basis. Franklin D. Richards moved to Ogden in the 1860s, while Lorenzo Snow settled in Brigham City and Ezra T. Benson in Cache Valley.

Many other men and women were uprooted from comfortable homes, from families, and from beloved surroundings, to be sent further into the wilderness to help stretch the borders of Zion. Without these selfless Latter-day Saints, Brigham's colonizing effort would never have progressed beyond the realm of thought. What was done in planting Mormon communities throughout the intermountain area was strictly a team effort that required not only sagacious leadership, but a large cadre of dedicated and industrious people who were willing to follow the course marked out by their leader irrespective of where it might take them.

Chapter Thirty-two

A Judicial Crusade

Beginning with Judge Perry E. Brocchus, Brigham Young and his people were oppressed by a series of arrogant and incompetent federal judges, all seemingly imbued with a sense of mission to subjugate and, if possible, to imprison the Mormon leader. All of them came with preconceived ideas about Brigham and how he should be handled. None of them, however, quite measured up to Judge James B. McKean in terms of industry, shrewdness, and malevolence.

President Ulysses S. Grant's appointment of this controversial man as the chief federal judge in Utah foreshadowed the most massive and agonizing exposure Brigham ever had to the vagaries of the judicial system of his day.

We may better understand Judge McKean by looking into the background of his presidential appointment. The judge was a man of unquestioned intellectual capacity, the son of a Methodist clergyman, who had carved out a better-than-average judicial reputation in New York. His deficiencies as a jurist were rooted in a somewhat volatile temperament, an alloy of impatience and obstinacy. This quality is clearly shown by a comment he made to President Grant at a time when he seemed unwilling to accept the appointment to the Utah bench: "I am a man of positive character, Mr. President, and in my endeavors to perform my duty in Utah I may become embroiled with the Mormons. No means exist there to execute my decrees, and thus I may stir up trouble to no purpose, and bring humiliation upon myself."[1] What likely inspired this statement was Judge McKean's recognition that the federal court in Utah lacked jurisdiction to impose sanctions under the Morrill Act of 1862, which would leave him powerless to deal with the most pressing problem outsiders associated with the Latter-day Saints—polygamy. This jurisdictional lack was not remedied, incidentally, until 1874 when the so-called Poland Act extended federal judicial control over all criminal, civil, and chancery cases, and placed the offices of territorial attorney general and marshal under federal authority. After being persuaded by Grant to accept the appointment, however, Judge McKean contrived an imaginative scheme to invest his court with jurisdiction to administer and apply the Morrill Act, even though Congress had not seen fit to give it that power.

President U. S. Grant's answer to Mr. McKean's reluctance reveals the depth of his misinformation about affairs in Utah and the excessive and extra-legal force he was prepared to use to bring Brigham Young and his people to heel: "Go there and make the laws respected. If your associates do not sustain you, I will choose men who will; and if civil process will not restrain lawlessness, I will support you with the army of the United States."[2]

With such a carte blanche charter under which to function, it is small wonder that within a short time after his appointment as Utah's chief federal justice in the spring of 1871, Mr. McKean undertook certain initiatives that loom up as landmarks in the history of American jurisprudence. He decreed the territorial district courts to be federal courts when the United States was a party and ruled that the proper officers of such courts were the United States district attorney and the United States marshal. Having thus neatly overcome the stumblingblock that had stymied his predecessors in their attempt to prosecute Brigham, the judge impaneled a grand jury in September 1871 from which all faithful members of the Church had been systematically excluded. This packed jury handed down an indictment against the Mormon leader that included sixteen counts of "lewdly and lasciviously associating and cohabiting with women, not being married to them." Brigham Young's lawyers promptly filed a motion to quash the indictment on the grounds that the jury had been illegally impaneled and that the instrument itself was defective.

During this time Brigham was in great pain from an attack of rheumatism, an ailment that afflicted him more frequently and with ever-increasing intensity as he grew older. It was chiefly on this account that he had built a home in St. George, where the mild weather offered comfort he could never find amidst the storms and cold of Salt Lake City winters. In September, 1871, Brigham was en route to St. George on his annual quest for relief from his rheumatic pains when, at Provo, word reached him of the action of the recently impaneled kangaroo jury. Not wanting to appear contemptuous of a court that deserved his contempt, the aging and crippled Mormon leader returned to face his new judicial tormentor, peaceably submitting to arrest on October 2, 1871.

Upon his arrival in Salt Lake City, Brigham found Mormon tempers running high. His followers were indignant at the charges against him and at the timing of the jury's action, which had upset their leader's long-held and widely publicized plans for a recuperative vacation in St. George. The prophet, however, approached the ordeal with the same calmness and deliberation that characterized most of his actions. Even the acerbic editor of the *Salt Lake Tribune,* who seldom found anything praiseworthy in Brigham's character or conduct, grudgingly wrote these words about the Mormon leader's appearance in court: "It was a decidedly novel spectacle yesterday afternoon to see the 'Lion of the Lord' sitting in the court room waiting for the coming of his earthly judge to try him. . . . His quietude, and an altogether seeming absence of a spirit chafing with rage at being brought to trial, evidently made a good impression. . . . Perhaps there was more respect and sympathy felt for Brigham Young, when he left the court room, feeble and tottering from his recent sickness, having respectfully sat in the presence of his judge three-quarters of an hour, after bail had been taken, than ever there was before in the minds of the same men."[3]

During Brigham Young's respectful submission to the court, its presiding officer, Judge McKean, unburdened himself of this extraordinary statement: "While the case at the bar is called *'The People versus Brigham Young,* its other and real title is *Federal Authority versus Polygamic Theocracy.'* The government of the United States, founded upon a written constitution, finds within its jurisdiction another government—claiming to come from God—*imperium in imperio*—whose policy and practice, in grave particulars, are at variance with its own. The one government arrests the other in the person of its chief, and arraigns it at the bar. A system is on trial in the person of Brigham Young. Let all concerned keep this fact steadily in view; and let that government rule without a rival which shall prove to be in the right."[4]

Judge McKean summarily brushed aside the vigorous objections of Brigham's counsel to these irrelevant and prejudicial remarks, binding the defendant over for trial and admitting him to bail in the amount of $5,000.

Not long afterward Brigham resumed his interrupted journey to St. George. There, on November 9, he presided at a ceremony whose spirit and purpose stood in sharp contrast to the acrid proceedings Judge McKean had conducted in his makeshift courtroom over Faust's stable. Brigham Young broke ground for the St. George Temple in the presence of five hundred Latter-day Saints, who were stirred by the music of Santa Clara's brass band, a St. George choir, and the remarks of Brigham Young and Erastus Snow.

Brigham spent a pleasant month in St. George transacting voluminous business and giving direction to the Church over his telegraph wire. He traveled to nearby Mormon communities and counseled the Saints on subjects ranging from the joys and blessings of those who inherit the celestial kingdom to the best method of growing corn.

Freed from the discomfort of winter storms and cold, Brigham had looked forward to working, thinking, and planning in balmy St. George throughout the winter. Then in the spring he would be prepared to return to his headquarters to face his judicial nemesis. He had been led to believe by Judge McKean that this schedule would be acceptable. But it was not to be. Moved by his own irascibility, by pressure from the government lawyers, and by persistent unfounded rumors in Salt Lake City that Brigham had gone south to evade the charges pending against him, Judge McKean arbitrarily set the trial for January 9, 1872. He did this deliberately, with full knowledge of the fatiguing effect such an arduous winter trip over rough unsurfaced roads would have on a seventy-year-old man wracked with rheumatic pains. Recognizing the order as Judge McKean's perverse and arbitrary way of asserting civil dominance over the Mormon leader, practically everyone with whom Brigham discussed the matter urged him not to go. This counsel did not spring from an intent that Brigham ignore the court, but from the belief that a higher court would absolve him of any guilt for disobeying under such aggravated circumstances. Had the defendant merely consulted his own wisdom and intelligence, he might well have followed this counsel. It certainly was founded upon good reasoning and was calculated to cast him in a favorable light with practically everyone except Judge McKean and his claque of Mormon-haters. But giving sway to an inner impulse that ordinarily governed him in such delicate matters, he rejected the counsel and elected to return. He told the brethren that "the voice of the Spirit" had directed him to go home. So often had he heard that voice and seen the results of obedience to it that he dared not ignore it in these stressful circumstances.

Following worship services on Sunday, December 17, 1871, the Lion of the Lord and his entourage departed from St. George for his uncertain face-off with the court that seemed determined to put him behind bars. More ominous, however, were reports that the

prosecution intended to broaden the scope of the proceedings to include a spurious charge of murder.
These reports gave those close to Brigham special concern. They could not help but compare Brigham's
plight to that of Joseph Smith when he submitted to
the Illinois officials at Carthage. The bloody martyrdom that had followed still lingered in the minds of the
Latter-day Saints, arousing bitter suspicion and distrust of the officials in Salt Lake City. The fact that the
murder charge was based solely on the testimony of a
confessed murderer, Bill Hickman, as to an incident
that allegedly occurred in the 1850s, provided some
hope to Brigham's followers, however.

At Kanarra, two days out of St. George, John D.
Parker, who had been one of Joseph Smith's guards,
"wept like a child" because Brigham adamantly insisted on going to Salt Lake City. A similar scene occurred
the next day at Cedar City when Brigham rejected similar counsel from Orrin P. Rockwell, another of Joseph
Smith's guards, and from his oldest son, Joseph A.
Young.

Over the years those close to Brigham had often
heard him refer to the "Light" that illuminated his
way. Ordinarily when he said, "Brethren, the Light
says so and so," all discussion ended.

To those who urged him not to return, the
Mormon prophet gave the answer: "The 'Light' says,
'Brigham return.' " Then, to calm their fears, he
added, "God will overrule all for the best good of
Zion."

Travel in those days was arduous under the most
favorable conditions. Amidst winter storms it was almost impossible. And Brigham's advanced age and
rheumatic distress shrouded this ordeal with a night-
marish quality that haunted him the remainder of his
days.

At Beaver the storm struck in force. It laid down a
foot of new snow that made travel extremely tedious.
At Cove Fort it was discovered that the telegraph lines
were down, cutting off communication with Salt Lake
City. As the party moved slowly toward Fillmore, the

storm increased in fury until, at Dog Valley, it became
so intense that the drivers could hardly see their teams
ahead of them or keep to the road, which, because of
an earlier thaw, was little more than a quagmire.

At Nephi, Brigham Young, by now in extreme
pain, transferred to an open buggy driven by Bishop
John Sharp, who had joined the party at that point.
The heavy mackinaw Brigham wore, the gloves,
muffs, fur cap, and thick lap robe did little to afford
protection against the vicious storm that raged until
the travelers reached Payson. At that point the storm
subsided. But there was no respite from the constant
jolting and lurching of the buggy until they reached
Draper, the then southern terminus of the Utah
Southern Railroad, where Brigham's counselor Daniel
H. Wells and others waited on a special train to take the
weary and pain-wracked Mormon leader home.

During the ride from Draper to Salt Lake City,
which, by comparison with his recent ordeal, was
smoothly luxurious, Brigham was briefed about the
developments in the judicial vendetta against the Mormon leaders. President Daniel H. Wells, mayor of Salt
Lake City; Hosea Stout, former attorney general of the
territory; and W. H. Kimball had all been arrested under the same contrived murder indictment that now
faced Brigham Young. Originally taken as a prisoner
to Camp Douglas, President Wells was admitted to bail
in the amount of $50,000 by Judge McKean, an action
that stunned the prosecuting attorney, who had insisted on a $500,000 bond as a condition to freeing the
mayor from custody. A possible reason for this unexpected softening of the Judge's attitude was the widely
publicized report of the editor of the *Indianapolis
Journal*, a Mr. Fishback, who was in the courtroom over
Faust's stable when Judge McKean delivered his discourse about the cosmic implications of the action
against Brigham Young. "It is unfortunate for the
nation," wrote Mr. Fishback, "that it is in the power of
such men as Judge McKean and the deputy district at-
torneys, Maxwell and Baskin, to precipitate a collision
between the federal authorities and the Mormons, in a

contest in which the government occupies a false and untenable position." This opinion of an objective gentile editor was circulated widely in the eastern centers where public opinion was forged, and doubtless had a moderating effect upon the crusading judge. "We are convinced," continued Mr. Fishback, "that the pending prosecutions are conceived in folly, conducted in violation of law, and with an utter recklessness as to the grave results that must necessarily ensue." Touching a vulnerable point, the judge's political standing in the eyes of the president who had appointed him, the editor concluded: "It is much to the credit of President Grant's administration that these deputy prosecutors [who, in turn, had been appointed by Mr. McKean] arrogate to themselves the entire credit of conceiving the disreputable trick to which they have resorted to effect their purpose."[5]

But the judge was volatile and wholly unpredictable. Whatever softening was shown when he admitted Daniel H. Wells to bail for only a tithe of what the prosecutor demanded had disappeared when Brigham Young appeared before him seeking freedom on bail. After hearing the arguments of counsel (in which one prosecutor sarcastically referred to precedents in bail cases involving the rebel Jefferson Davis and the traitor Aaron Burr) Mr. McKean denied bail to Brigham Young. He did relent, however, to the extent of permitting Brigham to remain in the custody of a U. S. marshal at a residence of his choosing. Brigham elected to stay in the Beehive House, a prisoner in his own home.

In the meantime, Judge McKean's quixotic crusade had begun to unravel. When the bills for witness, jury, and other fees of his self-appointed tribunal were presented for payment, the department of justice disallowed them. This was a crushing blow, especially to U. S. Marshal M. T. Patrick, who, in his zeal to help convict the Mormon leader, had advanced most of the $15,000 in expenses that had been incurred. Then followed a frantic attempt to obtain reimbursement elsewhere. Application was made to the U. S. Congress, which took the matter under advisement. The territorial auditor declined to pay on advice of the attorney general, who ruled that payment of such expenses could be made only on the order of the territorial marshal, an officer who had been supplanted by the U. S. marshal appointed by Judge McKean. And of course the territorial legislature yawned and turned a deaf ear to Judge McKean's plea for money. Faced with this financial crisis, it became necessary for the judge, who by now was in a towering rage, to dismiss both the grand and petit juries because his court had no money with which to pay their per diem allowances. In advising the jurors of their dismissal, the judge took the opportunity to unburden himself of still another vitriolic speech: "The high priesthood of the so-called Church of Jesus Christ of Latter-day Saints," he growled "who control the assembly, and all the officers of, or who are elected by, the assembly, refuse to permit the expenses of the United States courts to be paid unless they are allowed to control those courts." The territorial marshal merely responded that if Judge McKean wanted to hold courts for "territorial business" he should use the territorial marshal to call the jurors in the prescribed way. He assured the judge that "such jurors so drawn, lawful, good, and true men, can get their *per diem*, and the expenses of the courts paid."[6]

Within a matter of weeks after this incident, the Supreme Court of the United States reversed Judge McKean in a case (Engelbrecht) where a jury had been unlawfully drawn. "The effect of this decision," editorialized the *New York Tribune*, "is to make void all criminal proceedings in the territorial courts of Utah during the past year, and render necessary the immediate discharge of 138 prisoners who have been illegally held."[7]

Among these prisoners was the Lion of the Lord, who shortly after his release attended a meeting in the Tabernacle, where he greeted the Saints with a cheerful "Good Morning." After the congregation responded with one voice, "Good morning," this interchange occurred between the speaker and his audience: "How do you do?" "Very well." "How is your faith this morning?" "Strong in the Lord." "How do you think I look after my long confinement?" "First rate."

Then, after thanking and commending the deputy U. S. marshal who had guarded him, Brigham said: "I have no reflections to cast upon these courts. How much power, ability, or opportunity would I have to possess, do you think, if all were combined, to disgrace them as they have disgraced themselves. I have neither the power nor the ability, consequently I have nothing to say with regard to their conduct. It is before the world, it is before the Heavens continually."[8]

James B. McKean, undeterred by his futile attempt at jury-packing, soon turned his judicial trickery in another direction. The opportunity occurred in the celebrated divorce case involving Ann Eliza Webb Young, Brigham Young's last wife. Brigham was sealed to this vivacious and attractive woman in 1868. At the time, she was twenty-four years old and the mother of two sons, who were sired by her first husband, James L. Dee, from whom she was divorced. Five years after her marriage to the Mormon leader, Ann Eliza, feisty and capricious and unable to dominate the Young household as she would have liked, filed for divorce. In this she was encouraged by members of the so-called Utah ring, who continually sought means to diminish the influence and reputation of Brigham Young. As part of their trial strategy, the plaintiff's lawyers sought a living allowance of a thousand dollars a month for their client, in addition to other benefits. What made this case a novelty was the assumption upon which it was based—that Brigham and Eliza were legally married. Until now this was a fact the federal carpetbaggers in Utah were unwilling to concede. All their frenzied and extralegal efforts to convict Brigham Young of unlawful cohabitation were based on the premise that the Mormon leader had only one wife to whom he was lawfully married. All the other wives, according to this theory, had no legal standing whatsoever. Since Judge McKean had been in the vanguard of those who advanced this idea and had been the one who forfeited his reputation by wrenching the legal structure to accommodate his views, one would logically have expected him to reject Ann Eliza's request out of hand. It was not to be so. On the contrary, we now find him aggressively upholding the claim of a woman that not long before he would have rejected as coming from the mere paramour of a common criminal. The only logic one finds in examining the judicial conduct of Judge McKean is the single-minded consistency with which he pursued the humiliation of Brigham Young.

He found another opportunity to vent his hatred when, on March 11, 1875, the aging prophet appeared in his court on a charge of contempt, which arose from Brigham's refusal to comply with an earlier order in the Ann Eliza case, a refusal he made on advice of counsel in order to perfect an appeal.

It was with great difficulty that Brigham made his slow, painful way into Judge McKean's courtroom. The rheumatism that had afflicted him for several years had become progressively more severe and constant, so that he seldom enjoyed uninterrupted periods free from pain. As soon as the judge called the court to order, Brigham Young's counsel was on his feet requesting that his client be excused during the arguments because of his feeble health. The judge's only answer to this legitimate request was to say that the arguments doubtless would be brief. When it became apparent that this forecast was in error, Brigham's counsel renewed the request, which again was brushed aside without explanation. When the lengthy arguments had been presented, Judge McKean wrote out his decision, which was then read in open court. This decision adjudged Brigham Young guilty of contempt, levied a $25 fine, and ordered him imprisoned for twenty-four hours. The spirited arguments of Brigham's counsel about the inappropriateness of the jail sentence were unavailing. It mattered not that the theory of the plaintiff's case was fatally defective, that Brigham's counsel was attempting to perfect an appeal from the court's order, and that the defendant was a genuinely ill man, seventy-three years old, and shot through with rheumatic pains. Mr. McKean seemed intent only on demonstrating the predominate authority of his court over the Mormon leader and perhaps of vindicating his earlier defeat on the jury-packing issue. Whatever the reason, the judge adamantly clung to his decision.

Once the last attempt to dissuade Mr. McKean had failed, Brigham Young accepted the judgment with the same dignified calm that had marked his earlier demeanor in court. Under the guard of a deputy U. S. Marshal acting on orders from Judge McKean, Brigham went to the Beehive House where he selected and had packed the toiletries and clothing required during his absence. He comforted his wives and children and bid them farewell. Then his ever-present guard took Brigham to the prison. Accompanying Brigham were his personal physician, Seymour B. Young, the son of his brother Joseph; Daniel H. Wells, his counselor; and one of his clerks, Brother Rossiter.

At the prison he was first thrust into a cell shared by twelve men who were either convicted criminals or who were awaiting trial. Later, however, at the urging of his friends, Brigham was moved to a room adjacent to the warden's apartment, where he spent the night. The following day, after his sentence had been completed, the Mormon leader was released from prison and met by a party of friends and relatives who escorted him to the peace and security of his home.

Judge McKean, who had survived the public outcry that followed his jury-packing fiasco, was hardly prepared for the violent reaction to his order jailing Brigham Young. Even the judge's most ardent supporters could find little reason for the imprisonment other than the judge's blind craving for revenge. The hue and cry raised in the eastern press convinced President Ulysses S. Grant that Judge McKean was a luxury he could no longer afford, especially since his administration was under heavy attack from all sides because of charges of corruption arising from the "whisky ring" scandal. Five days after sentencing Brigham Young, Judge McKean was summarily dismissed from office. The Washington press release issued at the time announced that the removal was "caused by what the president deems fanatical and extreme conduct . . . and by several acts of McKean, which are considered ill advised and tyrannical, and in excess of his powers as a Judge."[9]

A whole parade of judges followed in the wake of Mr. McKean's dismissal, all involved in various aspects of the notorious Ann Eliza suit. The names of judges David B. Lowe, J. Alexander White, Jacob S. Boreman, and Michael Schaeffer will be found on various documents in this voluminous file. Included among them is one signed by Judge Boreman, who was cast in the same mold as Judge McKean, ordering the imprisonment of Brigham Young until the allowance *pendente lite* was paid. Later, in a habeus corpus proceeding, Judge White held this order to be void.

It was not until April, 1877, a few short months before Brigham Young's death, that this protracted litigation ended. At that time, following a trial on the merits, an order was entered decreeing that the polygamous marriage with Ann Eliza was void under the law.

Chapter Thirty-three

Adjustments and New Directions

Brigham enjoyed an interval of comparative peace between the censure of Judge McKean in the jury-packing case and the beginning of the Ann Eliza litigation. His enjoyment was heightened by the presence of his old friend and mentor, General Thomas L. Kane of Philadelphia, who arrived by train in November, 1872, with his wife and two sons. As the general's health was not good, Brigham persuaded him and his family to accompany the Youngs and their party on their annual visit to St. George, where the distinguished visitor might benefit from the sun and mild temperatures.

The enlarged party left Salt Lake City on December 12 and eleven days later arrived at their destination, having conducted meetings intermittently along the way. It did not take Brigham long to settle into the slow-paced, though still busy, routine that he always followed while in this remote, enjoyable place. After relaxing a few days and celebrating the Christmas season, Brigham began to travel around to the nearby communities to study their progress and to give encouragement and instruction. We sense clearly the spirit of peace he enjoyed during this visit and his pride in the development of the people from this excerpt from a letter, dated January 11, 1873, to Bishop Edward Hunter in Salt Lake City: "My health is much improved since I left your city. I am having a good rest, both mentally and physically, in this mild climate. We had a most beautiful rain a few days ago. The weather since has been delightful. Thermometer ranging from 56 to 68 degrees in the shade at noon. The brethren are sowing grain, pruning vineyards, working in their gardens, etc., while the birds are singing as though it were May."[1]

Freed temporarily from the crushing pressures that bore upon him constantly in Salt Lake City, Brigham was able to reflect upon the affairs of the Church in an unhurried, objective way during his pleasant winter in Dixie. He was now approaching his seventy-second birthday and had already lived beyond the life-expectancy of the time. As he considered the phenomenal growth of the Church, the rapid influx of converts, the burgeoning communities throughout the Mountain West, and the growing complexities of life brought about by the introduction of modern means of transportation and communication, the railroad and telegraph, he formulated a plan that would create waves of speculation and doubt, not only within the Church, but among the gentiles in the East as well.

Promptly upon his return to Salt Lake City in the latter part of February, 1873, he revealed the fruits of his winter meditations. He announced his resignation as the president of the Deseret National Bank and of Zion's Co-operative Mercantile Institution. On the heels of this startling news he advised the members of the Church at the annual conference in early April that he was relinquishing his role as trustee-in-trust, a responsibility he then placed upon George A. Smith, a counselor in the First Presidency. As if to emphasize the extraordinarily heavy load Brigham had carried over the years, twelve men were appointed to assist George A. Smith. Also, Brigham called five additional counselors to the First Presidency: Lorenzo Snow; Brigham Young, Jr.; Albert Carrington; John W. Young; and George Q. Cannon.

The immediate reaction to these unexpected announcements was surprise mingled with disbelief. So long had Brigham wielded the vast powers now being diffused among eighteen men that it took some time for the significance of what had happened to seep into the consciousness of the people. When it did, wide speculation was generated as to the reasons behind it. Was President Young ill? Had he been intimidated by his enemies? Had he lost the confidence and support of those in his inner circle of leadership? These and many other questions were asked by Saint and gentile alike. The editor of the New York *Herald,* for example, aware that Brigham Young and the Latter-day Saints were always hot copy, sent a wire to the Mormon leader asking about the reasons for his action. Apparently deciding that one answer published in a major newspaper would eliminate the need to make frequent, repetitive answers, Brigham was specific in a letter written to the *Herald* April 10, 1873: "For over forty years I have served my people, laboring incessantly, and I am now nearly seventy-two years of age and I need relaxation." Making it clear that his resignation did not affect his role as President of the Church but only relieved him from the direct burden of what he called "secular affairs," he added, "In that capacity I shall still exercise supervision over business, ecclesiastical and secular, leaving the minutiae to younger men." Brigham described economic conditions in Utah, extended an invitation to those with capital to invest there, and provided this summary of his stewardship during the years since the exodus: "The result of my labors for the last 26 years, briefly summed up, are: The peopling of this Territory by the Latter-day Saints of about 100,000 souls; the founding of over 200 cities, towns and villages inhabited by our people, which extend to Idaho in the north, Wyoming in the east, Nevada in the west, and Arizona in the south, and the establishment of schools, factories, mills and other institutions calculated to improve and benefit our community."[2]

In a letter to Albert Carrington not long after these major organizational changes took place, Brigham explained: "With relief from the great labors of business that have devolved upon me, I expect to devote my energies more fully to counseling the Saints, and will be left free to travel through the settlements, or remain at home, as wisdom shall dictate."[3]

As Brigham Young advanced in age and his death became more imminent, the issue of seniority in the Twelve became increasingly vital. The policy of succession in the presidency became fixed when Brigham, as President of the Twelve, succeeded Joseph Smith.

At this time, Orson Hyde had served as the President of the Twelve for many years. Yet there was a question about his status that grew from his having been dropped from the quorum on May 4, 1839, for an unjustified attack he made upon Joseph Smith. He was reinstated June 27, 1839. Over the years many Church leaders, including Brigham Young, had felt that Elder Hyde's seniority should date from his reinstatement, not from the time of his ordination in 1835. A similar question existed as to Orson Pratt, who was excommunicated August 20, 1842; rebaptized January 20, 1843; and ordained again as an Apostle on the same date and accepted as a member of the Quorum of the Twelve. Brigham Young had hesitated over the years to rectify this situation because to do so would strip Elder Hyde of his presidency of the Twelve and make him junior to John Taylor, Wilford Woodruff, and George A. Smith. It would also place Elder Pratt in the seventh position in the quorum instead of the second, where he had served for so long. Brigham knew well the impact such a radical change would have upon the brethren affected and their families. He knew also the false motives that would be imputed to him by those unacquainted with the background of such a decision and by his persistent enemies and detractors, who were constantly alert for reasons to attack him. But as he moved into his seventies and realized that his earthly ministry might end at any time, the need to act in this important and delicate matter became more and more compelling. The distasteful but necessary step was taken in June, 1875, at a meeting held in San Pete. "President Young brought up the subject of seniority," John Taylor later recorded, "and stated that John Taylor was the man that stood next to him; and that where he was not, John Taylor presided." Brigham also said at that time "that Brother Hyde and

Brother Pratt were not in their right positions in the Quorum."[4]

At the April conference in 1873, while wrestling with the problem of seniority in the Twelve, Brigham first began to expound his views upon what was later to be called the Order of Enoch, a people so unified in their purposes and so obedient to every principle and commandment that, Enoch-like, they would be worthy to enter heaven or to accept the Savior into a heavenly environment on earth. Being an activist rather than a mere theoretician, Brigham Young began to promote the idea of Enoch communities with all the energy and skill at his command. Within a few months after it was first touched upon, he elaborated the Enoch concept at a meeting held in Paris, Idaho: "I want you to be united. If we should build up and organize a community, we would have to do it on the principle of oneness, and it is one of the simplest things I know of. A city of one thousand or a million people could be united into a perfect family, and they could work together as beautifully as the different parts of a carding machine work together. Why, we could organize millions into a family under the order of Enoch."

Having thus enunciated the basic premise of his idea, Brigham went on to spell out the details, reflecting the mind of a leader who, with computer-like efficiency, carried in his head all the complicated details necessary to assemble a society without human precedent. "Brethren, if you will start here and operate together in farming, in making cheese, in herding sheep and cattle, and in every other kind of work, and get a factory here and a cooperative store, and operate together in sheep raising, store keeping, manufacturing, and everything else, no matter what it is, by and by, when we can plant ourselves upon a foundation that cannot be broken, we shall then proceed to arrange a family organization. . . . We can do this and keep up cooperation, and, when we can we will build up a city after the order of Enoch."[5]

With the same persistence and zeal he showed as a missionary and later as a colonizer, Brigham began to preach his new doctrine throughout the length and breadth of Mormondom. A short while after his visit to Idaho, we find him in Dixie with President George A. Smith, where they were "moved by the Holy Spirit to preach to the people more fully the principles of the United Order of Enoch." Brigham's itinerary gave little hint that he was slowing down. In early March, 1874, he held five meetings at Tokerville, four at Virgin, three at Rockville, two at Shunesburg, and one at Duncan's Retreat. Soon after, the wards at Tokerville, Virgin City, and Rockville were organized in the Order. "They entered immediately into measures to combine their labor and means, so as to produce the greatest food for the whole," George A. Smith reported in a letter to Joseph F. Smith, who was in England. "We receive applications daily from the different settlements to be organized. Brother Erastus Snow, Milo Andrus and A. M. Cannon have now gone to organize Pine valley, Pinto and Hebron, all thriving settlements that have sent in their requests to be organized."[6]

Brigham moved north the following month, preaching the new doctrine at every opportunity. At Nephi he made it plain that entry into the Order was wholly voluntary. He also defined the extent of the demands to be made upon those who joined: "As individuals, we do not want your farms, . . . we do not want your horses and cattle, we do not want your gold and your silver. . . . We want the time of this people called Latter-day Saints, that we can organize this time systematically, and make this people the richest people on the face of the earth."[7]

Chapter Thirty-four

Spiritual Stirrings

The few instances when Brigham Young divulged the content of spiritual manifestations he received centered mostly around the holy temples. He reported having seen both the Salt Lake and the St. George temples in vision before work on them commenced. He also advised some of his intimate associates that it had been made known to him that the site of the Manti Temple had been designated centuries before by one of the Book of Mormon prophets.

Many questioned the selection of the site at Manti, as it was on an incline requiring months of backbreaking work merely to level it in preparation for construction. The day before the dedication ceremony, Brigham told a companion, "Go tell the people we will dedicate the temple site tomorrow. And if no one else shows up, we will dedicate it alone."

Still later a fourth temple site, this one at Logan, Utah, was selected and dedicated under the direction of Brigham Young.

Work on the Salt Lake Temple was delayed because of many problems created by the political and military upheavals that rocked the territorial capital over the years. These were aggravated by inclement weather during the winter months and by the great difficulty in transporting the huge granite blocks from the quarry in the mouth of Little Cottonwood Canyon to the temple site. Brigham had undertaken the construction of a canal connecting the quarry with the temple site, with the thought of floating the stones on barges. Indeed, this ambitious project was well along when the railroad was extended to Salt Lake City, at which time a spur track was constructed to the quarry. Thereafter the stones were transported by flatcar.

By this time the temple had been under construction for twenty years, and it was apparent that because of its massive size and the extensive work left to be done, its completion was still many years in the future. This fact, coupled with Brigham's anxiety to complete a temple soon so that the Saints could enjoy the higher blessings of the gospel and vital proxy work could be performed, caused Brigham to push work on the St. George Temple aggressively. In balmy Dixie construction could go forward the year round, and materials were more accessible and easier to handle.

Timber for the St. George Temple was obtained from Mt. Trumball, a distance of sixty-five miles from the temple site. The rock quarry was much nearer, and since the stones used in the construction were much smaller than those used in the Salt Lake Temple, they were comparatively easy to fashion and transport.

Many workers from the north of the territory were called to labor at the temple site, the quarry, or Mt. Trumball. These men brought their own provisions with them, except that beef and potatoes were furnished by the temple work committee. At the height of construction, about a hundred men worked at the quarry, while as many more were employed in cutting, milling, and transporting the timber. These, added to the numerous artisans and craftsmen at work on the building itself and the sisters who were busy making rugs, drapes, and other niceties to decorate the interior, comprised an army of workers.

Brigham must have enjoyed watching the workmen at their tasks and seeing the beautiful temple rise. His fascination would have come not only from a contemplation of the uses to which the building would be put when completed, but from the joy a skilled artisan experiences in seeing his craft expertly applied by others.

Brigham frequently offered advice to the artisans about ways to improve the quality or quantity of their work, although he was careful to acknowledge the role of those in supervisory positions. In the early part of 1875, however, he became the temporary architect and superintendent of the project when William H. Folsom, the architect, took ill and had to return to Salt Lake City, and Miles Romney, who was a chief supervisor on the job, broke his leg.

During this period the aging prophet suffered as much from rheumatism as at any other period of his life. Seldom was he entirely free from pain. It took great effort merely to arise in the morning and to begin to move about. Once in motion, however, he persisted at whatever tasks were at hand and uncomplainingly bore the burdens of his physical infirmities. "President Young is in feeble health," George A. Smith wrote, "but able to ride out nearly every day. He goes to the Temple and instructs the workmen . . . [and] is our only architect."[1]

With the impetus provided by the volunteer laborers from the north and Brigham Young's encouragement and prodding, the work on the temple sped rapidly toward its conclusion. At odd hours during that period, Brigham Young, Wilford Woodruff, and other brethren who had received their endowments and other temple blessings from Joseph Smith counseled together as, for the first time, the wording of the sacred ordinances was reduced to writing. Then, in anticipation of the opening of the temple, many brethren and sisters were instructed in temple procedures so that the throngs of Latter-day Saints who had waited so long would be able to receive their blessings in the house of the Lord.

As the year 1876 drew to a close, an electric thrill ran through the territory as word circulated that the temple was nearing completion. During the last week of the year, following Christmas, workmen put the finishing touches on the lower part of the structure, so that by New Year's Day, 1877, this portion of the building was ready for the special dedicatory services Brigham Young had arranged. Twelve hundred expectant Latter-day Saints assembled in the temple on that day to participate in what, to them, was the most significant event to occur since the exodus.

Brigham Young called on Wilford Woodruff to offer the dedicatory prayer. Moreover, when the temple was finally completed at the time of the April general conference, Brigham Young asked his counselor Daniel H. Wells to offer the dedicatory prayer.

A diverse and picturesque congregation assembled in St. George for the April general conference in 1877. From the more affluent urban communities in the north came high Church and government leaders driving modern, factory-made buggies and wearing stylish clothing from well-stocked shops and department stores. From the rural communities ringing St. George came the sturdy farmers and ranchers with their families in more rustic vehicles and attired mostly in homemade clothes. From the south, across the intimidating Colorado River, came a handful of Indian missionaries in company with a few of their Lamanite converts who were far enough along in their progress to receive the temple ordinances. In this group were Andrew S. Gibbons and his stoically faithful wife, Rizpah. They brought with them Chief Tuba and his wife, Navajo converts, who were reported to have received their temple endowments "understandingly."[2] Brigham took Andrew Gibbons in a fatherly embrace and reminisced about their experiences on the Mormon trail thirty years earlier when the Indian missionary served as a twenty-two-year-old member in the gun division of Brigham's pioneer company. Throughout his life Brigham retained an interest in all those associated with him in various undertakings, especially the exodus.

April 6, the anniversary of the organization of the Church, fell on a Friday in the year 1877. Brigham Young selected that day to deliver the last general conference sermon of his life. He spoke in the upper room of the St. George Temple. "I would like to say a great deal during this conference to the Latter-day Saints," he began, "but I shall be able to talk but little, and therefore, when I do speak I wish you to listen, and this I believe you will do." Brigham then clarified certain principles of the United Order and mentioned many ways for the Saints to become more self-sufficient.

His main theme, however, was his vision of the destiny of the Church: "It has been asked if we intend to settle more valleys. Why certainly we expect to fill the next valley and then the next, and the next, and so on. It has been the cry of late, through the columns of the newspapers, that the 'Mormons' are going into Mexico! That is quite right, we calculate to go there. Are we going back to Jackson County? Yes. When? As soon as the way opens up. Are we all going? O no! of course not. The country is not large enough to hold our present numbers. When we do return there, will there be any less remaining in these mountains than we number today? No, there may be a hundred then for every single one that there is now. It is folly in men to suppose that we are going to break up these our hard earned homes to make others in a new country. We intend to hold our own here, and also penetrate the north and south, the east and the west, there to make others and to raise the ensign of truth. This is the work of God, that marvelous work and a wonder referred to by ancient men of God, who saw it in its incipiency, as a stone cut out of the mountains without hands, but which rolled and gathered strength and magnitude until it filled the whole earth. We will continue to grow, to increase and spread abroad, and the powers of earth and hell combined cannot hinder it. . . . I never mean to be satisfied until the whole earth is yielded to Christ and his people. . . .

"As to my health I feel many times that I could not live an hour longer, but I mean to live just as long as I can. I know not how soon the messenger will call for me, but I calculate to die in the harness."[3]

Chapter Thirty-five

The Final Days

The luxuriant evidence of spring with its greenery, pleasing aromas, and tuneful bird-choruses dominated St. George as Brigham and his entourage departed from the quiet Mormon community at the end of April. As the column wended its way upward toward the volcanic ridges to the northeast, a backward glance would have rewarded them with one of the most picturesque scenes anywhere. The uniform blocks, laid out with checkerboard precision, the stately poplars lining the wide streets, and the substantial homes surrounded by burgeoning gardens and orchards would have impressed upon their minds an image of domestic peace and security. And set against the background of the varicolored landscape beyond was the stately temple, gleaming white in the spring sunshine. If Brigham stole a glance or two backward, and we may be confident that he did, he may have wondered if he would again see this favored spot in mortality.

But if such thoughts arose in Brigham's mind, they would have had little opportunity to take root. Brigham still had many projects vying for his attention. He doubtless was already planning for the dedication of the Manti Temple site, which took place on April 25, 1977, en route to Salt Lake City.

Upon Brigham's arrival in Salt Lake City two days later, he was greeted with the heartening news that the Ann Eliza case had been decided in his favor. Thus ended a nagging worry that had disturbed his peace of mind for months.

Back at his desk Brigham set in motion the last ma-

jor administrative initiative of his career. It entailed
calling the members of the Twelve who had been living
in outlying areas to return to Church headquarters.
Thus, Charles C. Rich, Brigham Young, Jr., Lorenzo
Snow, and Franklin D. Richards, who had presided
over stakes north of Salt Lake City, and Orson Hyde
and Erastus Snow, who had presided in the south,
were released and others sustained in their places. In
releasing these Apostles to return to Salt Lake City,
Brigham told them that their ministry extended
beyond the boundary of a stake. In addition to reor-
ganizing the stakes over which these members of the
Twelve had presided, several new stakes were organized by divisions and the adjusting of stake boundaries. Operating from his headquarters between the
Beehive House and the Lion House, Brigham directed
these extensive administrative changes, taking charge
of some personally and sending others to handle the
rest.

Also, a schedule of meetings, speaking engage-
ments, and ceremonial duties kept Brigham heavily
occupied. For three successive Sundays following his
return from St. George, Brigham addressed capacity
crowds in the tabernacle, admonishing the people to
be faithful, diligent, and self-sufficient. During that
same period he inspected and counseled about the
construction of the Gardo House and the Salt Lake
Temple; entertained the U. S. minister to Madrid and
the Danish minister to Washington; traveled to Provo
to attend a board meeting of the Provo Manufacturing
Company; attended several meetings of the City
Council; and attended meetings with the officers and
directors of the Deseret National Bank, Deseret Telegraph Company, Salt Lake Railroad Company, ZCMI,
and the Utah Southern Railroad.

On May 16, Brigham, accompanied by his counselors and several members of the Twelve, traveled to
Logan, where, two days later, the Logan Temple site
was dedicated by Orson Pratt.

Brigham was reported as being "fatigued" on

Tuesday, May 29, following an interview and question-and-answer period with an "editorial party" from Nebraska.

During the following two days, Brigham's aging body rebelled at the way in which it was being driven. The result was a brief interlude of rest during which Brigham hardly left his room.

Up until the latter part of August, Brigham attended an incredible number of Church, civic, and cultural activities, including stake conferences, lectures, plays, and business meetings.

On Monday, August 20, Brigham handled his usual work and went to the theater in the evening, a routine he followed on Tuesday as well. Wednesday was a busy day in the office, during which a number of visitors called for counsel or to pay their respects. Nothing in Brigham's demeanor or conversation on Thursday, August 23, signified that it was his last workday. He handled his office duties with accustomed dispatch, affably conferring with his staff and those who stopped by. He rode out in the evening after dinner, as he occasionally did, enjoying the summer warmth of the valley. Later he attended a bishops' meeting and then retired rather early without voicing any complaint about illness or pain. At 11:00 P.M., however, he was seized suddenly with severe abdominal pains accompanied by violent retching and purging. Brigham's doctor, Seymour B. Young, was called immediately and diagnosed the ailment as "cholera morbus." After spending a restless and painful night, the patient requested medical relief at 5:00 A.M. A mild opiate was administered hypodermically into each foot to relieve the pain caused by muscle cramps. During the next two days, Brigham slept intermittently, suffering intense pain during his waking hours. Brigham bore his pain cheerfully, occasionally making humorous remarks to relieve the tension of family and friends.

Toward Saturday evening, an infection in his abdomen began to cause extensive swelling accompanied by excruciating pain. Opium was administered intermittently over the next two days, the dosage ranging from a half grain to a grain.

Sunday and Monday, Brigham moaned occasionally as if suffering extreme pain. He was administered to frequently during that period. Once when John W. Young pronounced a blessing upon him, the prophet aroused and responded with a firm "amen." On Monday, all of the prayer circles in the city were called to assemble in their accustomed places to pray for their leader. In St. George, Wilford Woodruff called his prayer circle together to implore the Lord in behalf of the prophet.

Early Tuesday morning, Brigham seemed to revive somewhat and got up twice with the aid of an attendant. At 4:00 P.M., he sank down in bed as if lifeless. Artificial respiration was administered off and on for nine consecutive hours, and hot poultices were placed over his heart to stimulate its action. This seemed to revive him somewhat, and in the afternoon he told the doctors and attendants he wanted to rest. At 8:00 P.M., however, he suffered a relapse and spent the night in a semi-comatose state. By Wednesday morning, it was apparent the end was near. He was administered to at intervals throughout the day, but was given no narcotics. At 2:00 P.M., he was administered to for the last time and responded with an "amen" in a clear and distinct voice. The end came at 4:00 P.M., Wednesday, August 29, 1877.

Although his body lay lifeless in the casket, Brigham Young's powerful personality dominated the funeral services conducted in the Tabernacle on Sunday, September 2, 1877, four days after his death. An amazing document, dictated by Brigham in 1873 and read at his funeral in obedience to direction it contained, outlined the procedure to be followed in preparing for and conducting his last rites. No detail was overlooked, not even the specifications for his coffin, which Brigham decreed should be "made of plump one and one-quarter inch boards, not scrimped in length, but two inches longer than I would measure, and from two to three inches wider than is commonly made for a person of my breadth and size. . . . Place me on a little comfortable cotton bed, with a good suitable pillow for size and quality; my body dressed in my temple clothing, and laid nicely into my coffin, and the coffin to have the appearance that if I wanted to turn a little to the right or to the left, I should have plenty of room to do so. The lid can be made crowning."

He expressed the wish that all his family attend the funeral who "conveniently" could do so, but directed that those who did attend were to "wear no crepe on their hats or on their coats." Further, he ruled that "the females [were] to buy no black bonnets, nor black dresses, nor black veils." He did relent, however, by giving "liberty" to those who already owned such items to wear them. The services were to consist of singing and praying, with remarks by any of his friends who "really desire" to speak.

Brigham's instructions for interment were: "Take my remains on a bier, and repair to the little burying ground, which I have reserved on my lot east of the White House on the hill, and in the southwest corner of this lot, have a vault built of mason work large enough to receive my coffin. . . . Then place flat rocks over the vault sufficiently large to cover it, that the earth may be placed over it—nice, fine, dry earth—to cover it until the walls of the little cemetery are reared, which will leave me in the southeast corner. This vault ought to be roofed over with some kind of temporary roof. There let my earthly house or tabernacle rest in peace, and have a good sleep, until the morning of the first resurrection; no crying or mourning with anyone as I have done my work faithfully and in good faith."[1]

Key to Abbreviations

CHC   *A Comprehensive History of The Church of Jesus Christ of Latter-day Saints, Century One,* B. H. Roberts

HC   *History of The Church of Jesus Christ of Latter-day Saints,* Joseph Smith

JD   *Journal of Discourses*

MH 1   *Manuscript History of Brigham Young, 1801-1844,* compiled by Elden J. Watson

MH 2   *Manuscript History of Brigham Young, 1846-1847,* compiled by Elden J. Watson

MS   *Millennial Star*

Notes

Introduction
1. HC 7:578.
2. HC 7:585.
3. Ibid.
4. HC 7:585-86.

Chapter 1
1. MH 1:1.

Chapter 2
1. JD 2:249.
2. *Deseret News,* Mar. 31, 1858, p. 1.
3. JD 1:90.
4. MS 25:424.
5. Ibid.
6. MS 25:438.

Chapter 3
1. MS 25:439.
2. JD 5:97.

Chapter 4
1. JD 2:128.
2. Ibid.
3. MS 25:439.
4. Ibid.
5. Ibid.
6. HC 1:297.

Chapter 5
1. MS 25:454.

Chapter 6
1. D&C 103:22.
2. JD 2:10.
3. JD 10:20.

Chapter 7
1. D&C 18.
2. JD 9:89.
3. HC 2:181.
4. Ibid.
5. JD 9:89.
6. HC 2:182.
7. Ibid.
8. D&C 18.
9. HC 2:188-89.
10. HC 2:195.

Chapter 8.
1. JS-V 1:1-3.
2. HC 2:428.
3. HC 2:435.
4. JD 4:297.
5. MS 25:487.
6. Ibid.
7. MS 25:518.
8. HC 3:2.

Chapter 9
1. HC 3:23.
2. D&C 115:7, 8, 10, 11.
3. D&C 118:4, 5.
4. HC 4:xxx.
5. Parley P. Pratt, *Autobiography of Parley Parker Pratt,* p. 191.
6. HC 3:180.
7. HC 3:295.
8. MS 25:568.
9. Ibid.

Chapter 10
1. MH 1:57.
2. MH 1:53-54.
3. MH 1:58-59.
4. MH 1:66.
5. MH 1:67.

Chapter 11
1. Matthias F. Cowley, *Wilford Woodruff,* p. 120.
2. MS 25:743.
3. JD 4:35.
4. MS 26:7.
5. JD 14:81.
6. HC 4:512.
7. HC 4:250.
8. MH 1:103.

Chapter 12
1. MS 26:88.
2. D&C 126:1-3.
3. HC 4:402-3.
4. JD 18:241.
5. MS 26:167.
6. Ibid.

7. Mary Ann Angell to Brigham Young, Aug. 16, 1843; cited in S. Dilworth Young, *Here Is Brigham,* p. 332.
8. HC 6:188.
9. Ibid.
10. HC 6:340.
11. MS 26:343.
12. MS 26:359.

Chapter 13
1. HC 7:233.
2. HC 7:236.
3. William E. Hunter, *Edward Hunter, Faithful Steward,* p. 79.
4. HC 7:240.
5. HC 7:256.
6. HC 7:249.
7. CHC 2:505.
8. HC 7:463.
9. HC 7:403.
10. HC 7:398.
11. *Nauvoo Neighbor,* Oct. 1, 1845, p. 3.
12. Thomas Ford, *A History of Illinois,* p. 304.
13. MH 2:19-20.
14. MH 2:25.
15. MH 2:27.
16. MH 2:29.

Chapter 14
1. Wallace Stegner, *The Gathering of Zion,* p. 52.
2. William Mulder and A. Russell Mortensen, *Among the Mormons,* pp. 182-83.
3. MH 1:61.
4. Stegner, *Gathering of Zion,* p.106.

Chapter 15
1. Brigham Young to Charles C. Rich, Jan. 4, 1847, in *Journal History of the Church,* Historical Department, The Church of Jesus Christ of Latter-day Saints, Salt Lake City; hereafter cited as Church Archives.

Chapter 16
1. Journal of William Clayton, Church Archives.
2. Ibid.
3. Journal of Wilford Woodruff, Church Archives.
4. Journal of William Clayton, Church Archives.
5. Ibid.

6. Ibid.
7. Ibid.
8. Ibid.
9. Journal of Orson Pratt, Church Archives.
10. CHC 3:200.
11. CHC 3:201.
12. Wallace Stegner, *The Gathering of Zion,* p. 167.
13. CHC 3:224.

Chapter 17
1. Brigham Young to Charles C. Rich, Aug. 2, 1847; cited in Leonard J. Arrington, *Charles C. Rich,* p. 118.
2. Preston Nibley, *Brigham Young: The Man and His Work, p. 103.*
3. *Ibid.*
4. *Ibid., p. 102.*
5. *Ibid., p. 104.*

Chapter 18
1. *Preston Nibley, Brigham Young: The Man and His Work,* p. 107.
2. Ibid., p. 108.
3. Ibid., p. 109.

Chapter 19
1. Journal of Wilford Woodruff, Church Archives.
2. Ibid.
3. CHC 3:310, 312.
4. CHC 3:319.
5. MS 10:314.
6. Preston Nibley, *Brigham Young: The Man and His Work,* p. 120.
7. Ibid., p. 121.
8. Journal of Thomas Bullock, Sept. 3, 1848, p. 104, Church Archives.

Chapter 20
1. James S. Brown, *Life of a Pioneer,* pp. 121-22.
2. CHC 3:410.

Chapter 21
1. CHC 3:349-50.
2. CHC 3:349.

Chapter 22
1. Hubert Howe Bancroft, *History of Utah,* p. 456.
2. Journal of Wilford Woodruff, Church Archives.
3. CHC 3:522.
4. CHC 3:523.
5. CHC 3:534.

Chapter 23
1. *Deseret News,* Feb. 19, 1853.
2. JD 6:268.
3. JD 12:31, 32.
4. Clarissa Young Spencer and Mabel Harmer, *Brigham Young at Home,* p. 143.
5. CHC 4:64.

Chapter 24
1. JD 4:87.
2. JD 4:43, 44, 45.
3. JD 4:43.

Chapter 25
1. CHC 4:99.
2. Manuscript History of Brigham Young, Church Archives, pp. 1099, 1102-3.

Chapter 26
1. Clarissa Young Spencer and Mabel Harmer, *Brigham Young at Home,* p. 17.
2. Ibid., pp. 35, 36.
3. Ibid., pp. 18-19.
4. Richard F. Burton, *The City of the Saints,* pp. 263-66.

Chapter 27
1. Hubert Howe Bancroft, *History of Utah,* p. 511.
2. Ibid., pp. 507-9.
3. CHC 4:155.
4. Bancroft, *History of Utah,* p. 567.
5. CHC 4:161.
6. CHC 4:164.
7. CHC 4:178.
8. CHC 4:179.

Chapter 28
1. CHC 4:490.
2. Hubert Howe Bancroft, *History of Utah,* p. 573.

Chapter 30
1. JD 12:290.
2. Samuel Bowles, *Our New West,* p. 260.
3. Deseret News, Nov. 3, 1869, p. 457.
4. JD 12:59.

5. *Deseret News,* editorial, June 21, 1871.
6. Hubert Howe Bancroft, *History of Utah,* p. 646.
7. *Deseret News,* June 21, 1871, p. 236.

Chapter 31
1. Preston Nibley, *Brigham Young: The Man and His Work,* pp. 423-24.

Chapter 32
1. CHC 5:320.
2. Ibid.
3. CHC 5:396-97.
4. *Deseret News,* Oct. 18, 1871, p. 429.
5. CHC 5:400-401.
6. CHC 5:410.
7. CHC 5:412-13.
8. *Deseret News,* May 1, 1872, p. 168.
9. CHC 5:446-47.

Chapter 33
1. Preston Nibley, *Brigham Young: The Man and His Work,* pp. 488-89.
2. Ibid., pp. 491-92.
3. Ibid., p. 494.
4. John Taylor, *Succession in the Priesthood,* pamphlet, Church Archives, p. 17.
5. Nibley, *Brigham Young,* pp. 496-97.
6. Ibid., pp. 502-3.
7. Ibid., p. 506.

Chapter 34
1. Preston Nibley, *Brigham Young: The Man and His Work,* p. 512.
2. Helen Bay Gibbons, *Saint and Savage,* p. 195.
3. JD 18:355-57.

Chapter 36
1. Preston Nibley, *Brigham Young: The Man and His Work,* pp. 536-37.

Bibliography

Bancroft, Hubert Howe. *History of Utah*. Salt Lake City: Bookcraft, 1964.

Bowles, Samuel. *Our New West*. New York: Hartford Publishing Co., 1869.

Brown, James S. *Life of a Pioneer*. Salt Lake City: Geo. Q. Cannon & Sons Co., 1900. Reprinted by AMS Press Inc., New York, 1971.

Burton, Richard F. *The City of the Saints*. New York: Alfred A. Knopf, 1963.

Cowley, Matthias F., comp. and ed. *Wilford Woodruff*. Salt Lake City: Bookcraft, 1964.

Ford, Thomas. *A History of Illinois*. 2 vols. Chicago: R. R. Donnelly & Sons Co., 1945.

Gibbons, Helen Bay. *Saint and Savage*. Salt Lake City: Deseret Book Co., 1965.

Hunter, William E. *Edward Hunter, Faithful Steward*. Salt Lake City: Mrs. William E. Hunter, 1970.

Journal of Discourses. 26 vols. London: Latter-day Saints' Book Depot, 1854-86.

Manuscript History of Brigham Young. Historical Department, The Church of Jesus Christ of Latter-day Saints, Salt Lake City, Utah.

Mulder, William and Mortensen, A. Russell. *Among the Mormons*. Lincoln: University of Nebraska Press, 1973.

Nibley, Preston. *Brigham Young: The Man and His Work*. Salt Lake City: Deseret News Press, 1937.

Pratt, Parley P. *Autobiography of Parley Parker Pratt*. 5th ed. Edited by Parley P. Pratt, Jr. Salt Lake City: Deseret Book Company, 1961.

Roberts, B.H. *A Comprehensive History of The Church of*

Jesus Christ of Latter-day Saints, Century One. 6 vols. Salt Lake City: The Church of Jesus Christ of Latter-day Saints, 1930.

Smith, Joseph. *History of The Church of Jesus Christ of Latter-day Saints.* 7 vols. 2nd ed. rev. Edited by B. H. Roberts. Salt Lake City: The Church of Jesus Christ of Latter-day Saints, 1932-51.

Spencer, Clarissa Young and Harmer, Mabel. *Brigham Young at Home.* Salt Lake City: Deseret Book Co., 1940.

Stegner, Wallace. *The Gathering of Zion.* New York: McGraw-Hill Book Company, 1964.

Watson, Elden J., comp. *Manuscript History of Brigham Young, 1801-1844.* Salt Lake City: Elden J. Watson, 1968.

————. *Manuscript History of Brigham Young, 1846-1847.* Salt Lake City: Elden J. Watson, 1971.

Young, S. Dilworth. *Here Is Brigham.* Salt Lake City: Bookcraft, 1964.

Index